FRED BASSET YEARBOOK 2016

Copyright © Alex Graham Limited, 2015

Drawings by Michael Martin

Summersdale Publishers Ltd
46 West Street
Chichester
West Sussex
PO19 1RP
UK

www.summersdale.com

Printed and bound in the Czech Republic

ISBN: 978-1-84953-758-2

Substantial discounts on bulk quantities of Summersdale books are available to corporations, professional associations and other organisations.
For details contact Nicky Douglas by telephone: +44 (0) 1243 756902, fax: +44 (0) 1243 786300 or email: nicky@summersdale.com.

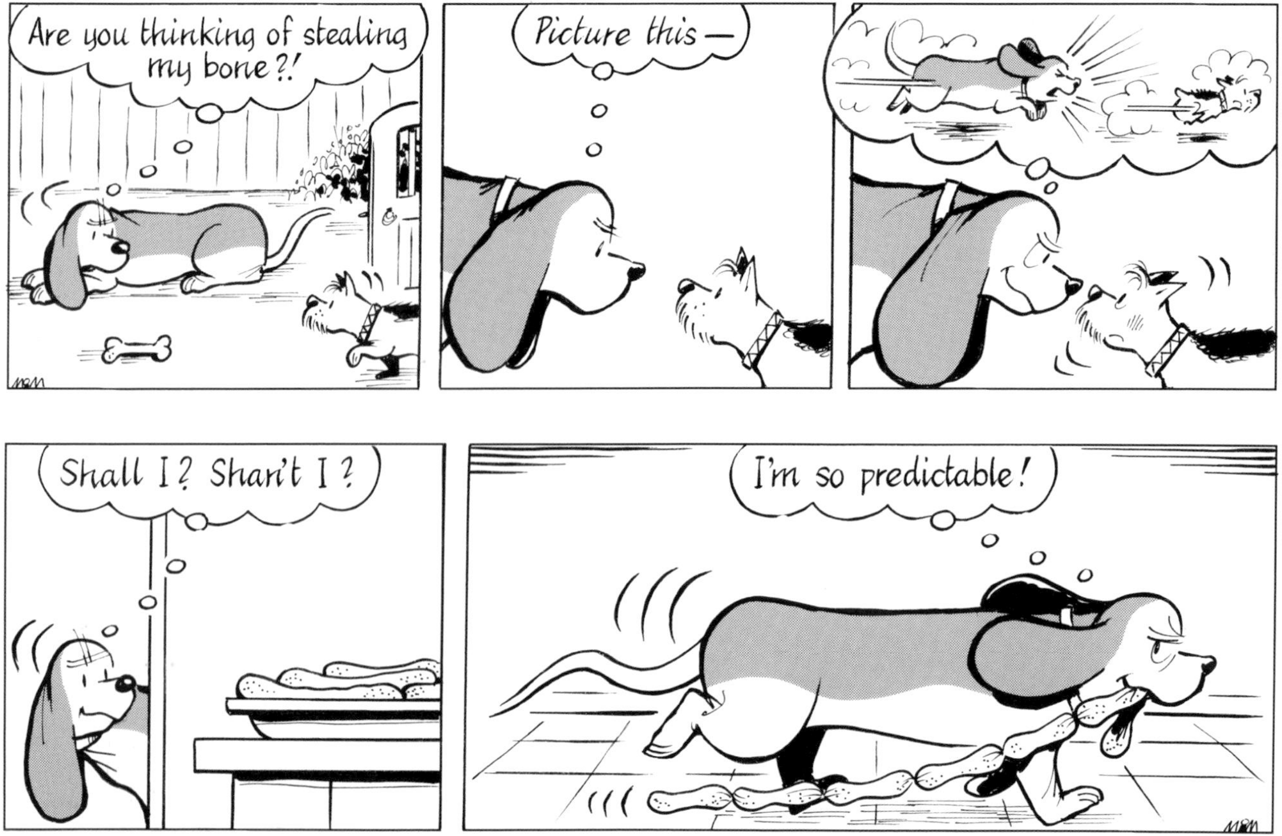
Are you thinking of stealing my bone?!
Picture this—
Shall I? Shan't I?
I'm so predictable!

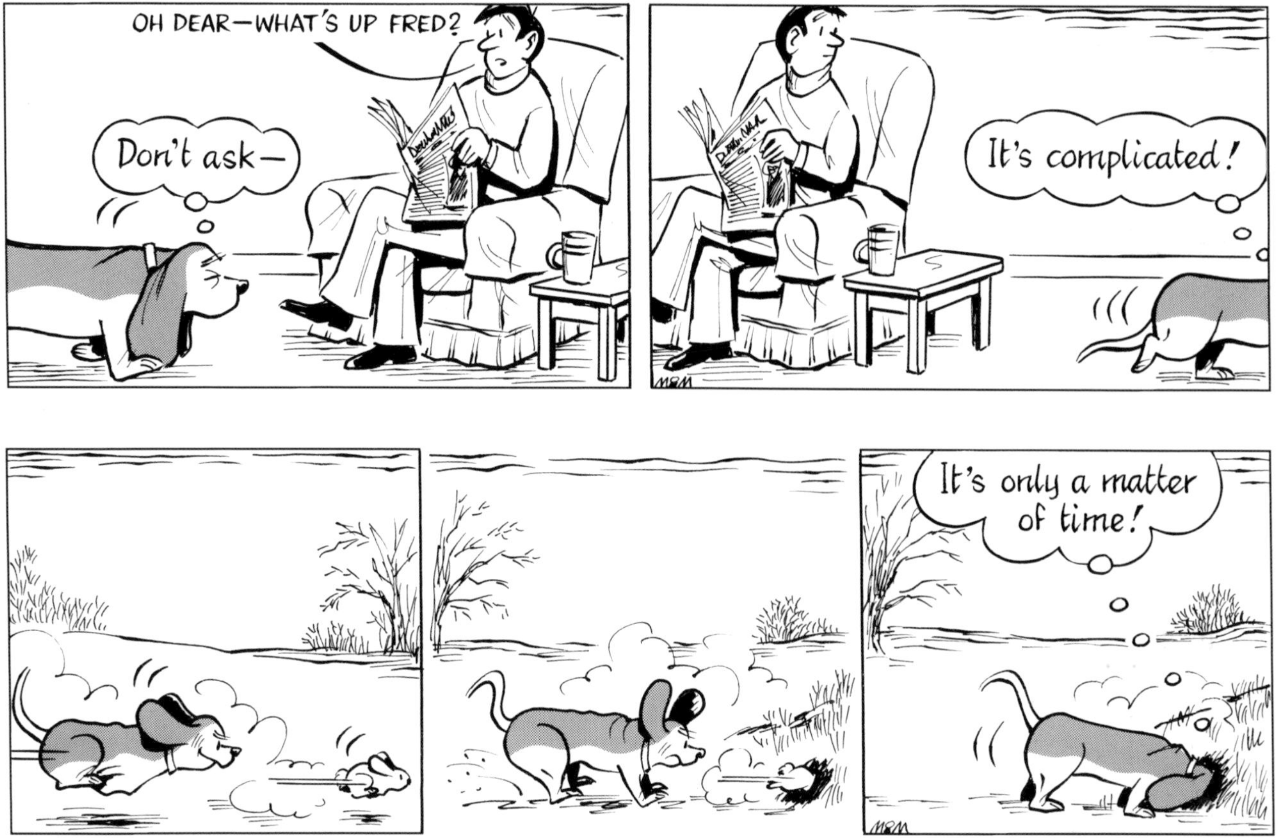
OH DEAR—WHAT'S UP FRED?
Don't ask—
It's complicated!
It's only a matter of time!

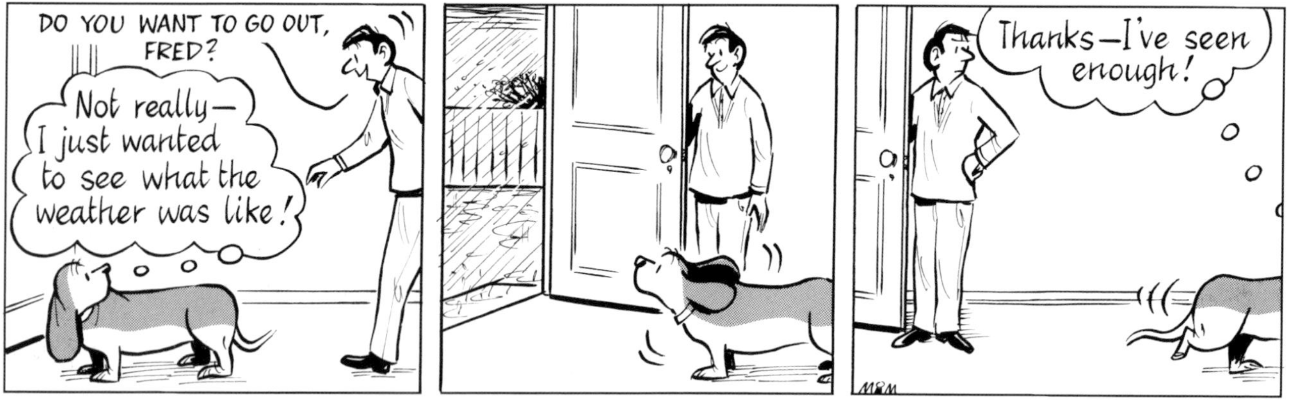
DO YOU WANT TO GO OUT, FRED?
Not really— I just wanted to see what the weather was like!
Thanks—I've seen enough!
M&M

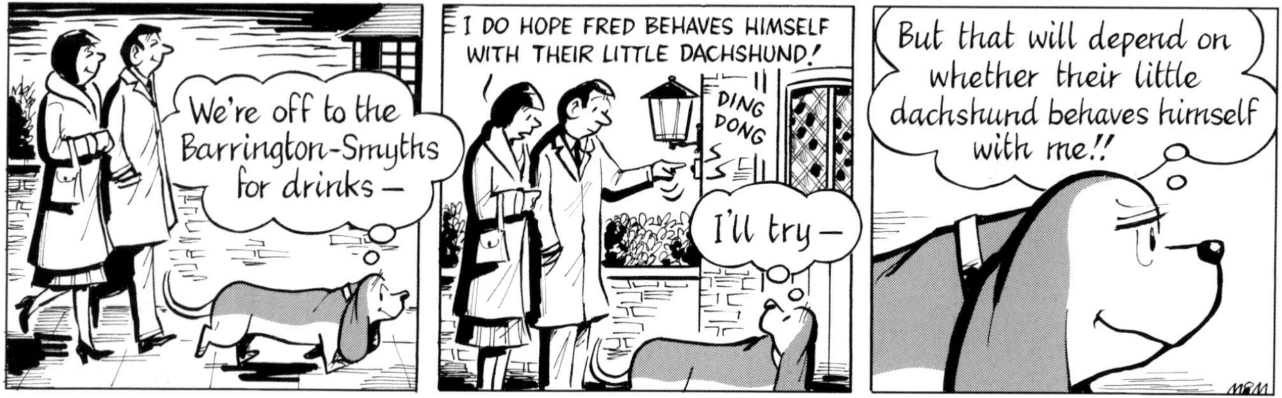
We're off to the Barrington-Smyths for drinks—
I DO HOPE FRED BEHAVES HIMSELF WITH THEIR LITTLE DACHSHUND!
DING DONG
I'll try—
But that will depend on whether their little dachshund behaves himself with me!!
M&M

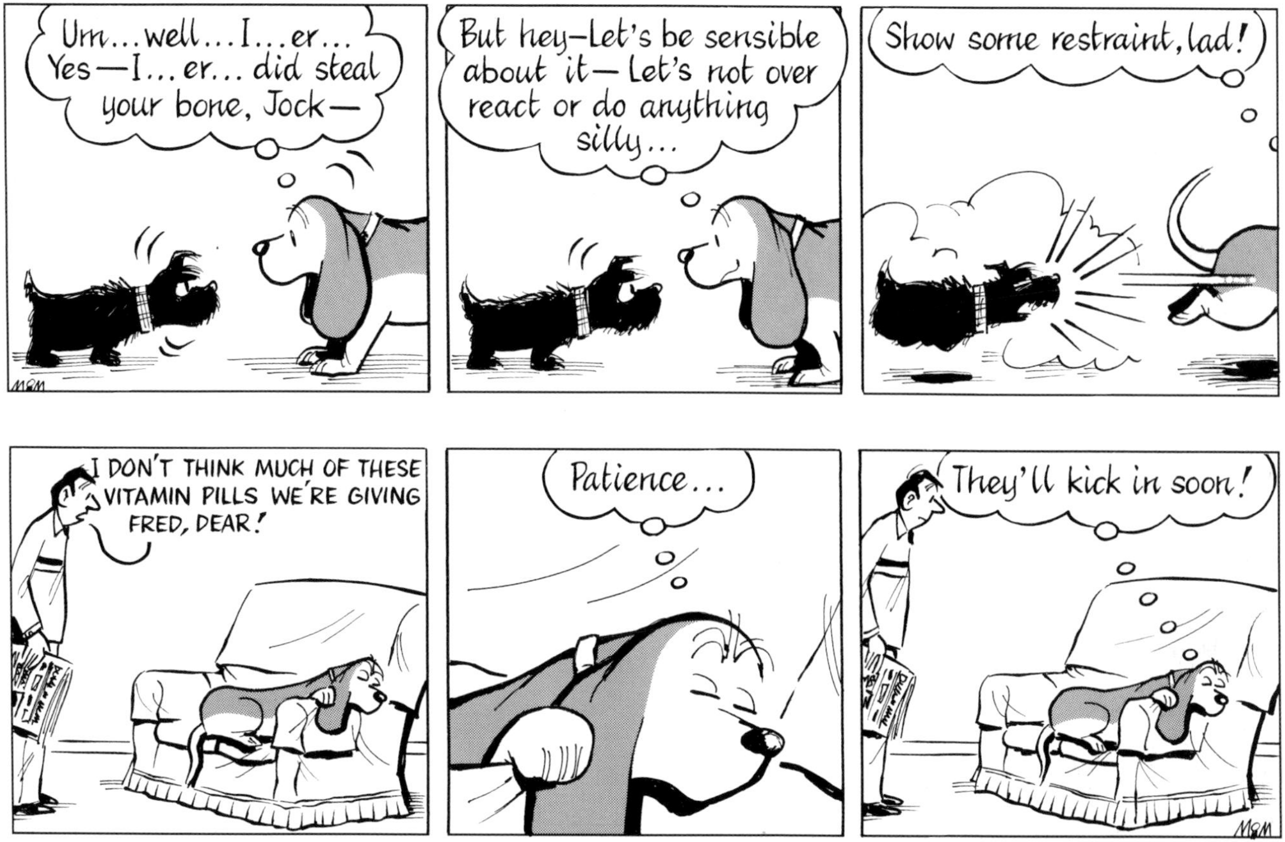
Um... well... I... er... Yes—I... er... did steal your bone, Jock—
But hey—Let's be sensible about it—Let's not over react or do anything silly...
Show some restraint, lad!
I DON'T THINK MUCH OF THESE VITAMIN PILLS WE'RE GIVING FRED, DEAR!
Patience...
They'll kick in soon!
M&M

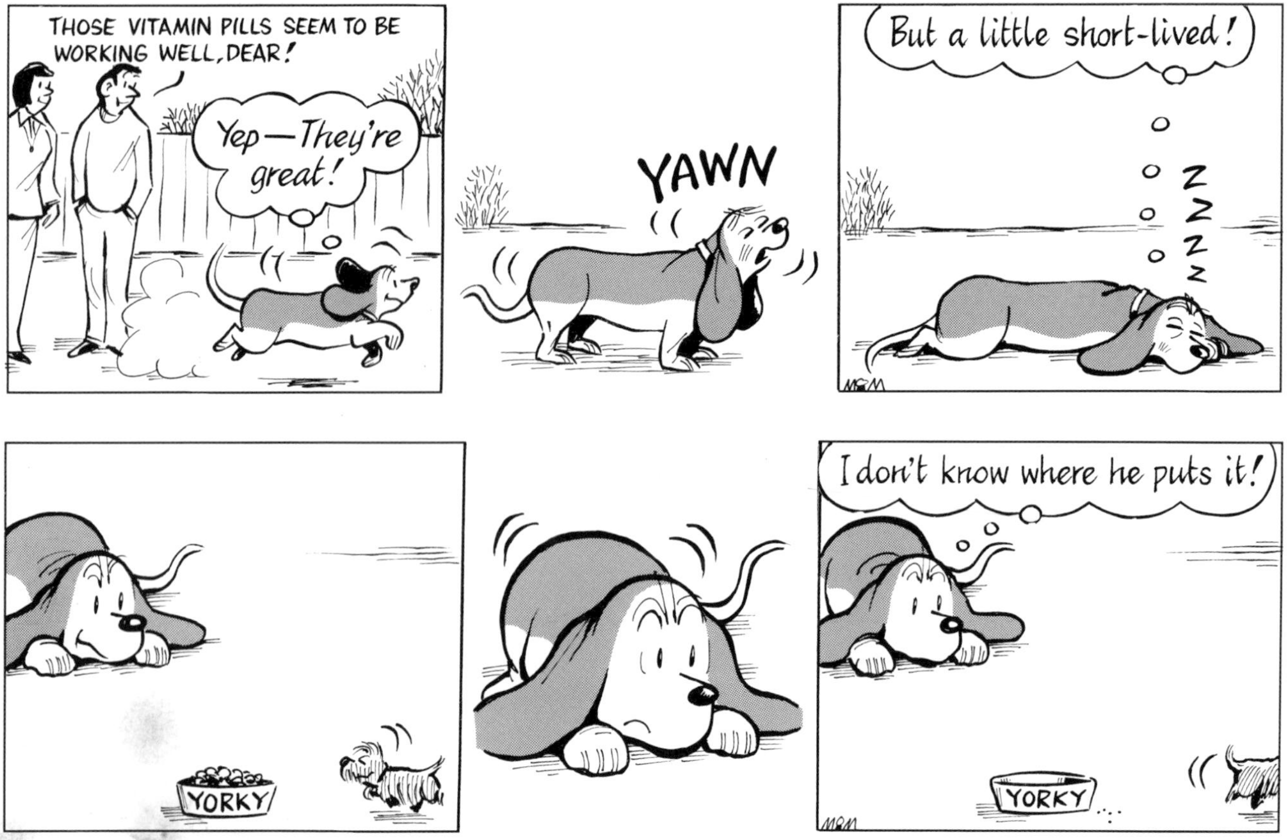
THOSE VITAMIN PILLS SEEM TO BE WORKING WELL, DEAR!
Yep—They're great!
YAWN
But a little short-lived!
Z Z Z Z
MGM
YORKY
I don't know where he puts it!
YORKY
MGM

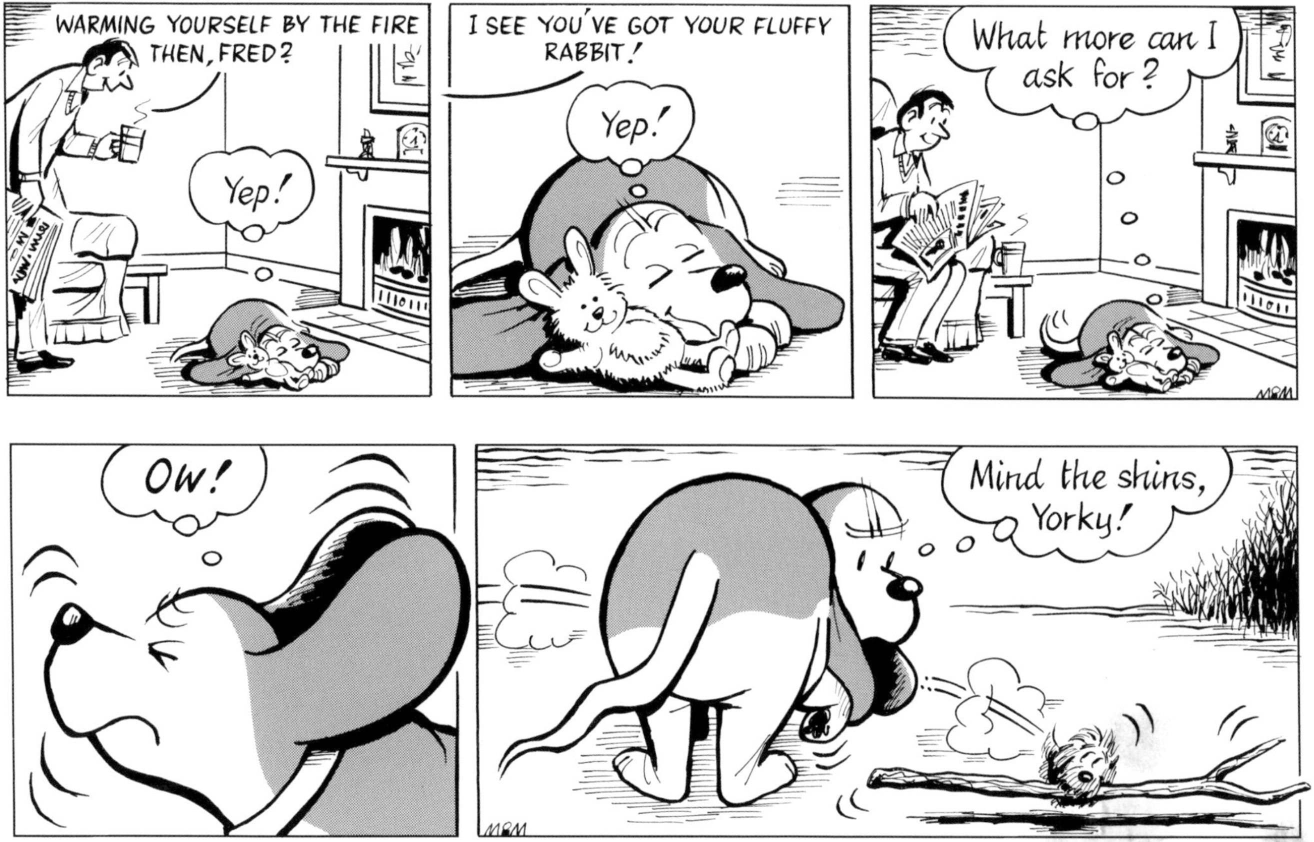

WARMING YOURSELF BY THE FIRE THEN, FRED?
Yep!
I SEE YOU'VE GOT YOUR FLUFFY RABBIT!
Yep!
What more can I ask for?
Ow!
Mind the shins, Yorky!

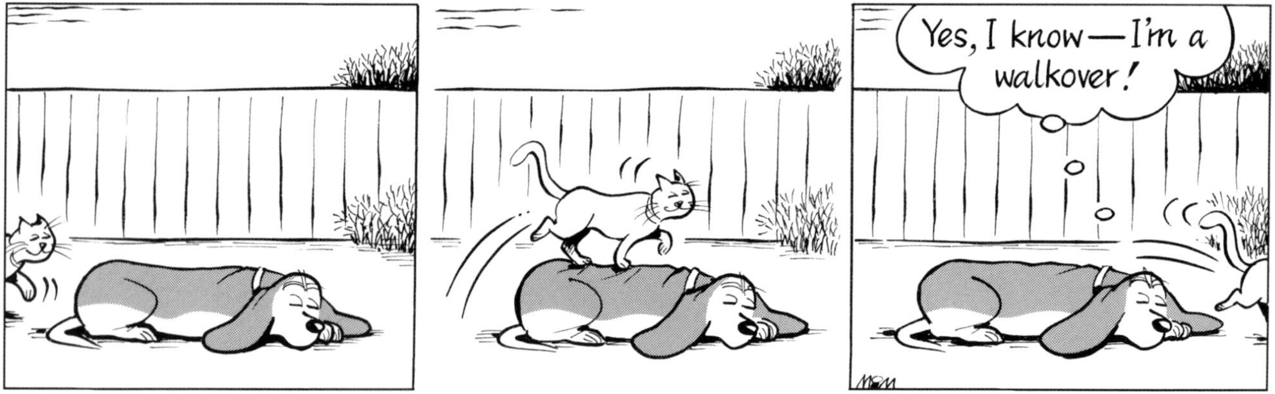
Yes, I know—I'm a walkover!

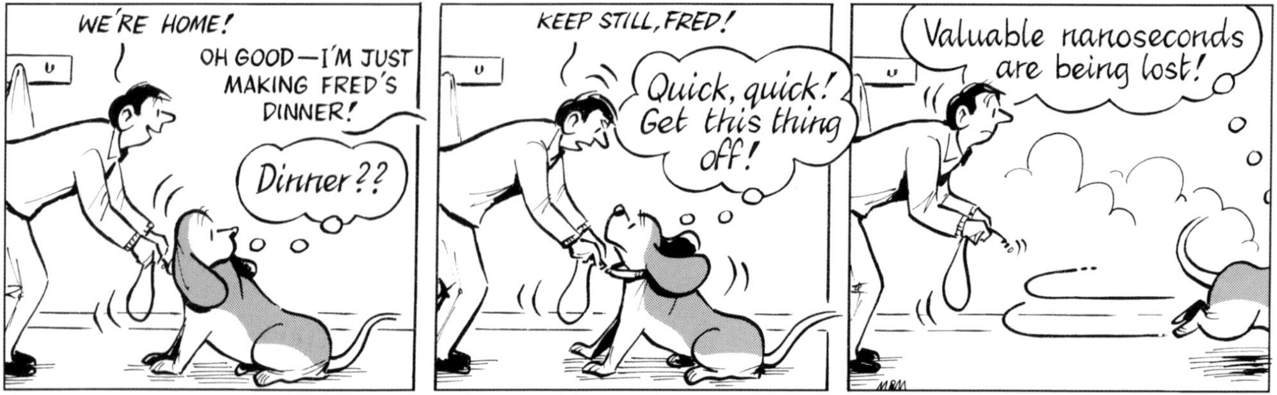
WE'RE HOME!
OH GOOD—I'M JUST MAKING FRED'S DINNER!
Dinner??
KEEP STILL, FRED!
Quick, quick! Get this thing off!
Valuable nanoseconds are being lost!

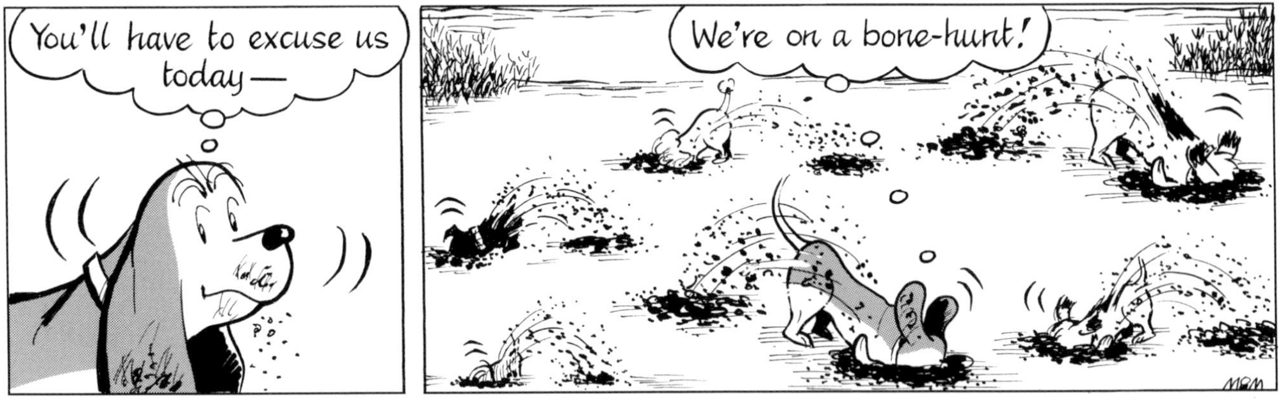
You'll have to excuse us today—
We're on a bone-hunt!
MSM

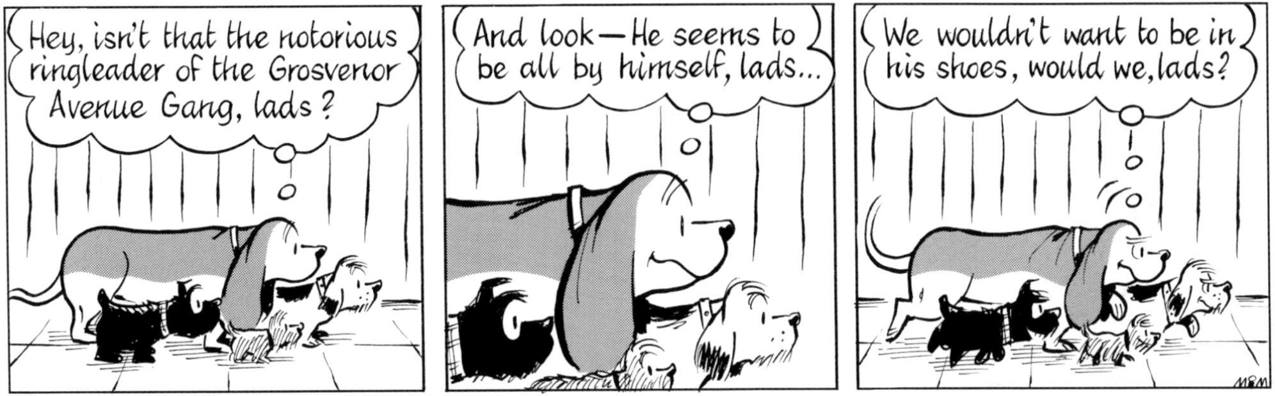
Hey, isn't that the notorious ringleader of the Grosvenor Avenue Gang, lads?
And look—He seems to be all by himself, lads...
We wouldn't want to be in his shoes, would we, lads?
MSM

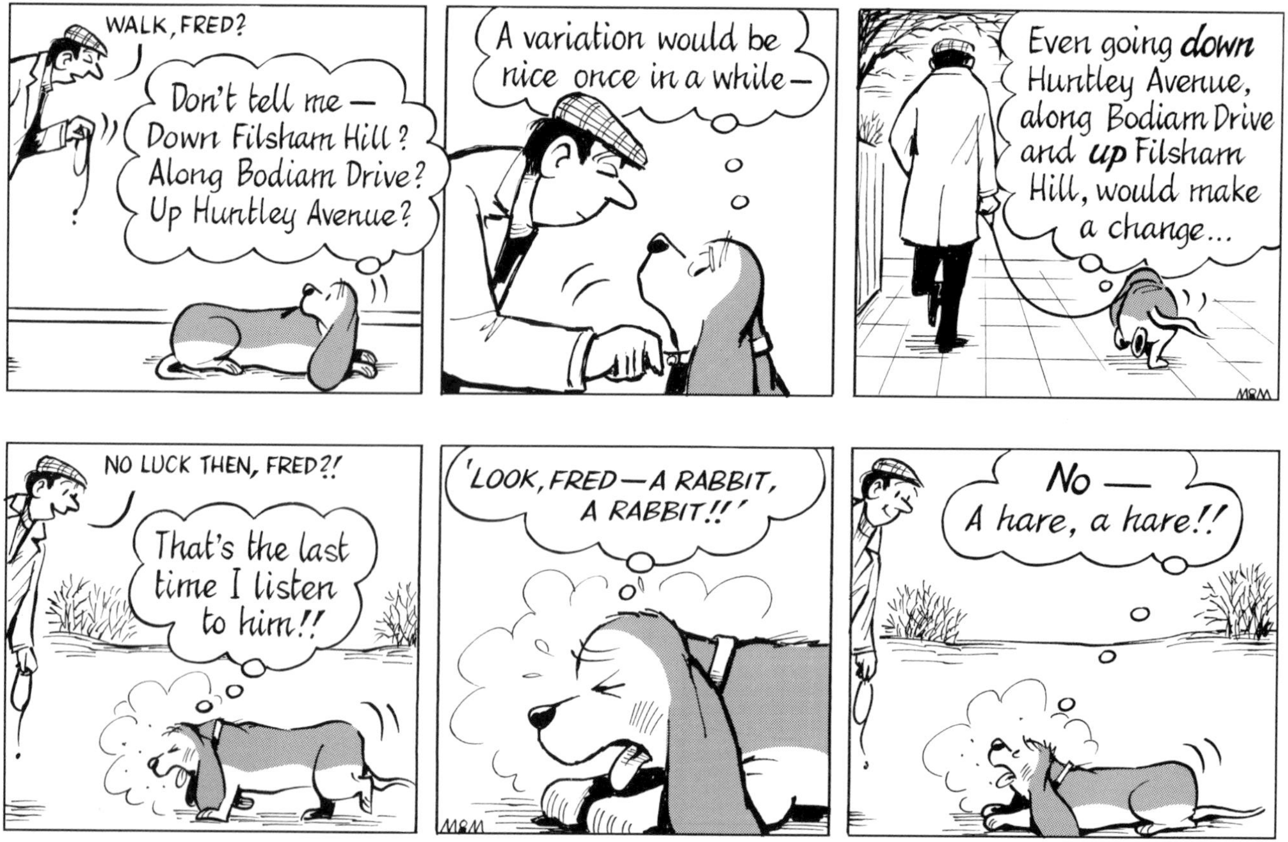
WALK, FRED?
Don't tell me — Down Filsham Hill? Along Bodiam Drive? Up Huntley Avenue?
A variation would be nice once in a while —
Even going **down** Huntley Avenue, along Bodiam Drive and **up** Filsham Hill, would make a change...
M&M
NO LUCK THEN, FRED?!
That's the last time I listen to him!!
'LOOK, FRED — A RABBIT, A RABBIT!!'
M&M
No — A hare, a hare!!

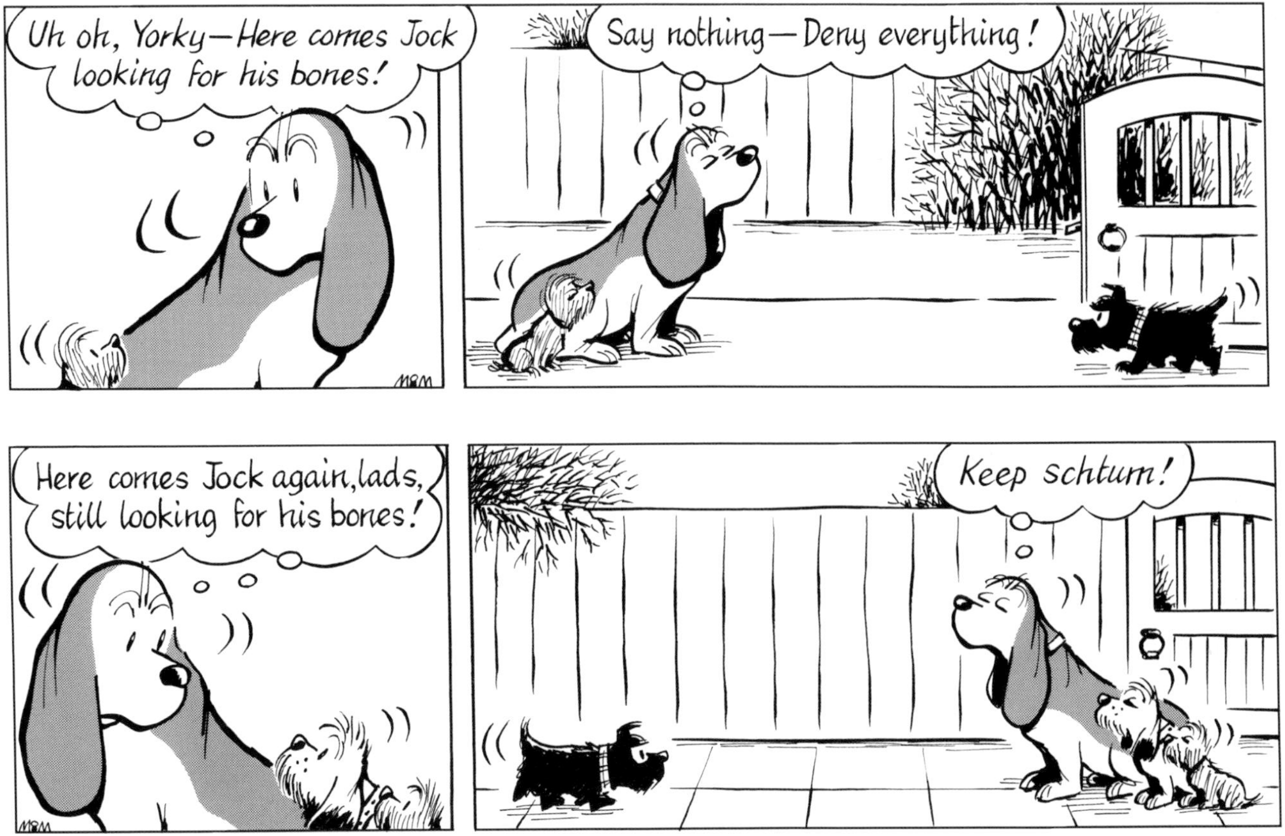

Uh oh, Yorky—Here comes Jock looking for his bones!
Say nothing—Deny everything!
Here comes Jock again, lads, still looking for his bones!
Keep schtum!

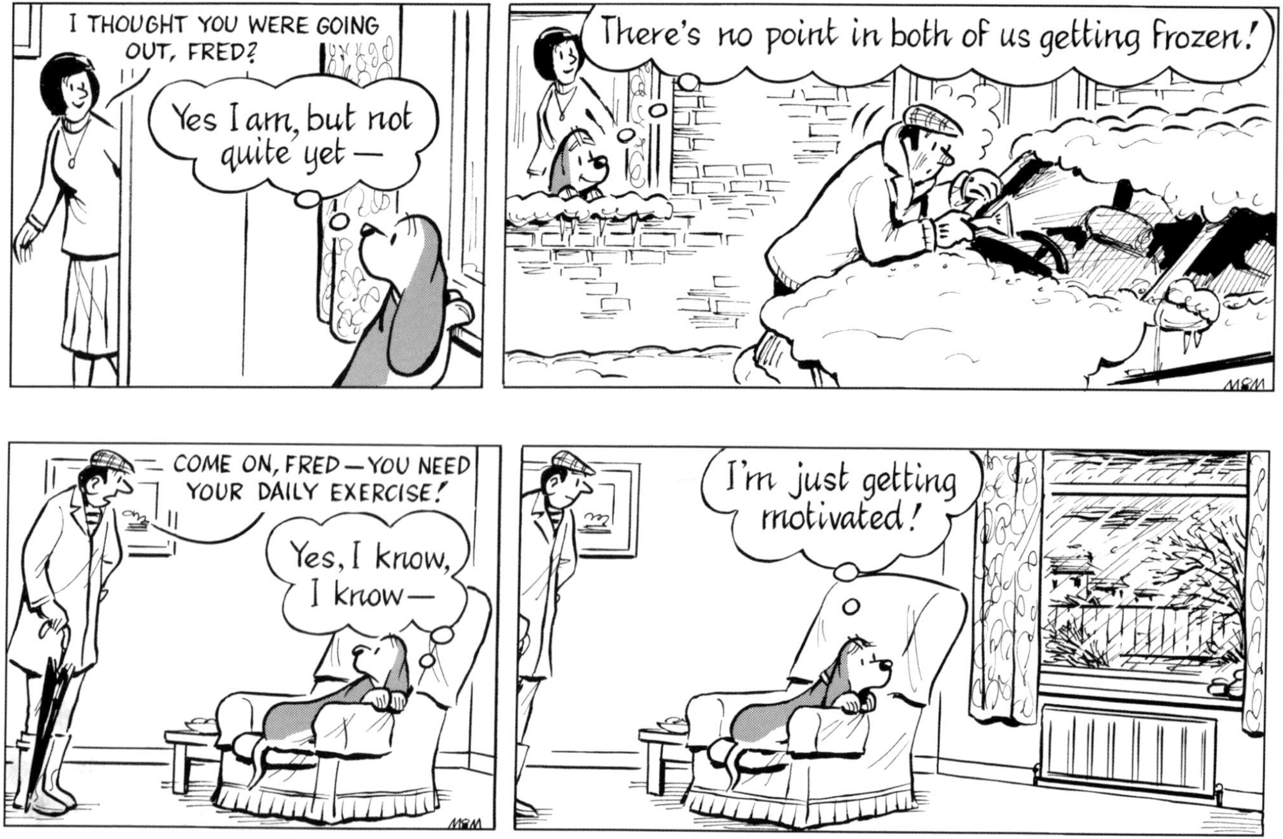

I THOUGHT YOU WERE GOING OUT, FRED?
Yes I am, but not quite yet —
There's no point in both of us getting frozen!
M&M
COME ON, FRED — YOU NEED YOUR DAILY EXERCISE!
Yes, I know, I know —
M&M
I'm just getting motivated!

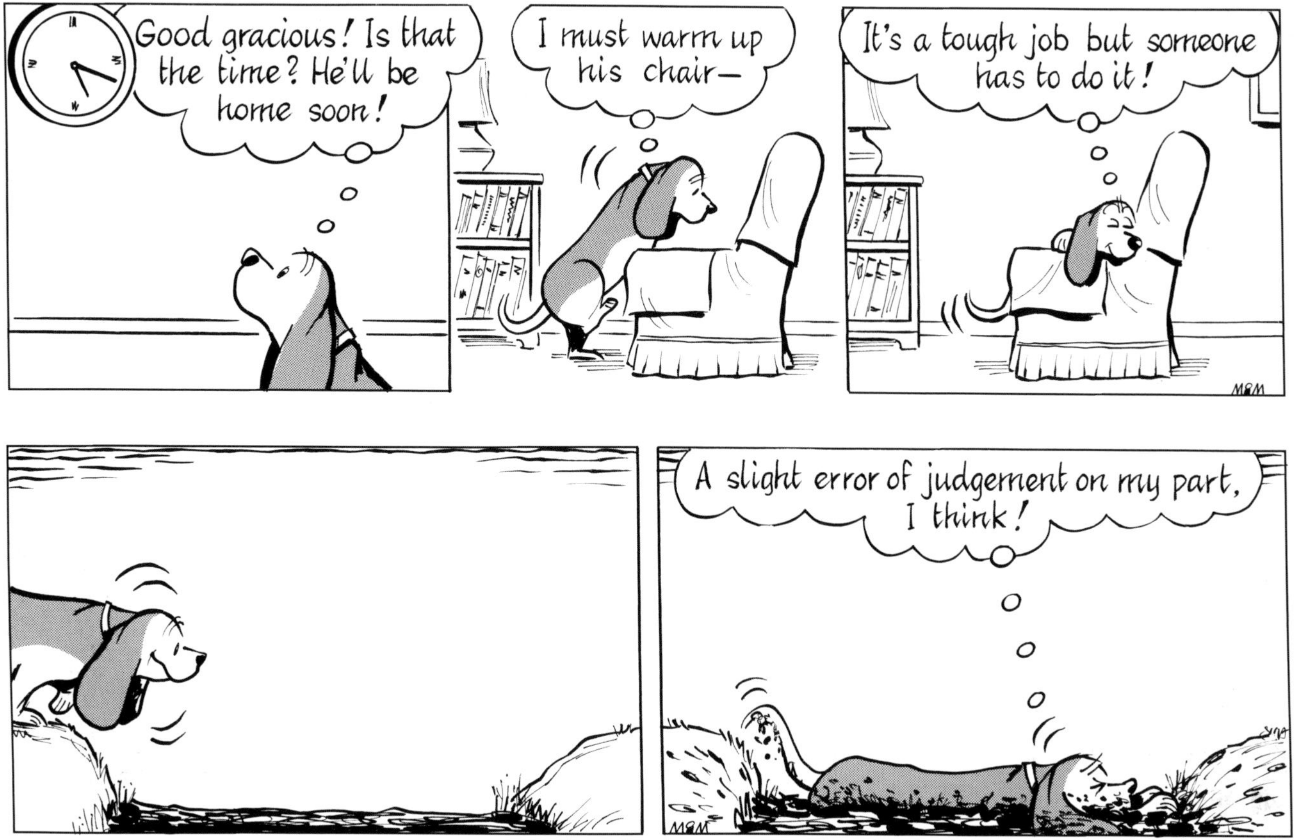
Good gracious! Is that the time? He'll be home soon!
I must warm up his chair—
It's a tough job but someone has to do it!
A slight error of judgement on my part, I think!

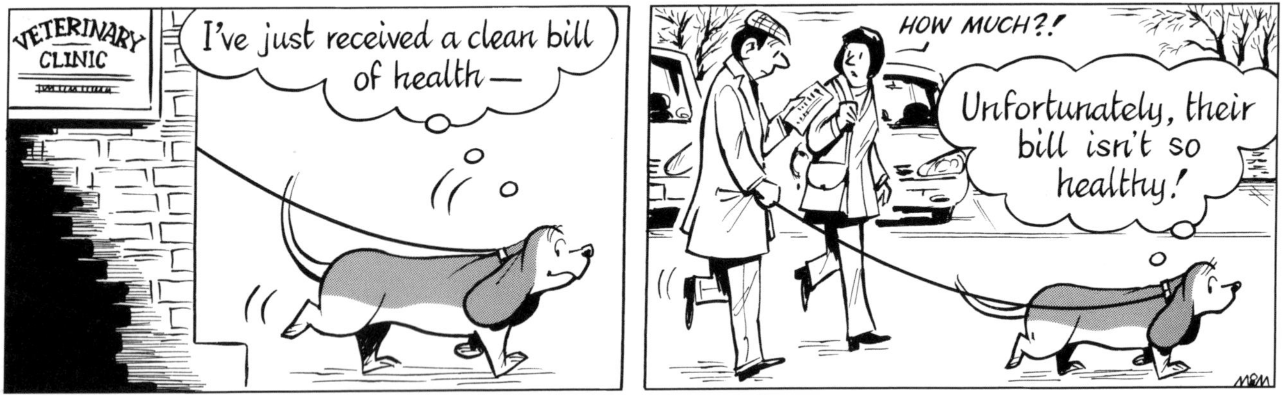
VETERINARY CLINIC
I've just received a clean bill of health —
HOW MUCH?!
Unfortunately, their bill isn't so healthy!
MBM

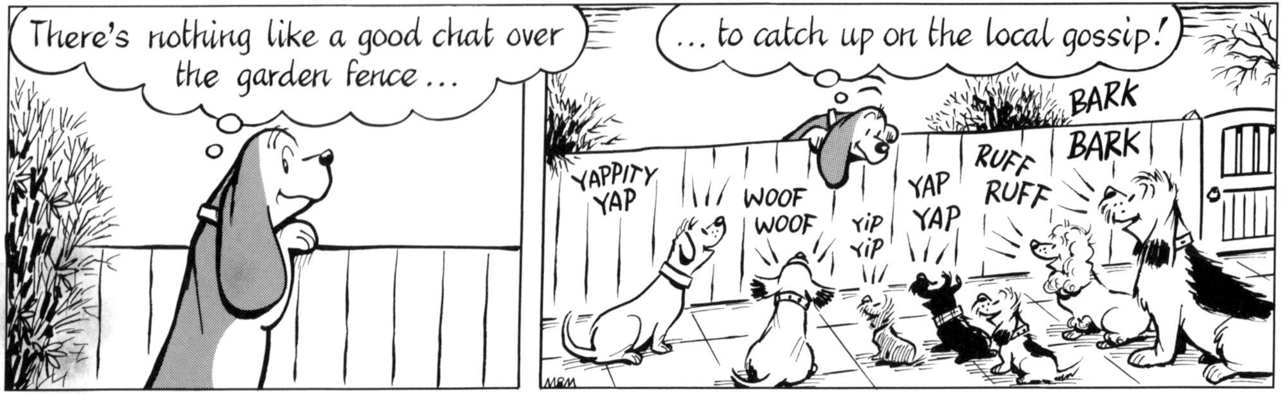
There's nothing like a good chat over the garden fence ...
... to catch up on the local gossip!
BARK
BARK
YAPPITY YAP
WOOF WOOF
YIP YIP
YAP YAP
RUFF RUFF
MBM

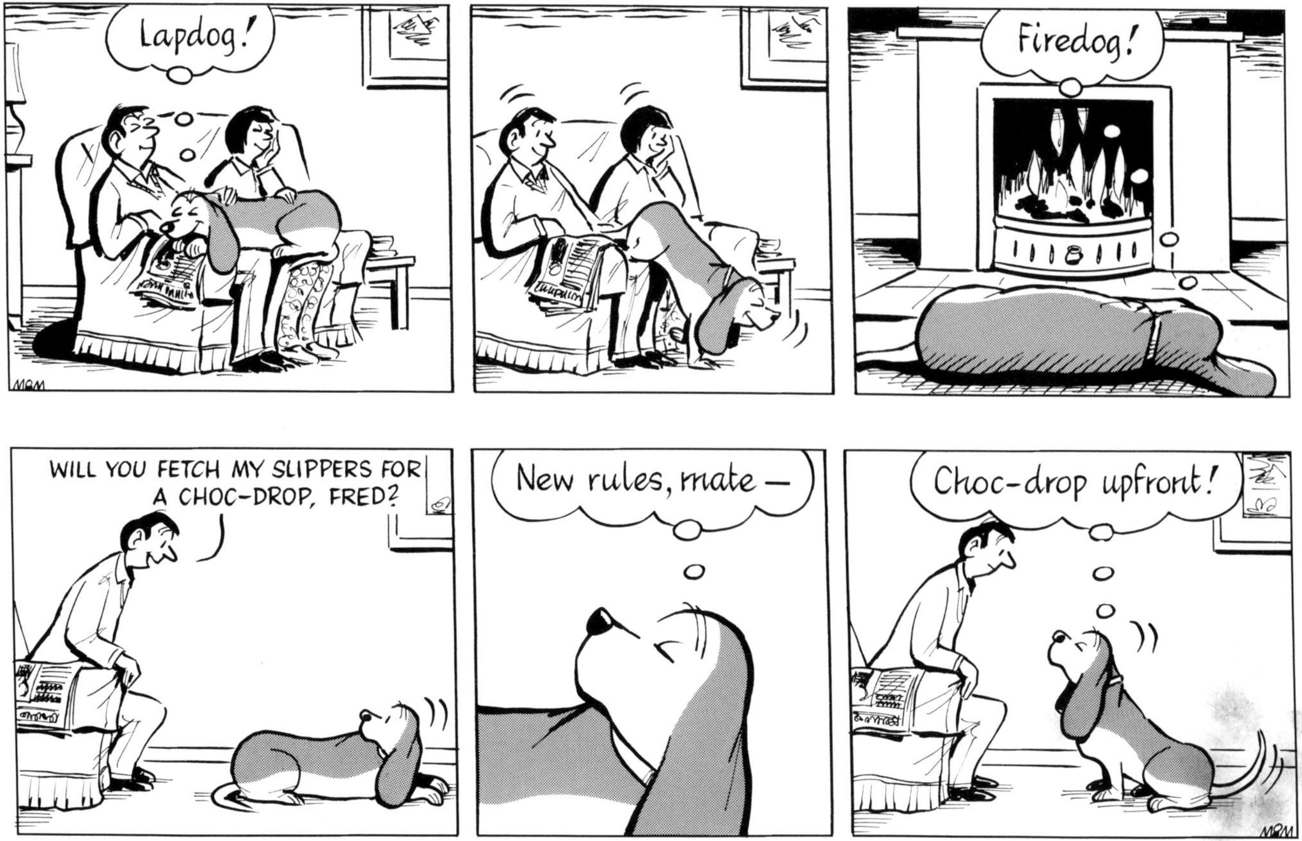
Lapdog!
Firedog!
WILL YOU FETCH MY SLIPPERS FOR A CHOC-DROP, FRED?
New rules, mate –
Choc-drop upfront!

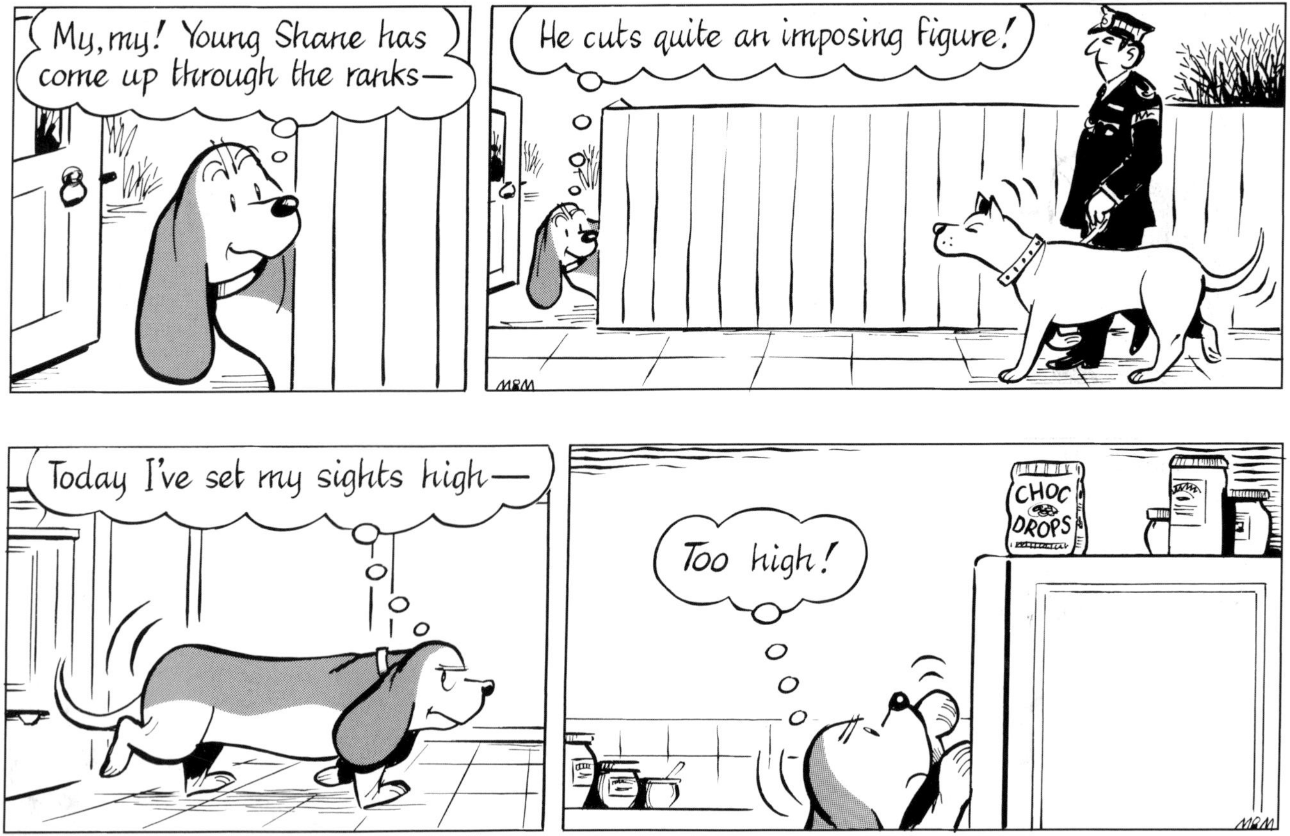
My, my! Young Shane has come up through the ranks—
He cuts quite an imposing figure!
MSM
Today I've set my sights high—
CHOC DROPS
Too high!
MSM

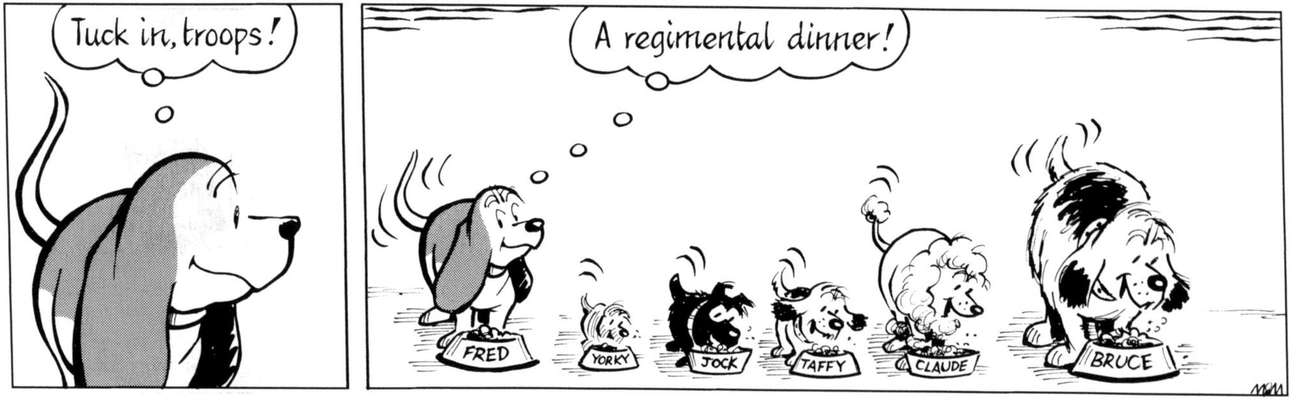
Tuck in, troops!
A regimental dinner!
FRED
YORKY
JOCK
TAFFY
CLAUDE
BRUCE
M&M

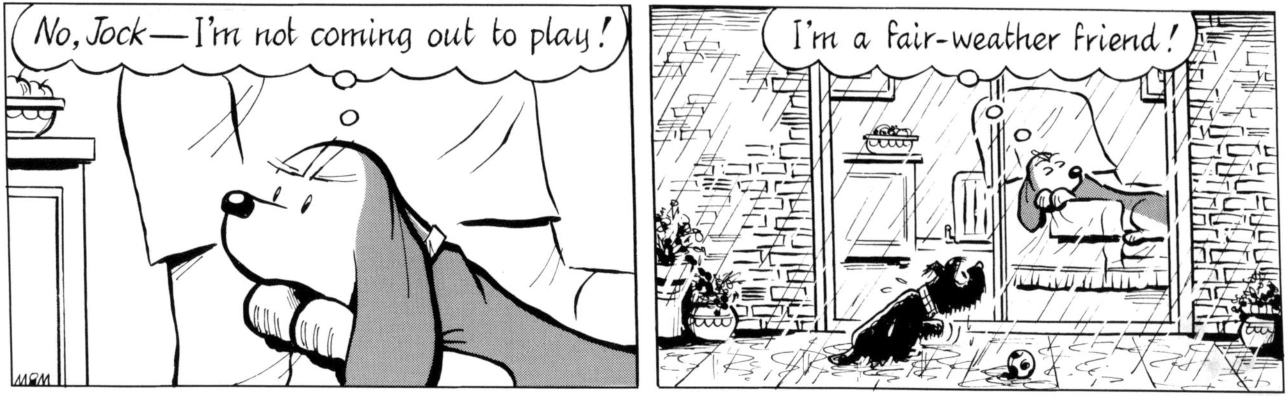
No, Jock—I'm not coming out to play!
M&M
I'm a fair-weather friend!

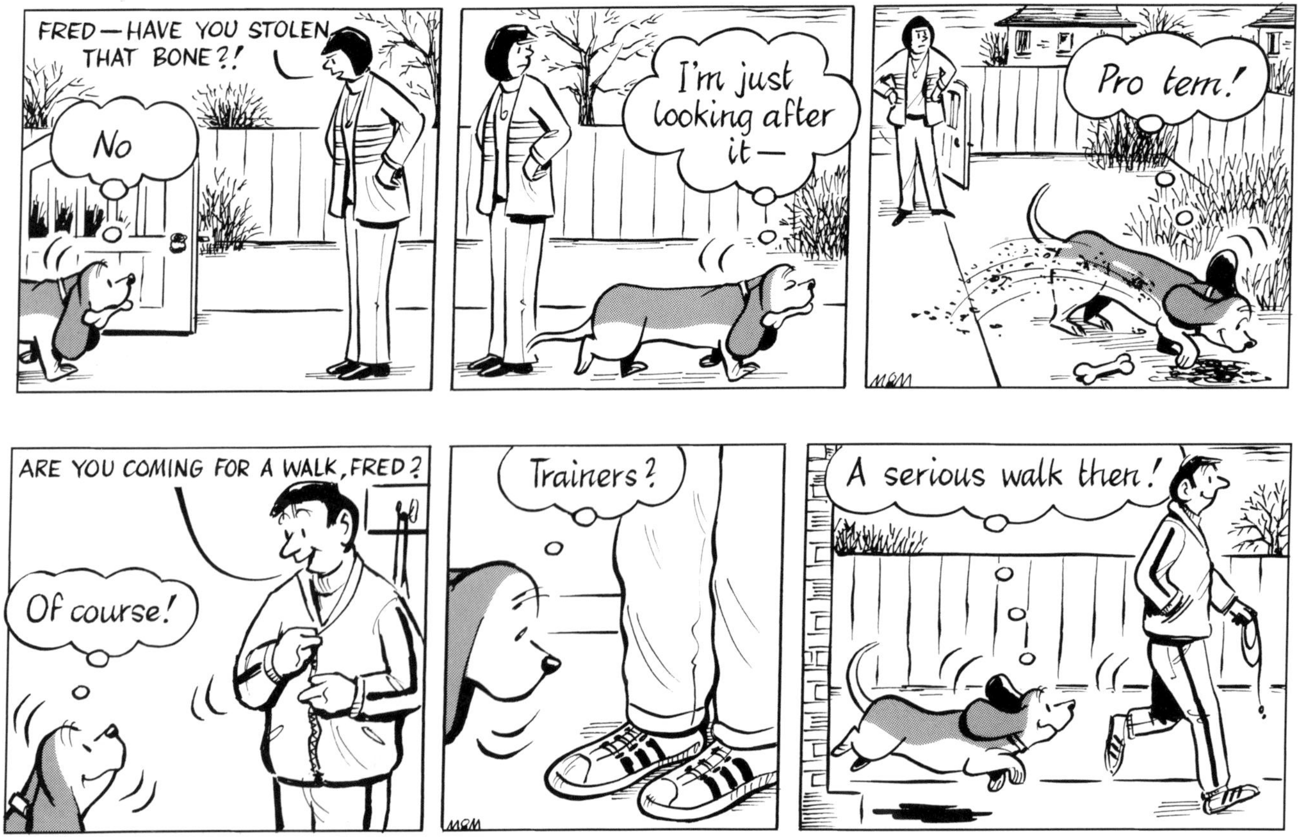
FRED—HAVE YOU STOLEN THAT BONE?!
No
I'm just looking after it—
Pro tem!
MGM
ARE YOU COMING FOR A WALK, FRED?
Of course!
Trainers?
A serious walk then!
MGM

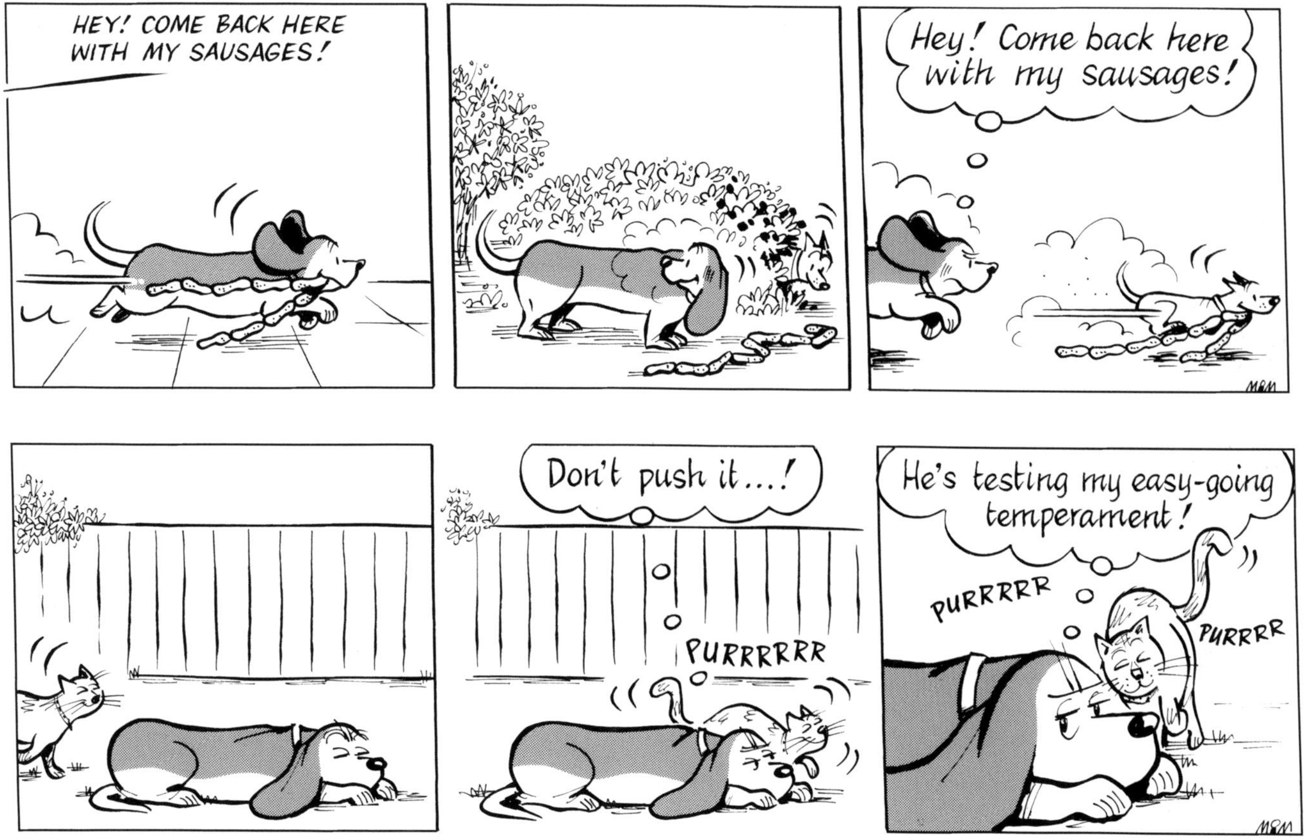
HEY! COME BACK HERE WITH MY SAUSAGES!
Hey! Come back here with my sausages!
MRM
Don't push it....!
PURRRRRR
He's testing my easy-going temperament!
PURRRRR
PURRRR
MRM

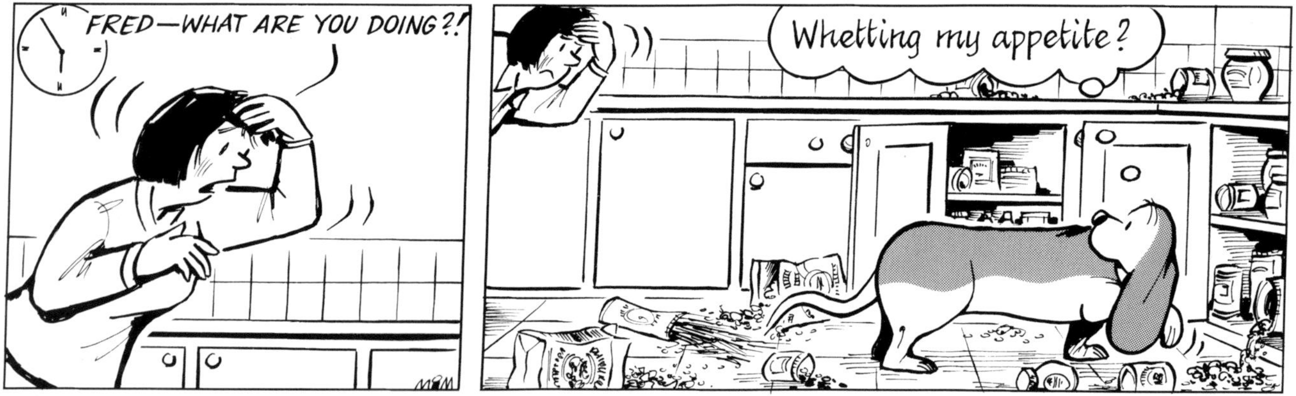
FRED—WHAT ARE YOU DOING?!
Whetting my appetite?
M&M

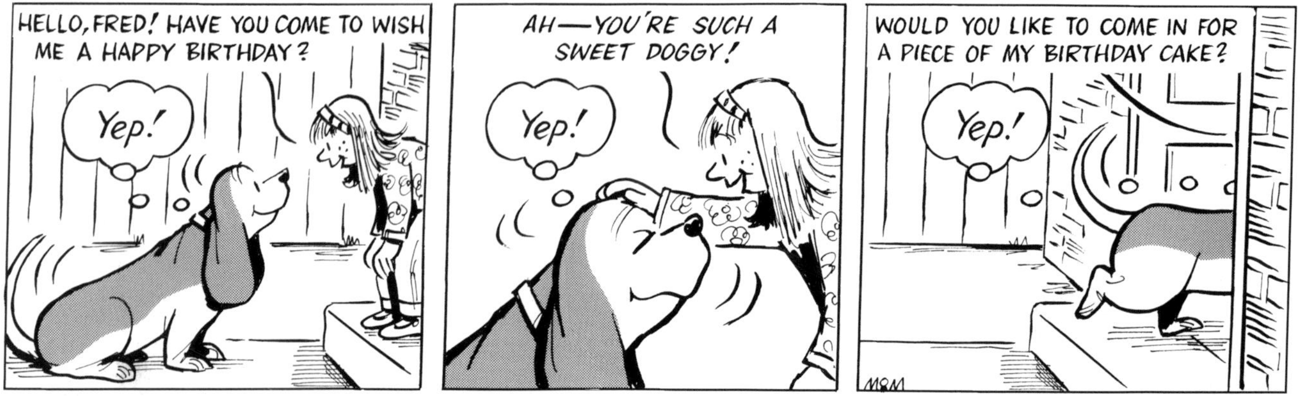
HELLO, FRED! HAVE YOU COME TO WISH ME A HAPPY BIRTHDAY?
Yep!
AH—YOU'RE SUCH A SWEET DOGGY!
Yep!
WOULD YOU LIKE TO COME IN FOR A PIECE OF MY BIRTHDAY CAKE?
Yep!
M&M

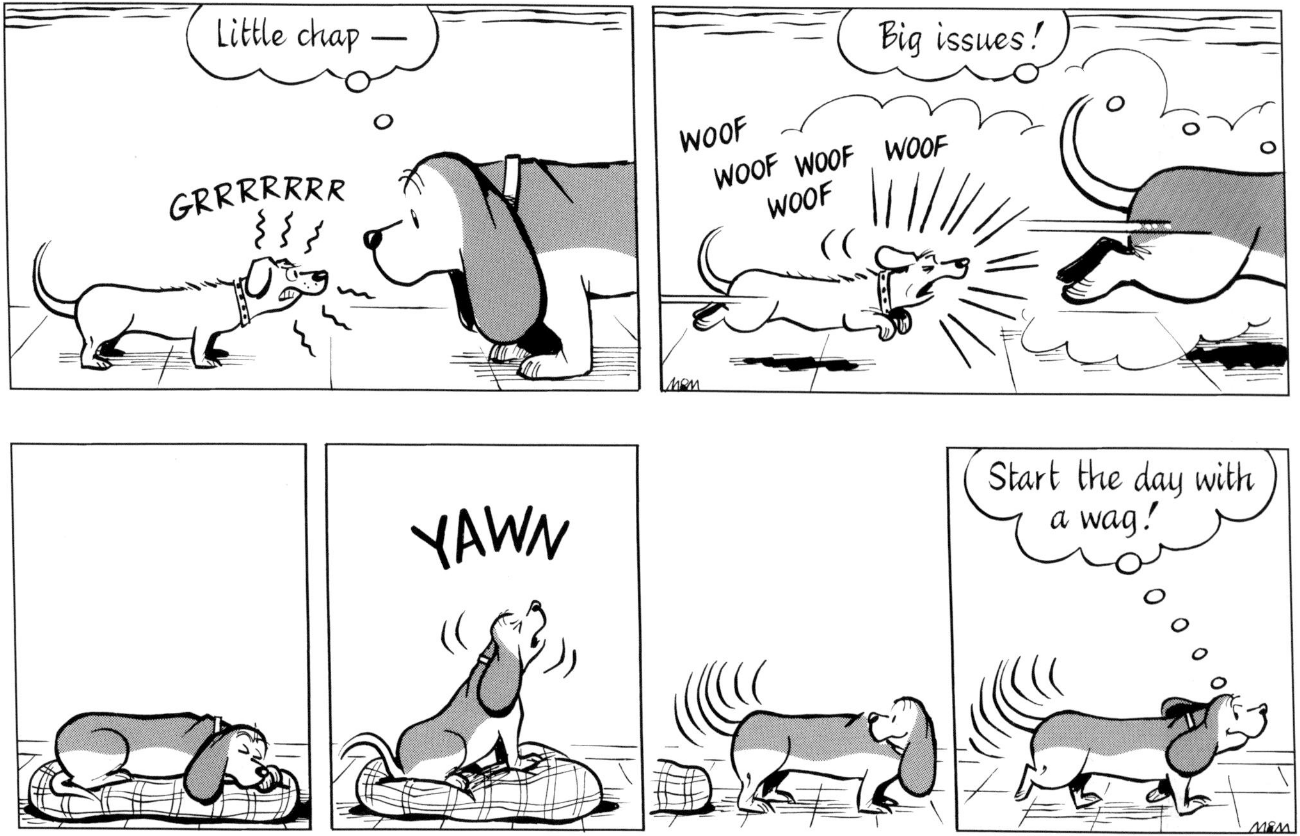
Little chap —
GRRRRRRR
Big issues!
WOOF
WOOF WOOF
WOOF
WOOF
YAWN
Start the day with a wag!
MBM

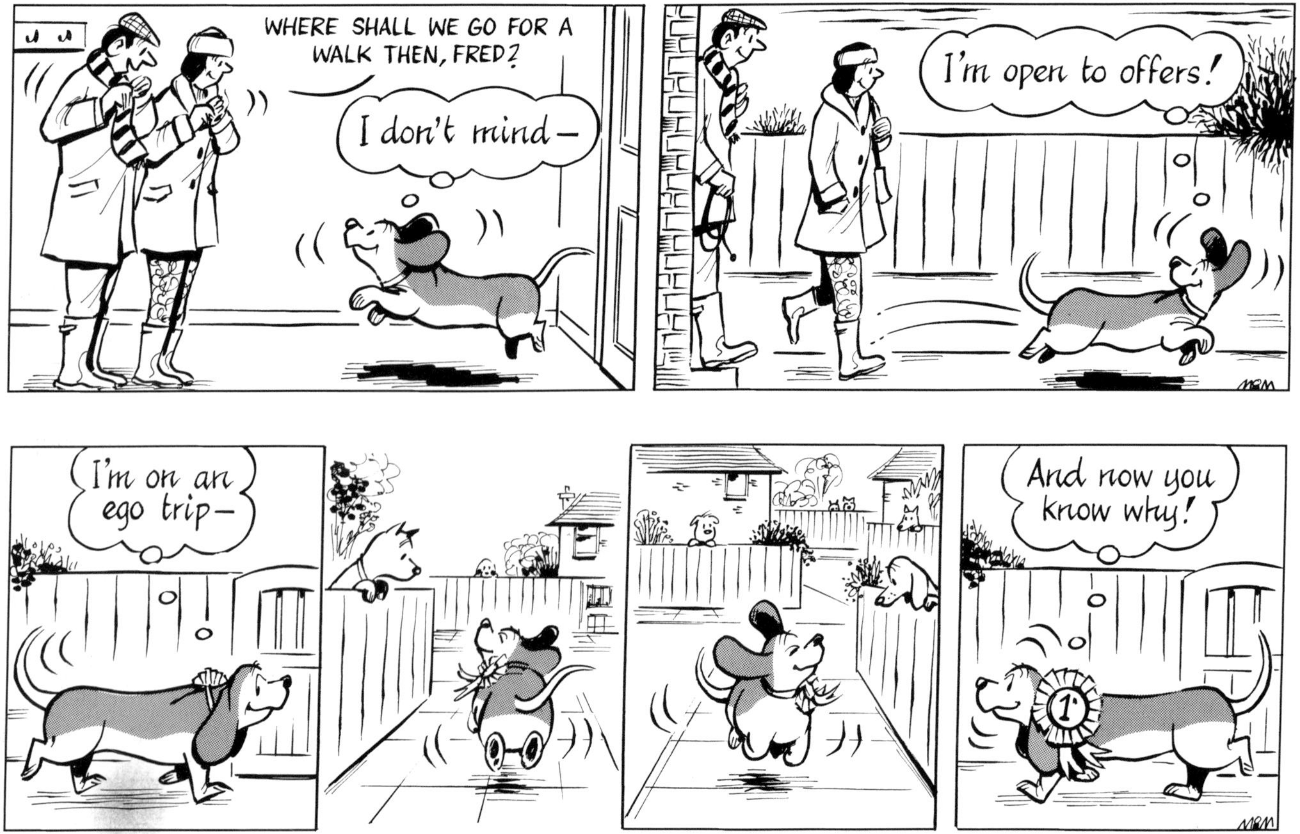
WHERE SHALL WE GO FOR A WALK THEN, FRED?
I don't mind–
I'm open to offers!
MBM
I'm on an ego trip–
And now you know why!
1st
MBM

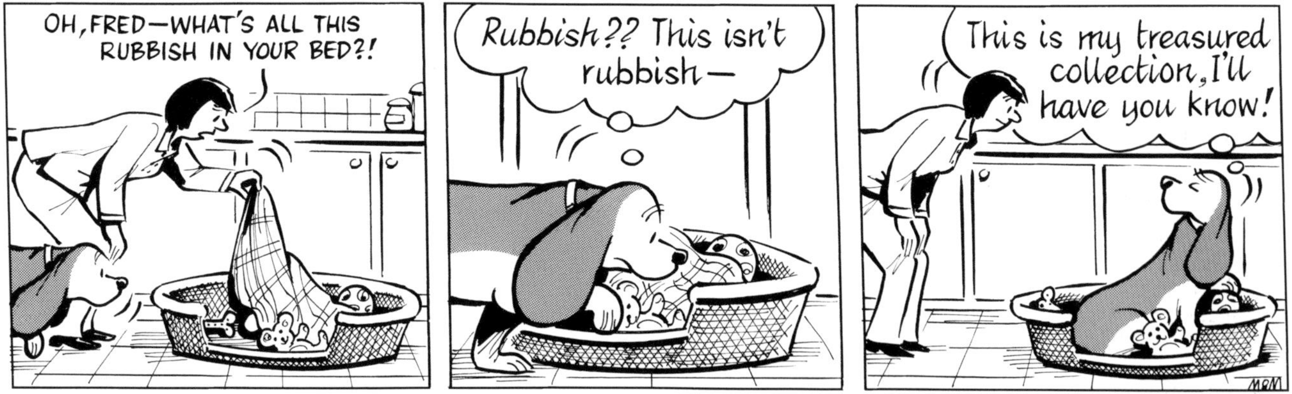
OH, FRED—WHAT'S ALL THIS RUBBISH IN YOUR BED?!
Rubbish?? This isn't rubbish—
This is my treasured collection, I'll have you know!

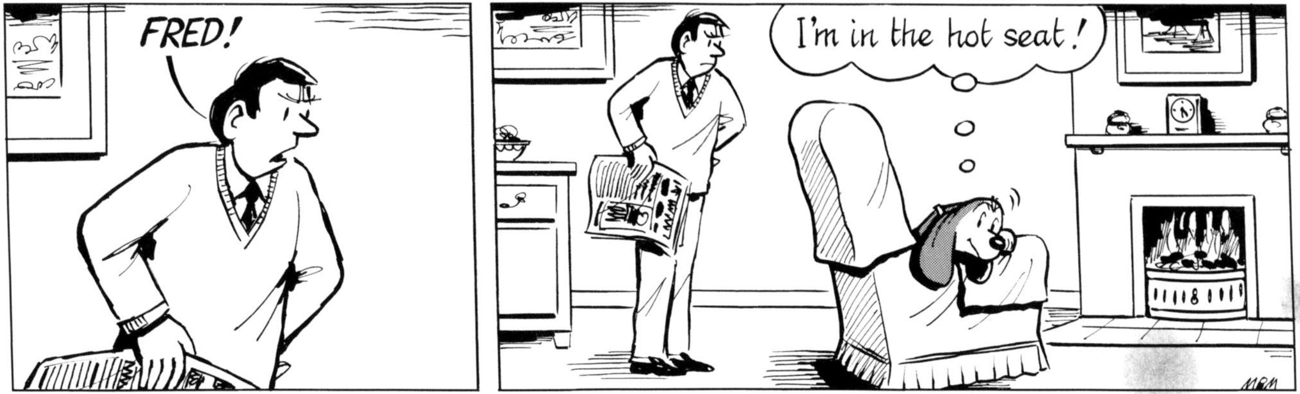
FRED!
I'm in the hot seat!

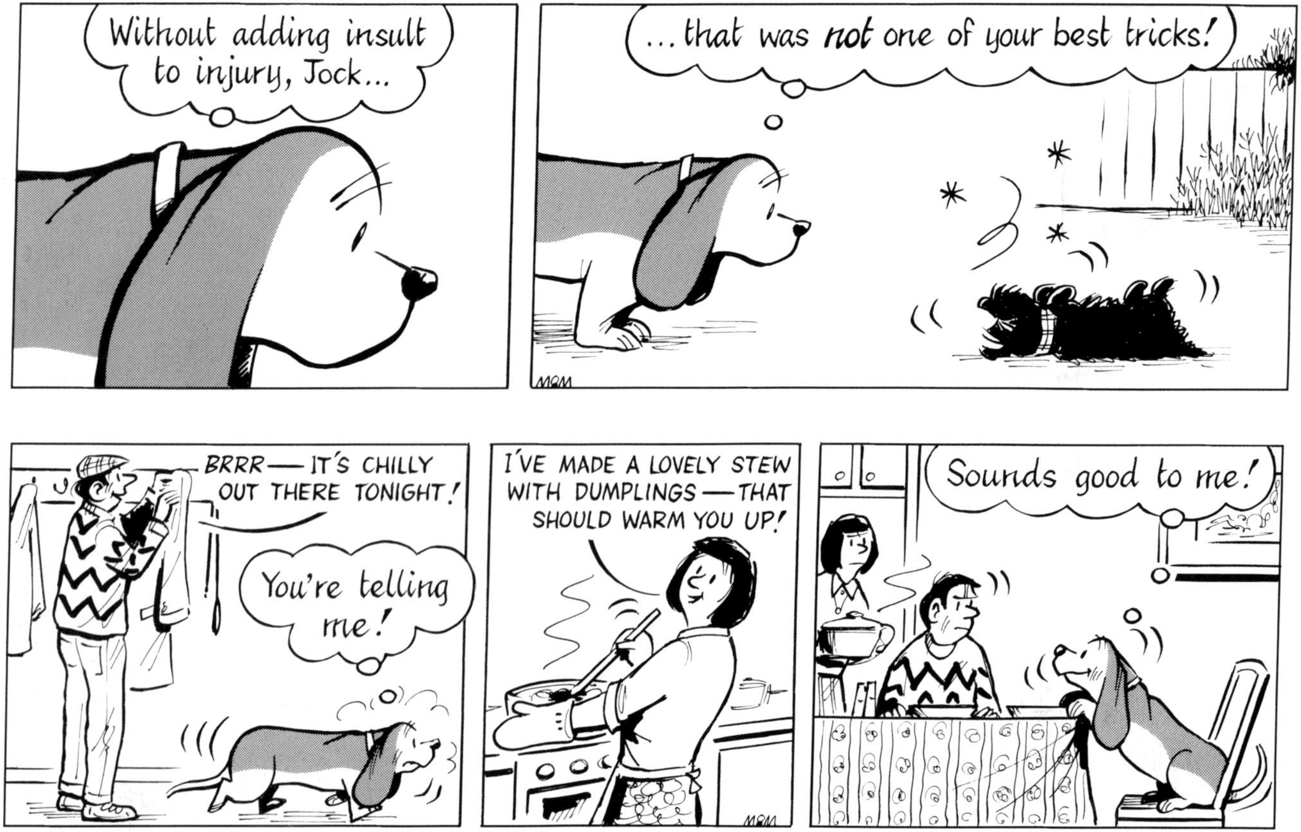
Without adding insult to injury, Jock...
...that was **not** one of your best tricks!
M&M
BRRR—IT'S CHILLY OUT THERE TONIGHT!
You're telling me!
I'VE MADE A LOVELY STEW WITH DUMPLINGS—THAT SHOULD WARM YOU UP!
M&M
Sounds good to me!

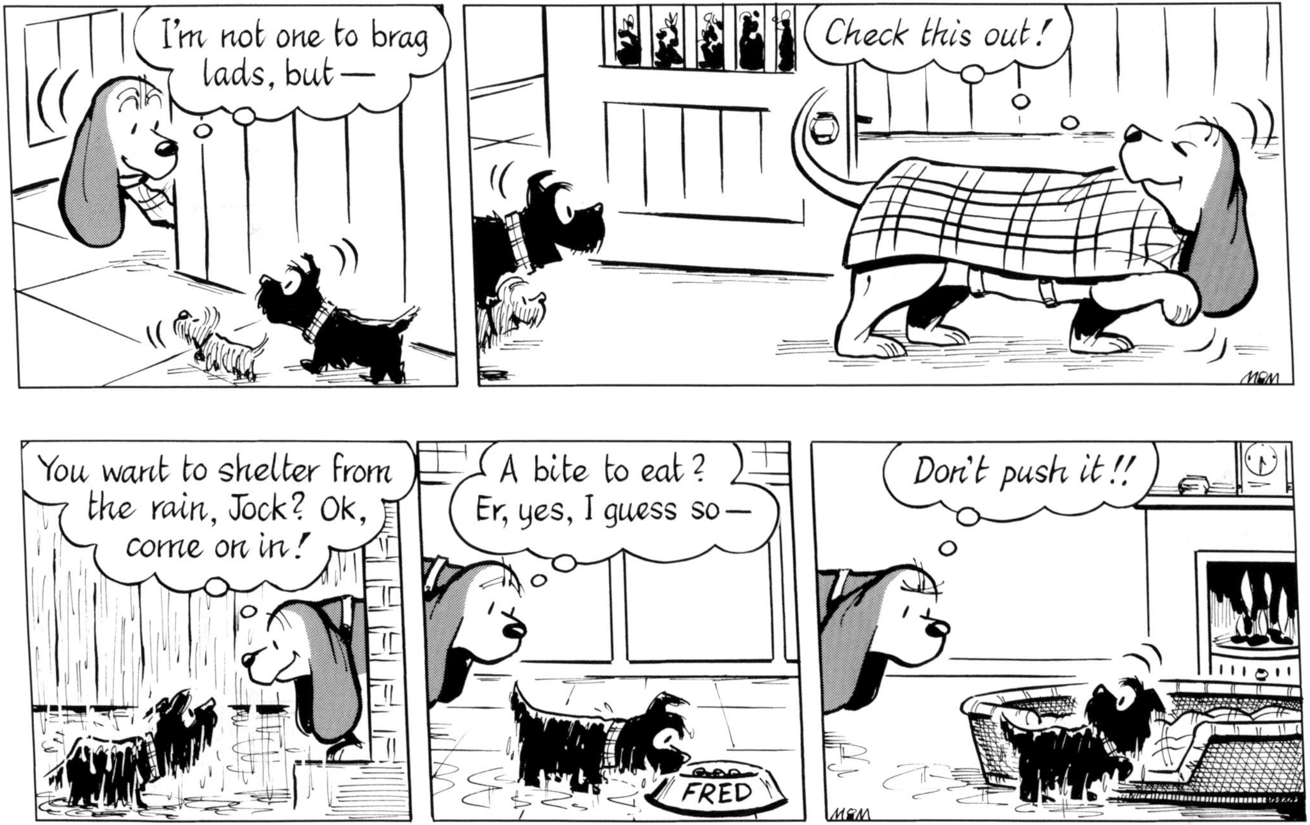
I'm not one to brag lads, but—
Check this out!
You want to shelter from the rain, Jock? Ok, come on in!
A bite to eat? Er, yes, I guess so—
FRED
Don't push it!!
MGM

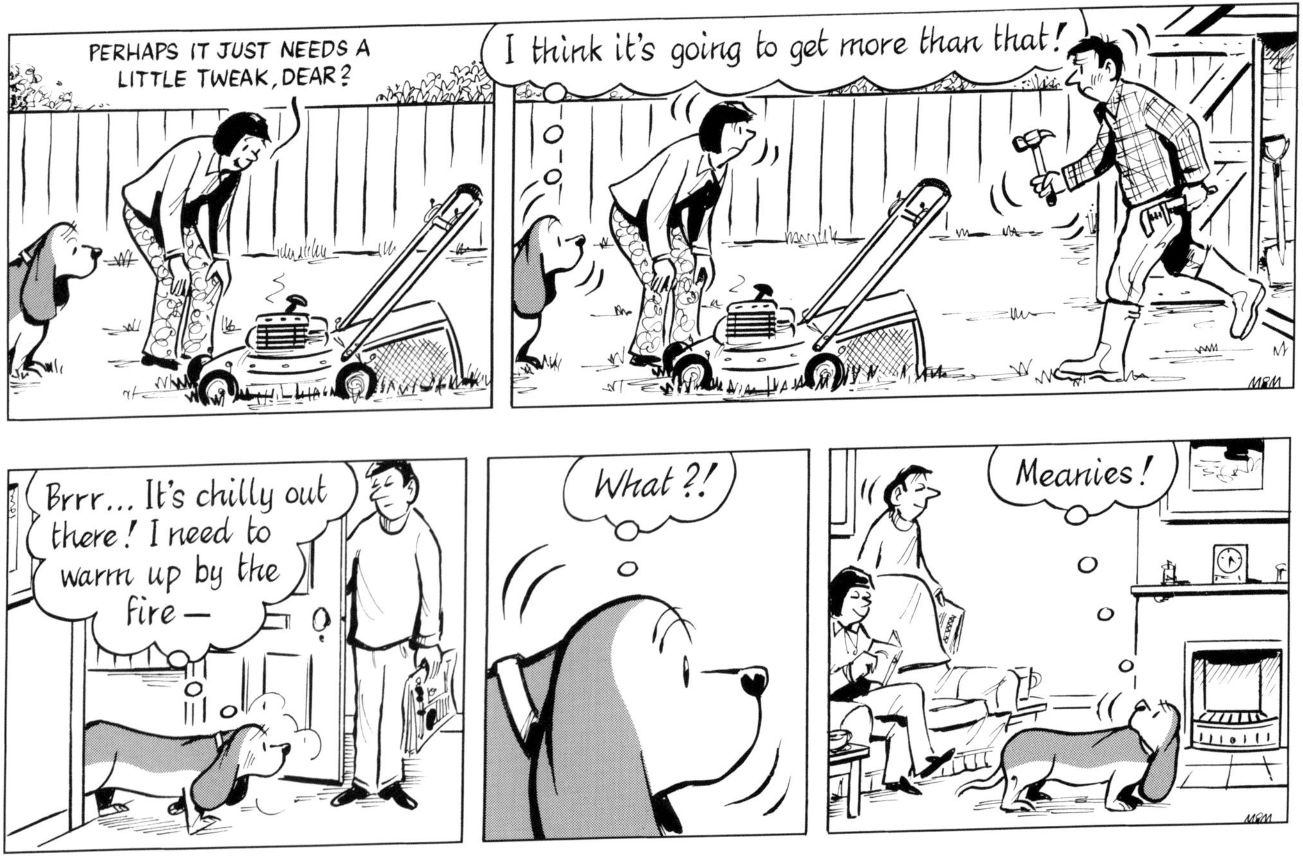
PERHAPS IT JUST NEEDS A LITTLE TWEAK, DEAR?
I think it's going to get more than that!
MGM
Brrr... It's chilly out there! I need to warm up by the fire—
What?!
Meanies!
MGM

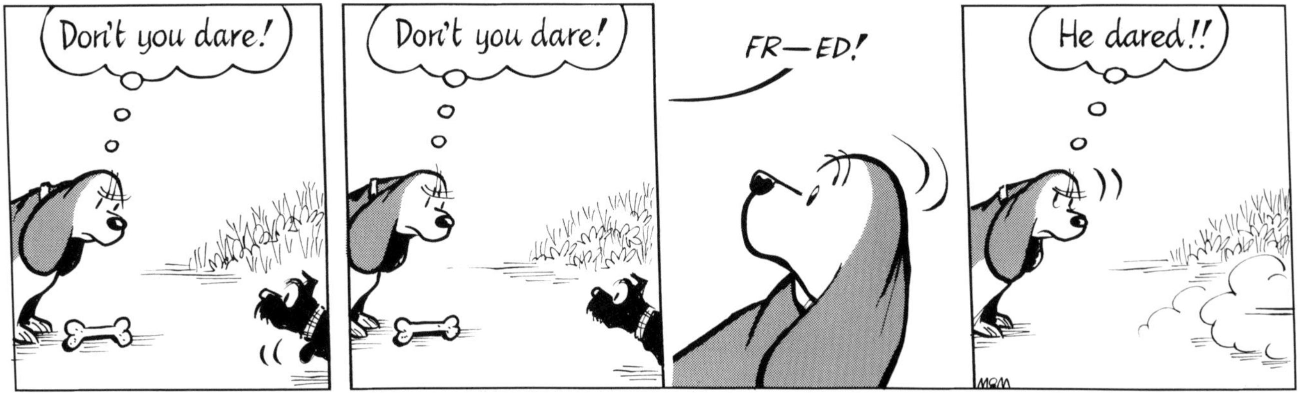
Don't you dare!
Don't you dare!
FR—ED!
He dared!!

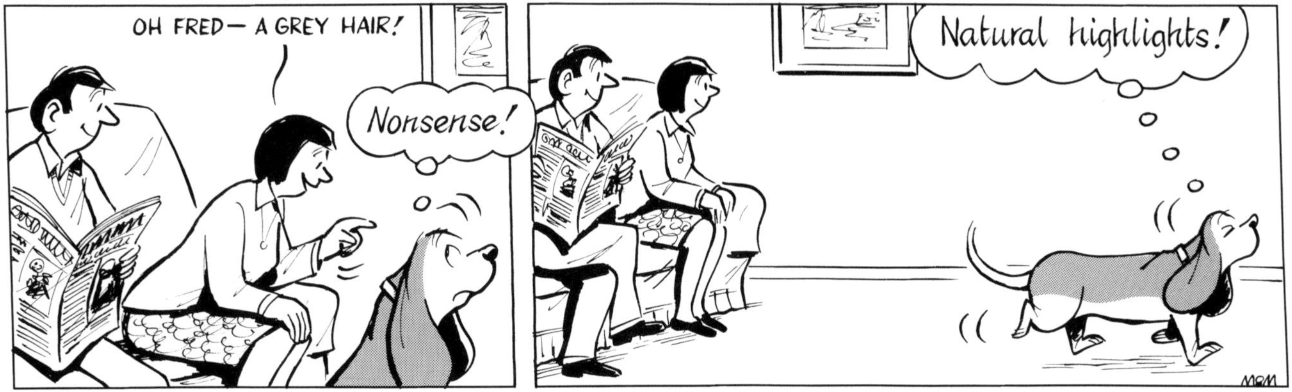
OH FRED— A GREY HAIR!
Nonsense!
Natural highlights!

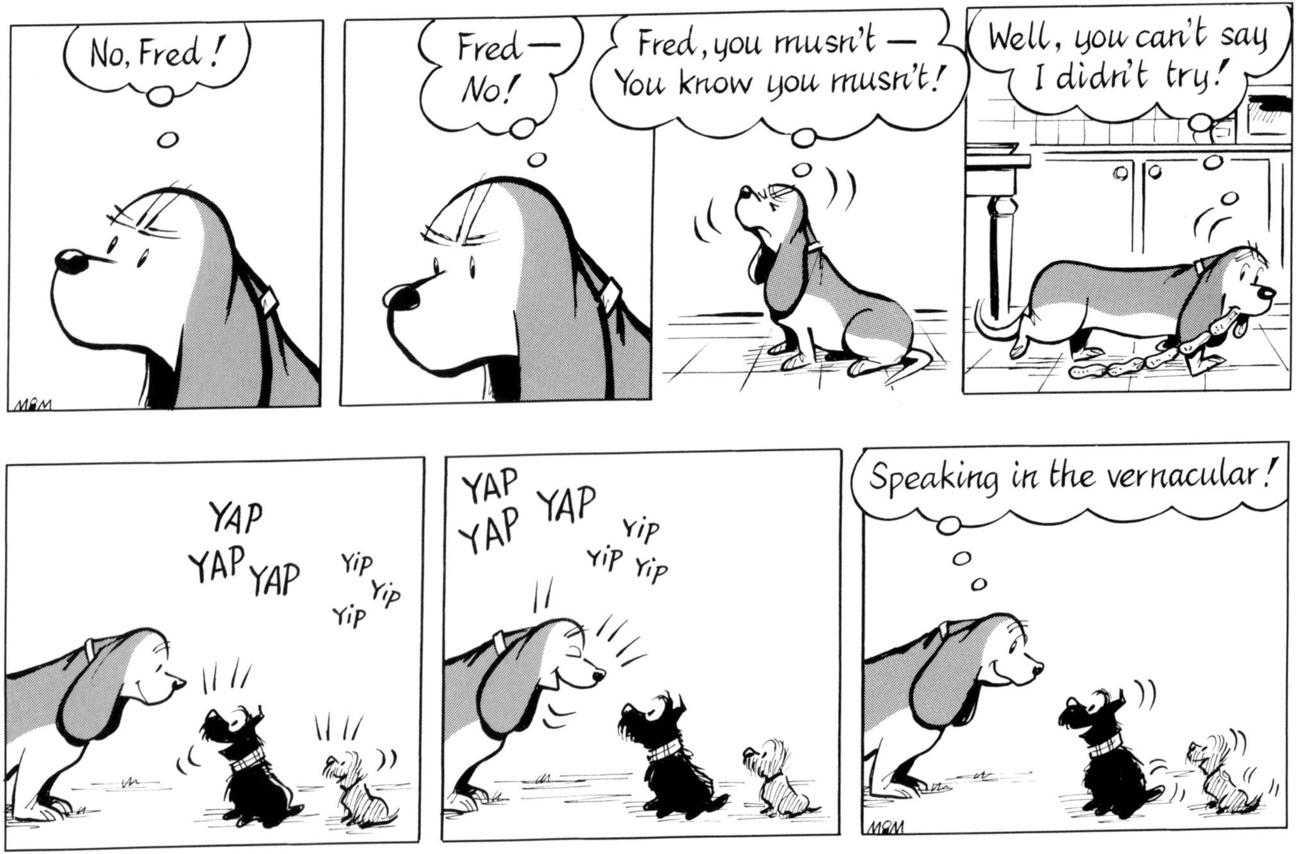
MBM
No, Fred!
Fred — No!
Fred, you mustn't — You know you mustn't!
Well, you can't say I didn't try!
YAP YAP YAP
Yip Yip Yip
YAP YAP YAP
Yip Yip Yip
Speaking in the vernacular!
MBM

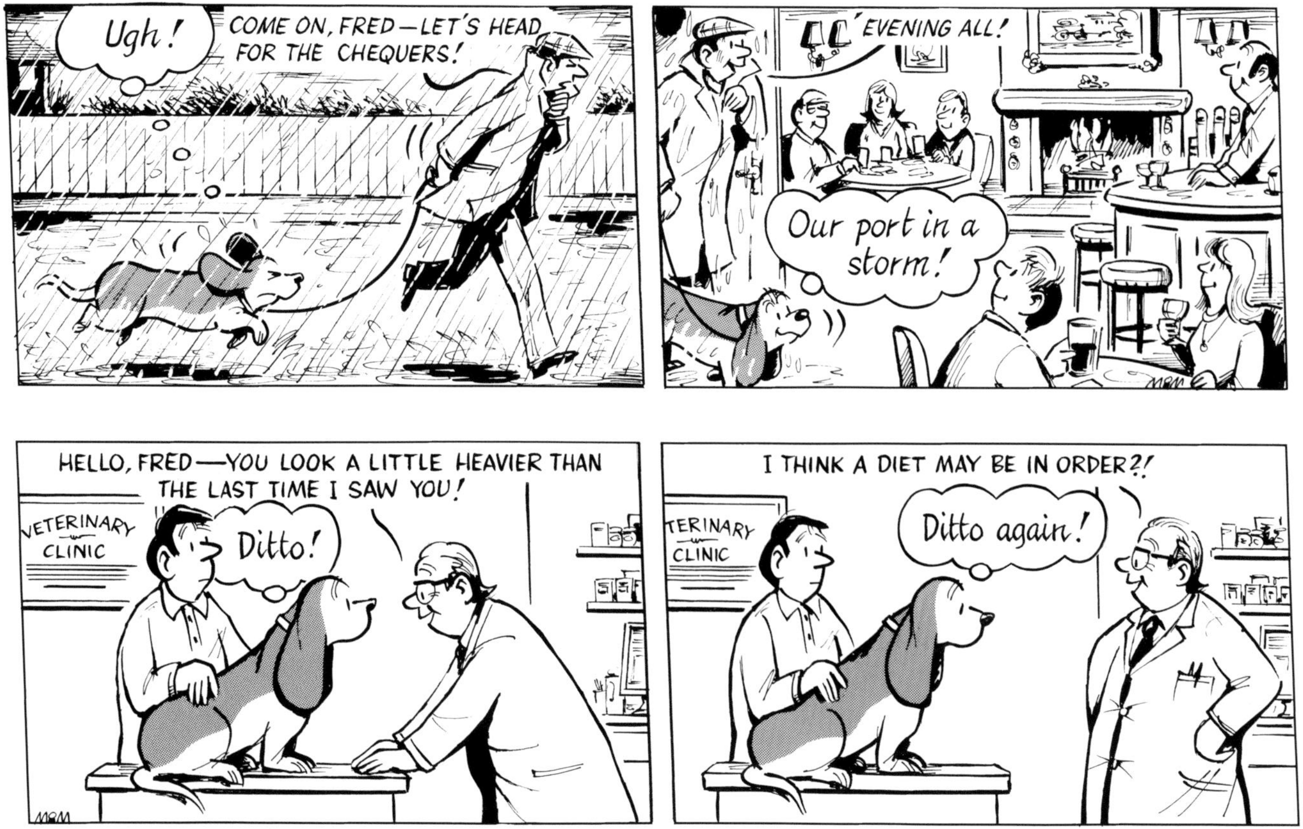
Ugh!
COME ON, FRED—LET'S HEAD FOR THE CHEQUERS!
'EVENING ALL!
Our port in a storm!
HELLO, FRED—YOU LOOK A LITTLE HEAVIER THAN THE LAST TIME I SAW YOU!
VETERINARY CLINIC
Ditto!
I THINK A DIET MAY BE IN ORDER?!
TERINARY CLINIC
Ditto again!

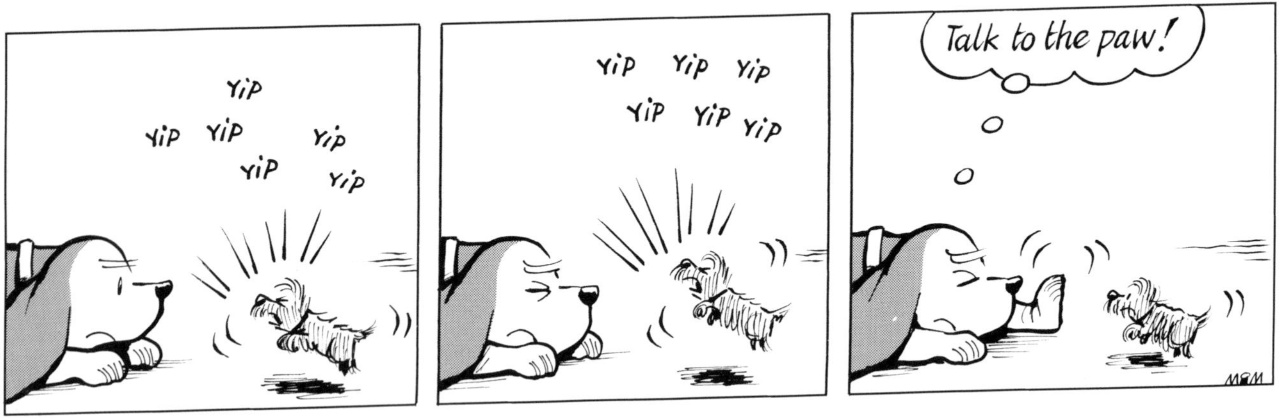
YIP
YIP YIP YIP
YIP YIP
YIP YIP YIP
YIP YIP YIP
Talk to the paw!
M&M

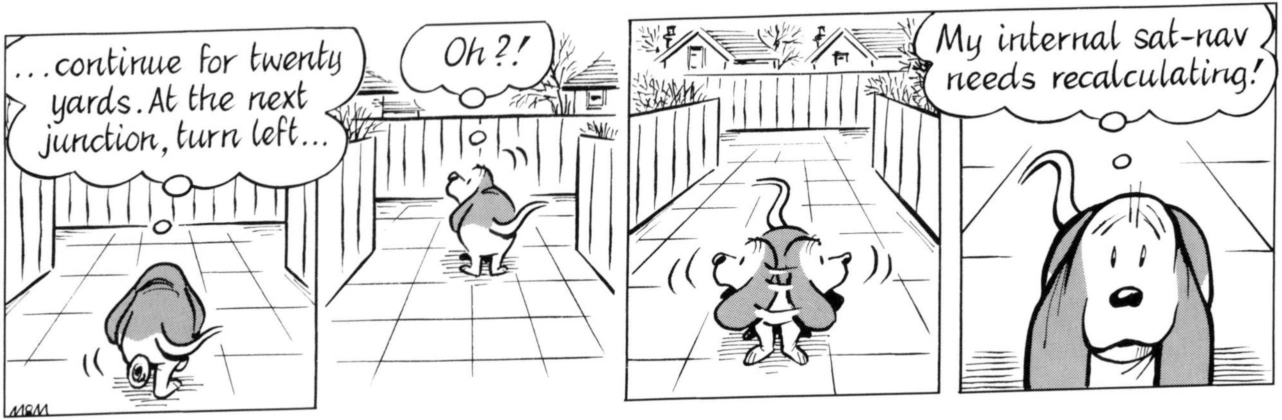
...continue for twenty yards. At the next junction, turn left...
M&M
Oh?!
My internal sat-nav needs recalculating!

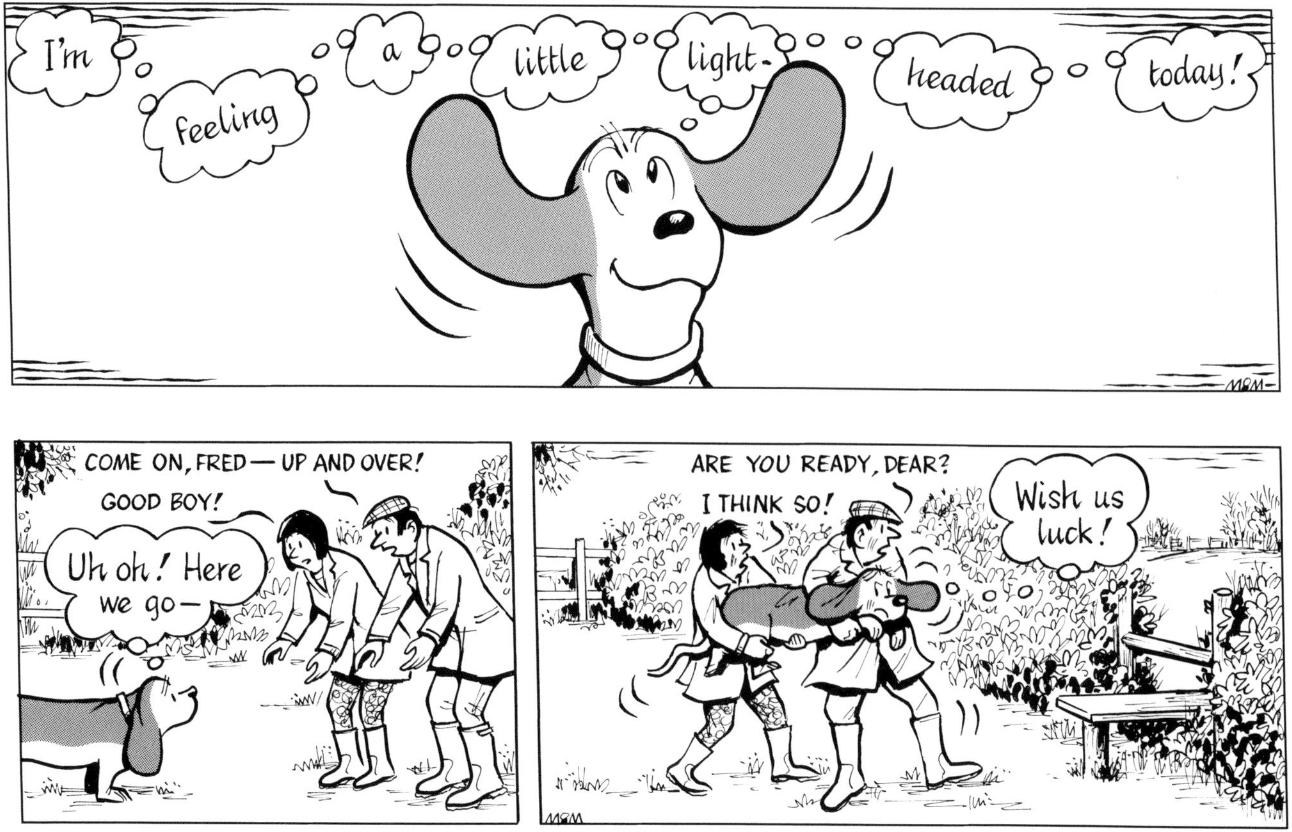
I'm feeling a little light-headed today!
MSM
COME ON, FRED — UP AND OVER!
GOOD BOY!
Uh oh! Here we go—
MSM
ARE YOU READY, DEAR?
I THINK SO!
Wish us luck!

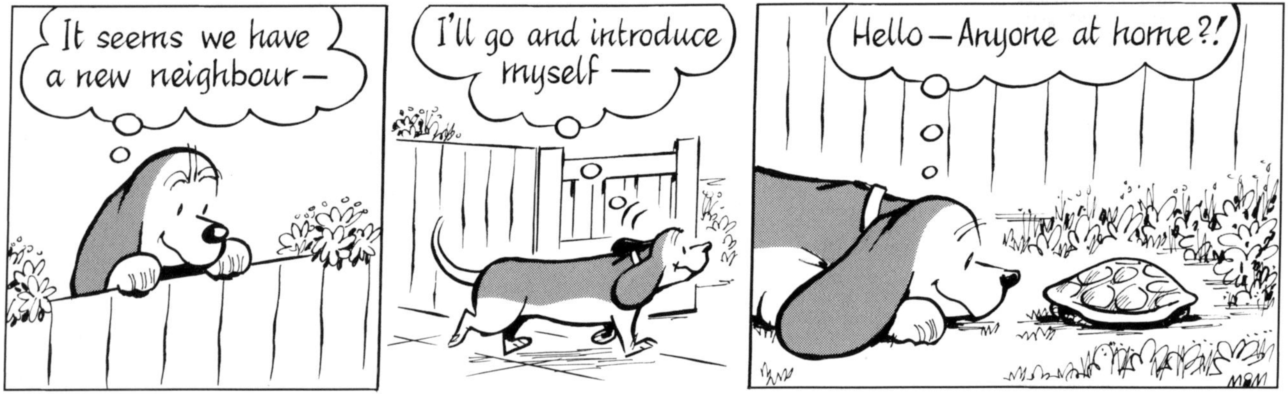
It seems we have a new neighbour –
I'll go and introduce myself —
Hello – Anyone at home?!
MBM

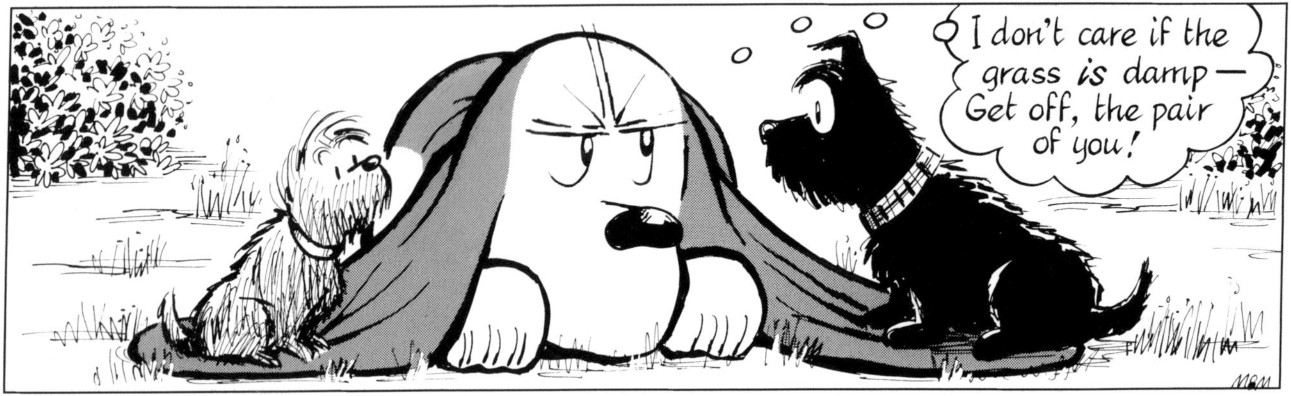
I don't care if the grass *is* damp – Get off, the pair of you!
MBM

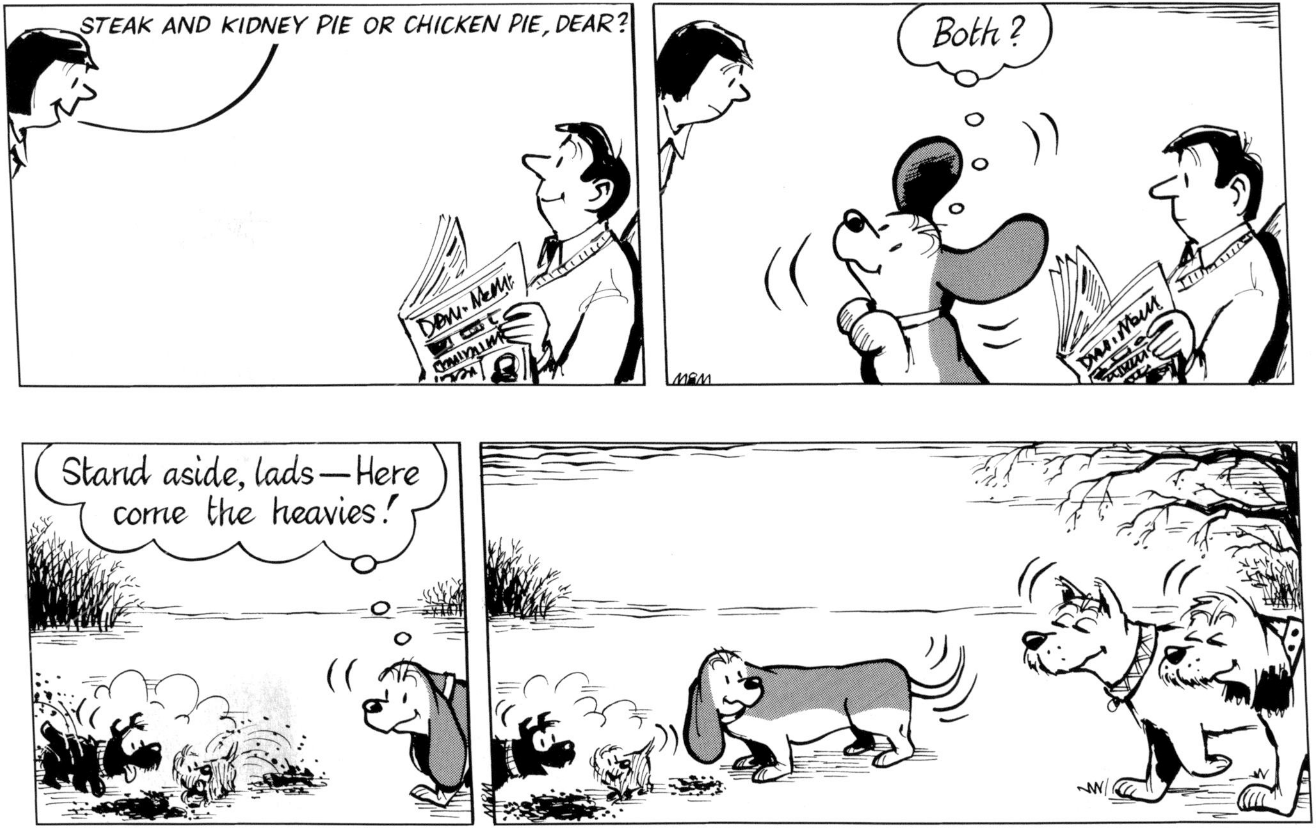
STEAK AND KIDNEY PIE OR CHICKEN PIE, DEAR?
Both?
Stand aside, lads—Here come the heavies!

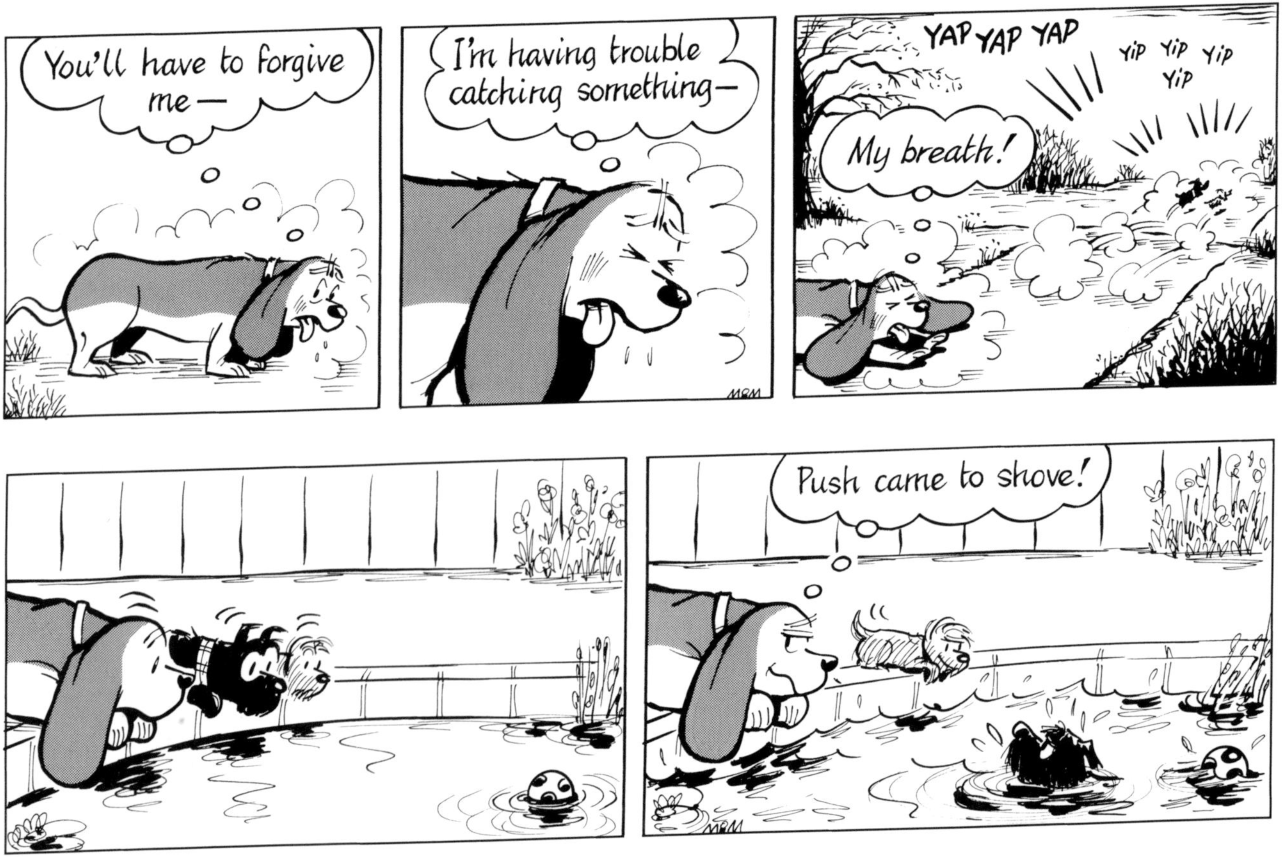
You'll have to forgive me—
I'm having trouble catching something—
YAP YAP YAP
Yip Yip Yip Yip
My breath!
Push came to shove!

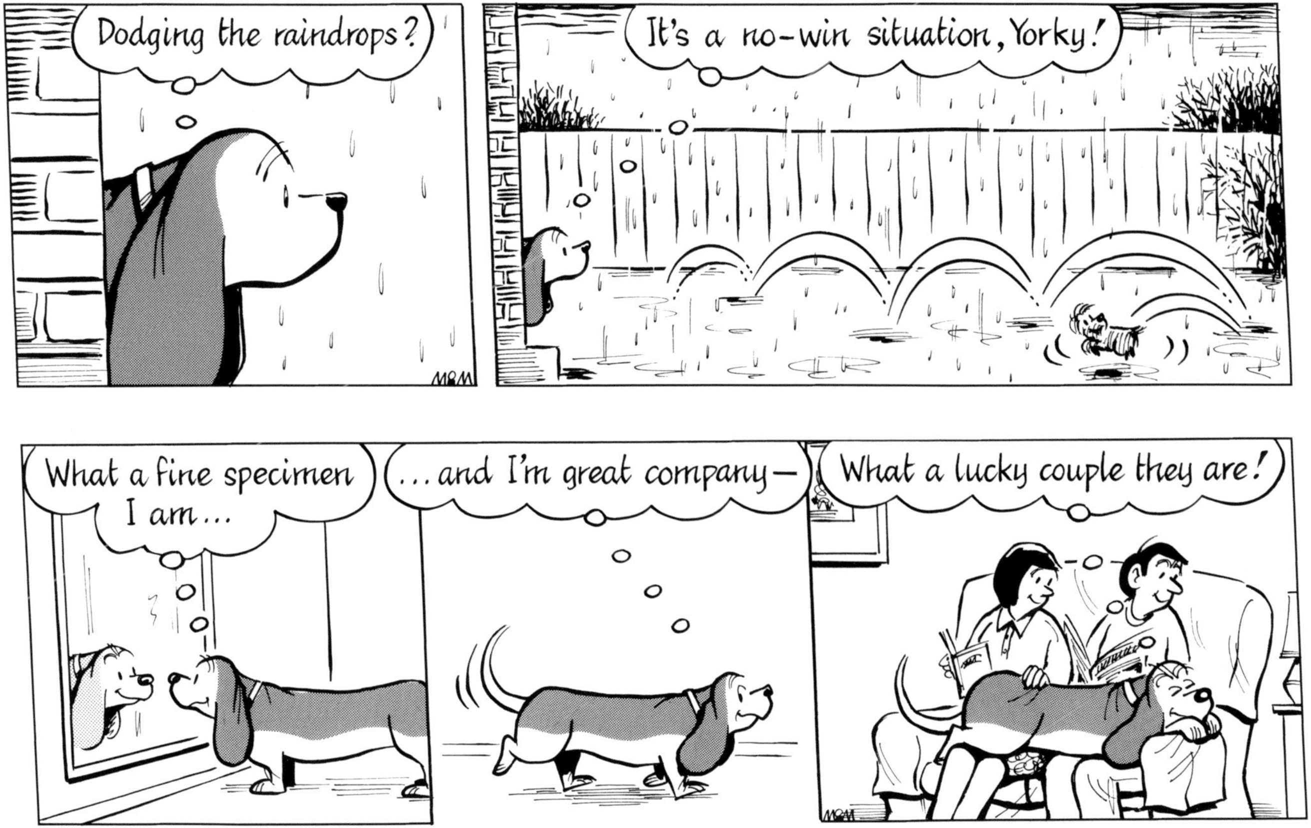

Dodging the raindrops?
It's a no-win situation, Yorky!
What a fine specimen I am...
...and I'm great company—
What a lucky couple they are!
MGM

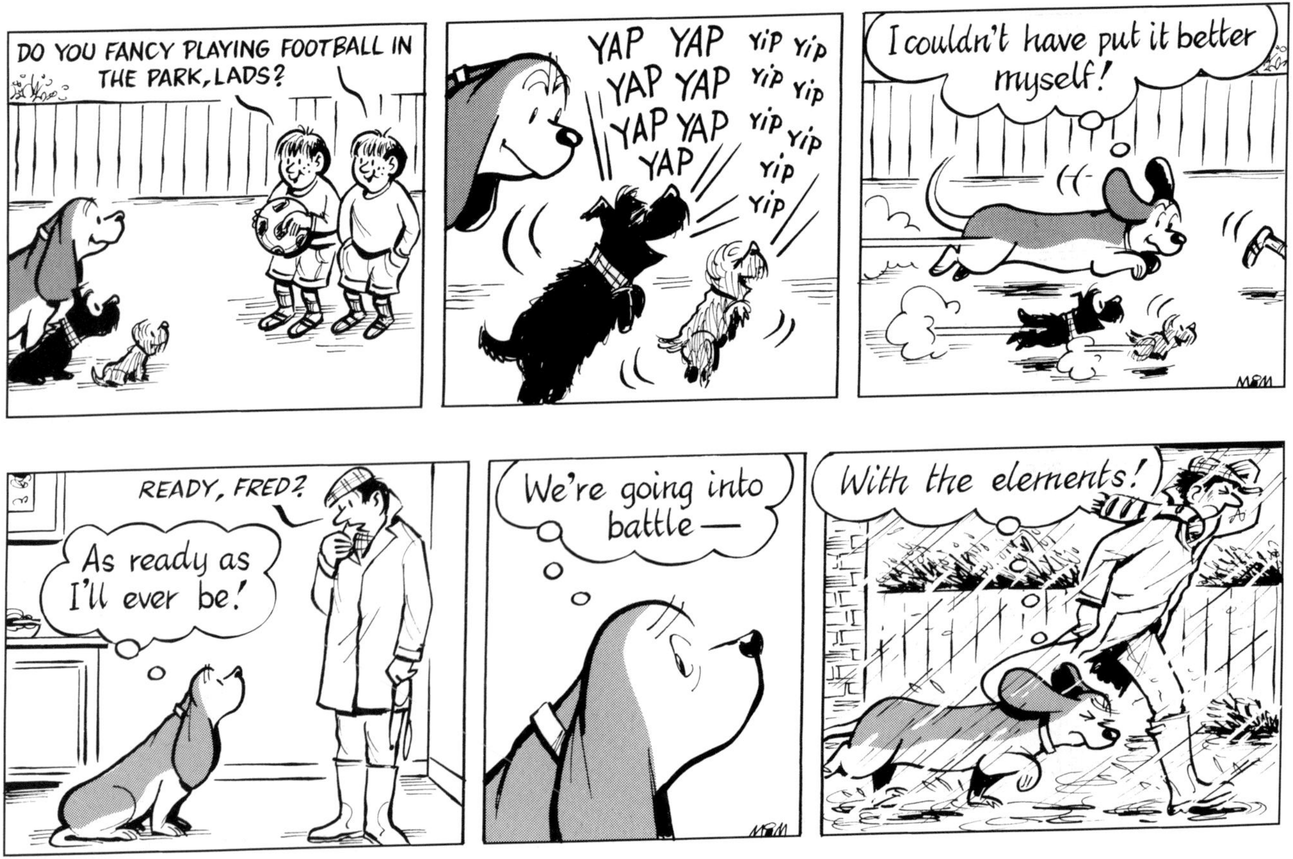
DO YOU FANCY PLAYING FOOTBALL IN THE PARK, LADS?
YAP YAP YAP YAP YAP YAP YAP
YIP YIP YIP YIP YIP YIP YIP YIP
I couldn't have put it better myself!
MSM
READY, FRED?
As ready as I'll ever be!
We're going into battle —
MSM
With the elements!

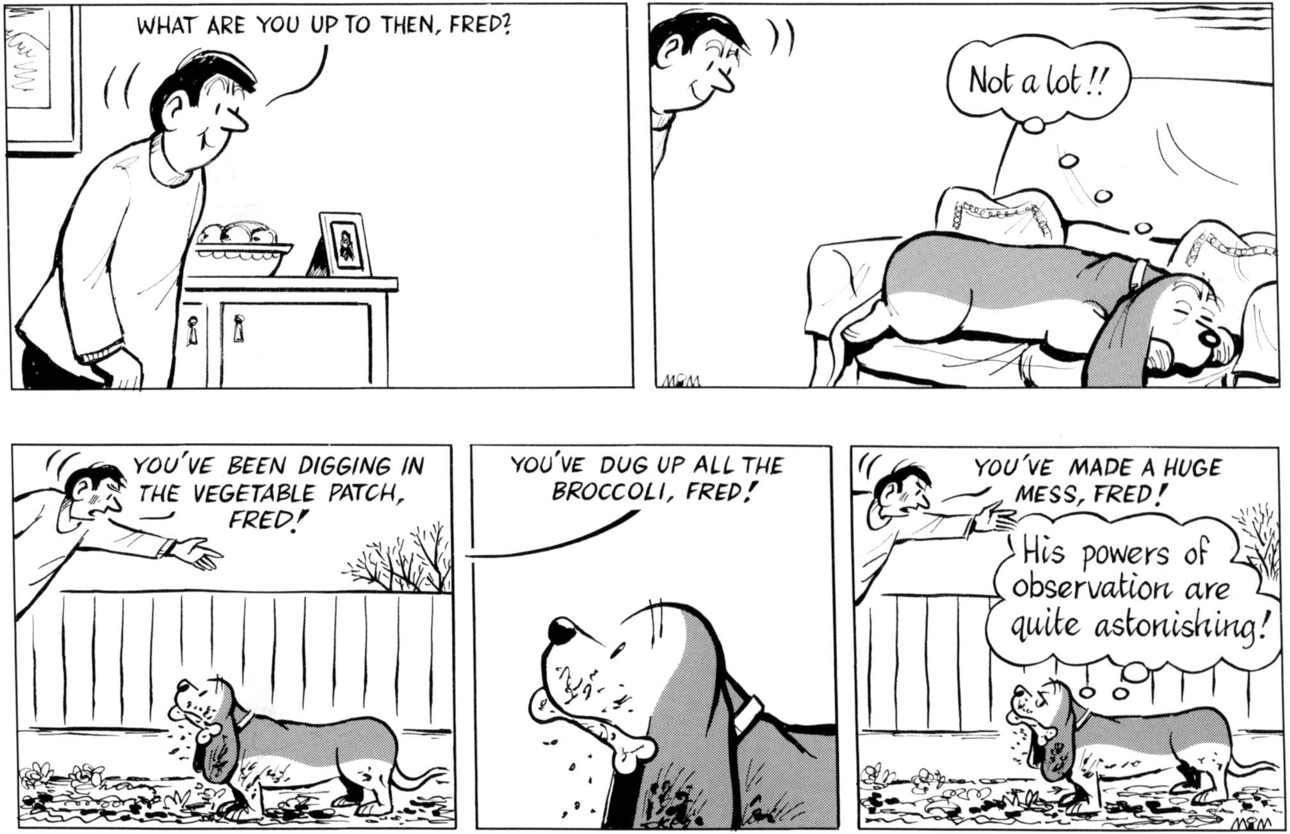

WHAT ARE YOU UP TO THEN, FRED?
Not a lot!!
YOU'VE BEEN DIGGING IN THE VEGETABLE PATCH, FRED!
YOU'VE DUG UP ALL THE BROCCOLI, FRED!
YOU'VE MADE A HUGE MESS, FRED!
His powers of observation are quite astonishing!

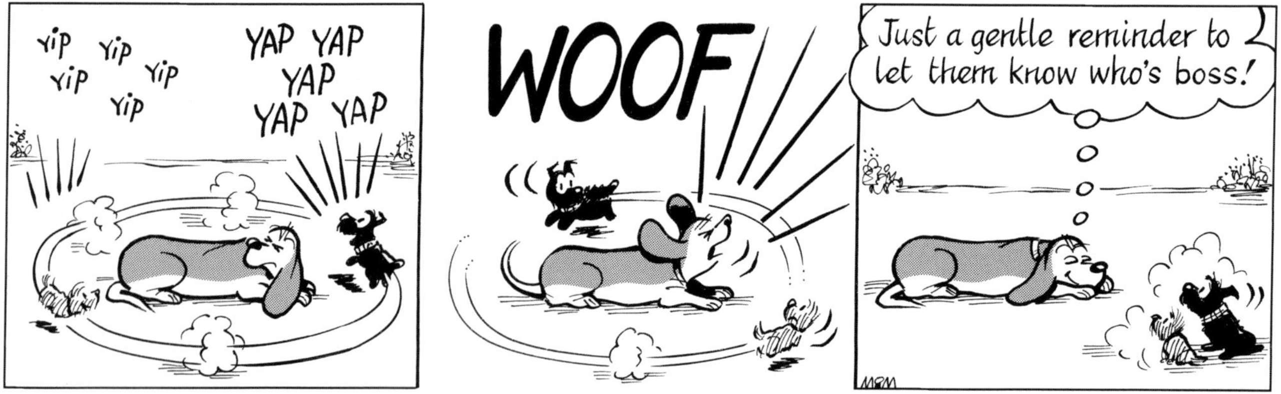
YIP YIP YIP YIP YIP
YAP YAP YAP YAP YAP
WOOF
Just a gentle reminder to let them know who's boss!

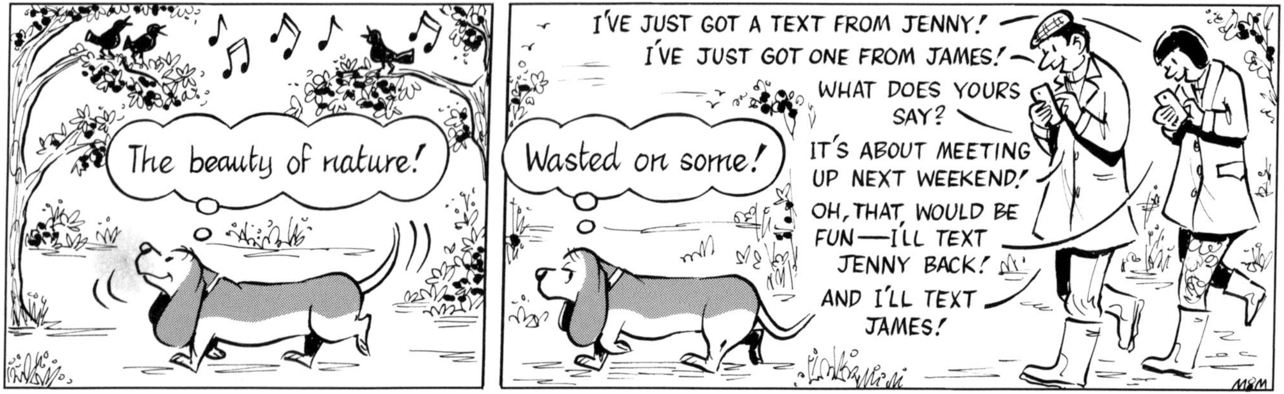
The beauty of nature!
Wasted on some!
I'VE JUST GOT A TEXT FROM JENNY!
I'VE JUST GOT ONE FROM JAMES!
WHAT DOES YOURS SAY?
IT'S ABOUT MEETING UP NEXT WEEKEND!
OH, THAT WOULD BE FUN—I'LL TEXT JENNY BACK!
AND I'LL TEXT JAMES!

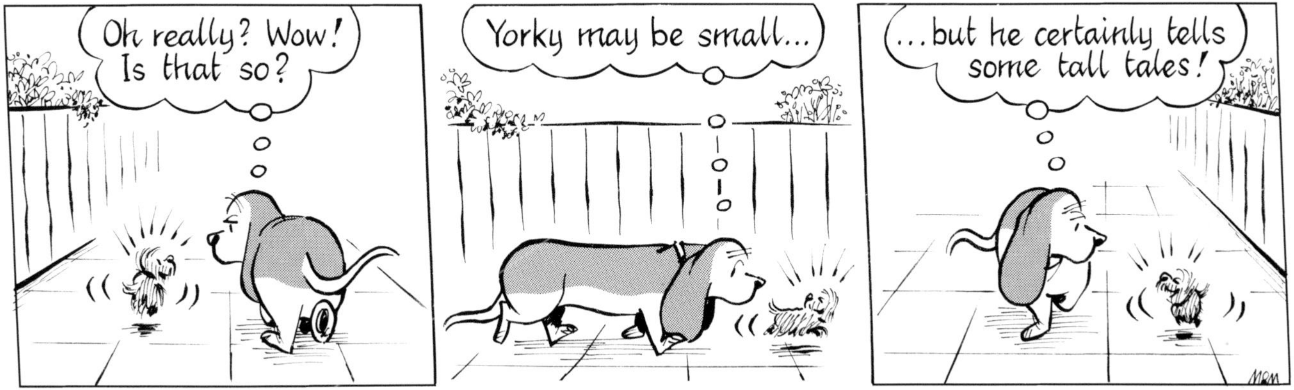
Oh really? Wow! Is that so?
Yorky may be small...
...but he certainly tells some tall tales!
MGM

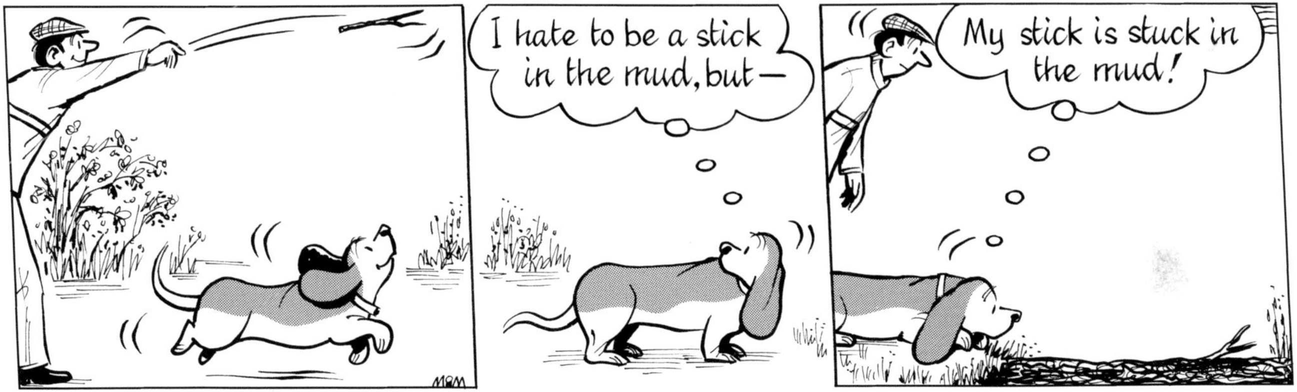
MGM
I hate to be a stick in the mud, but—
My stick is stuck in the mud!

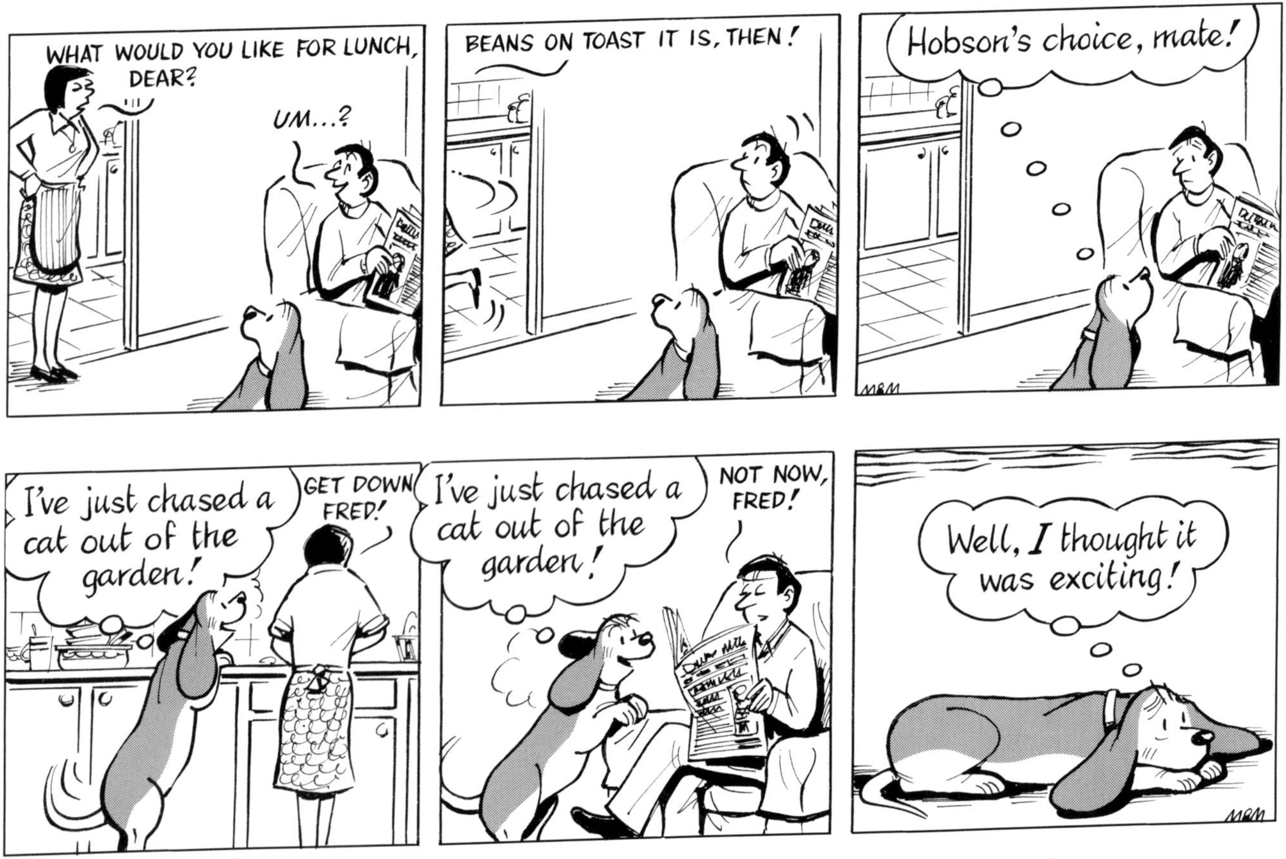
WHAT WOULD YOU LIKE FOR LUNCH, DEAR?
UM...?
BEANS ON TOAST IT IS, THEN!
Hobson's choice, mate!
MBM
I've just chased a cat out of the garden!
GET DOWN FRED!
I've just chased a cat out of the garden!
NOT NOW, FRED!
Well, *I* thought it was exciting!
MBM

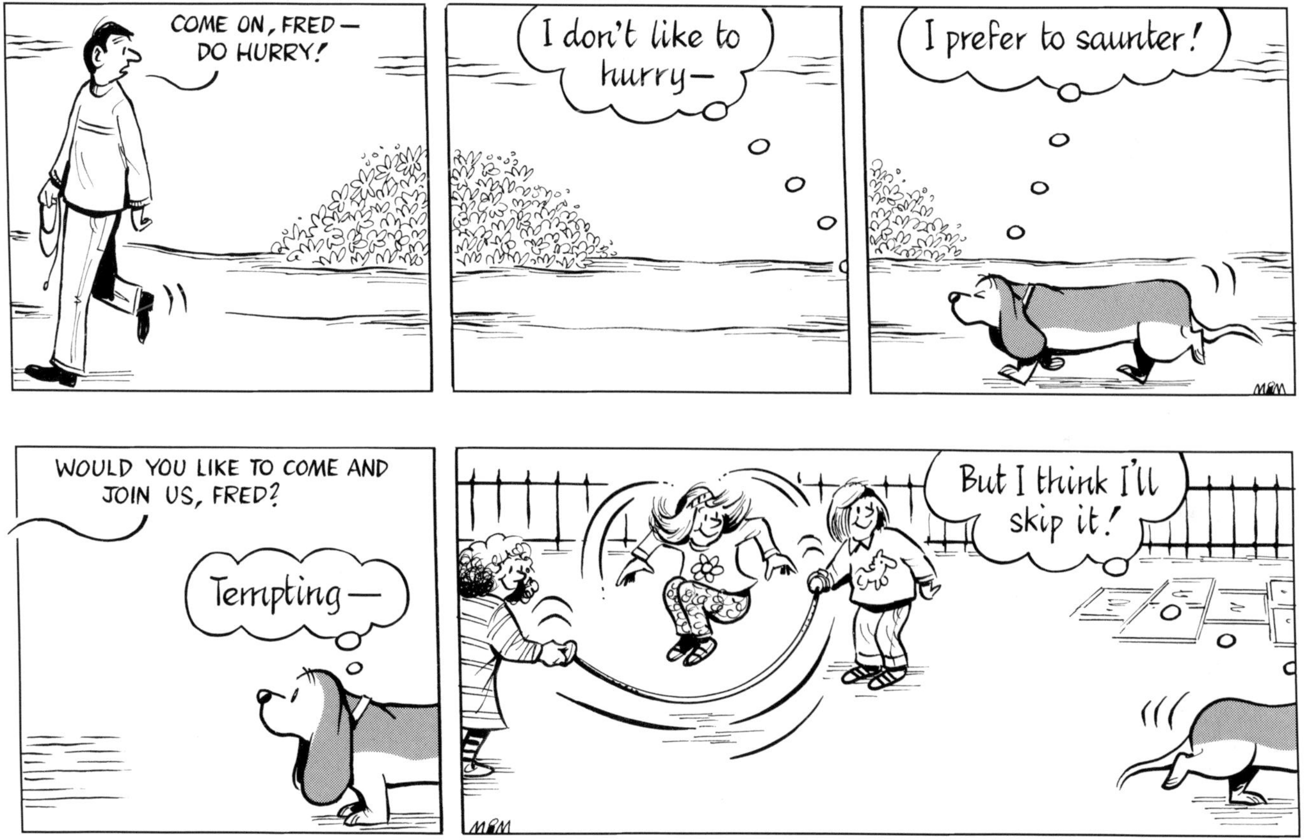
COME ON, FRED — DO HURRY!
I don't like to hurry —
I prefer to saunter!
MBM
WOULD YOU LIKE TO COME AND JOIN US, FRED?
Tempting —
But I think I'll skip it!
MBM

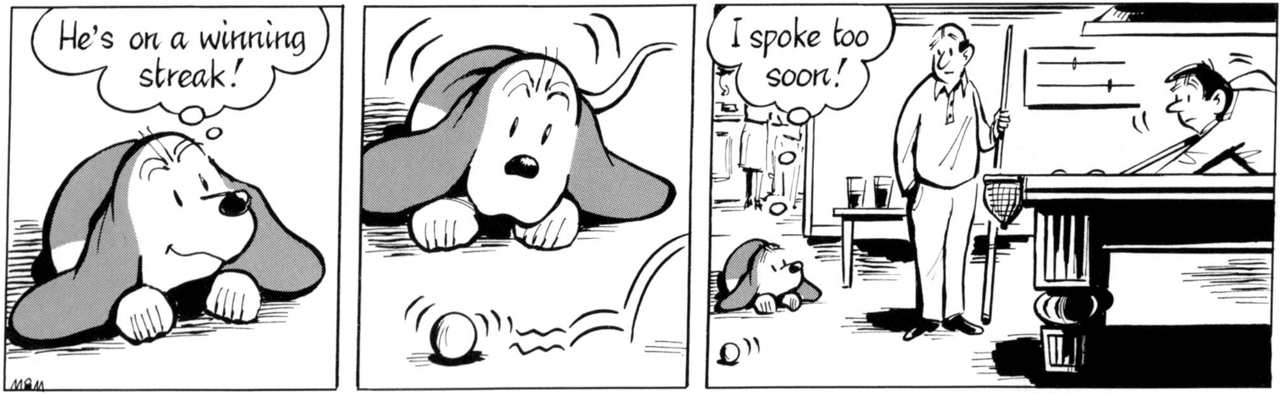
He's on a winning streak!
I spoke too soon!
M&M

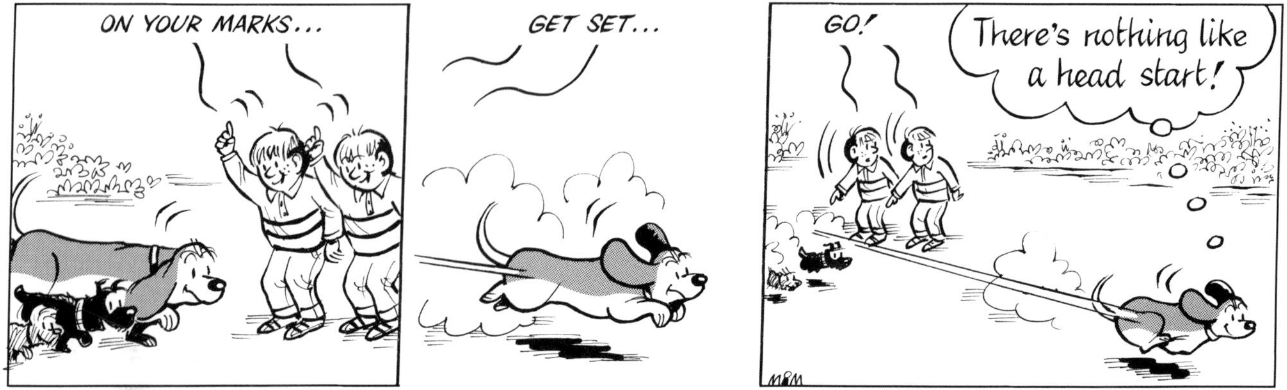
ON YOUR MARKS...
GET SET...
GO!
There's nothing like a head start!
M&M

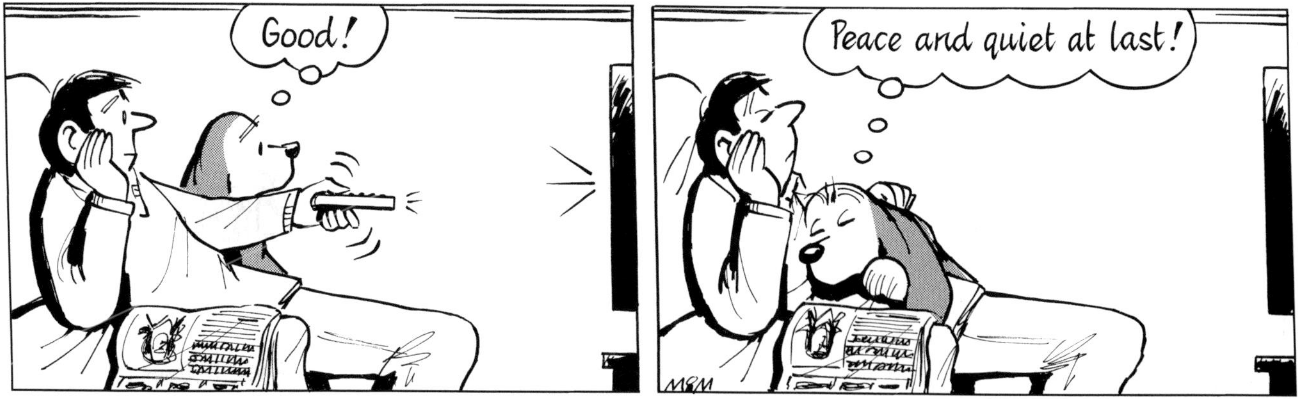
Good!
Peace and quiet at last!
M&M

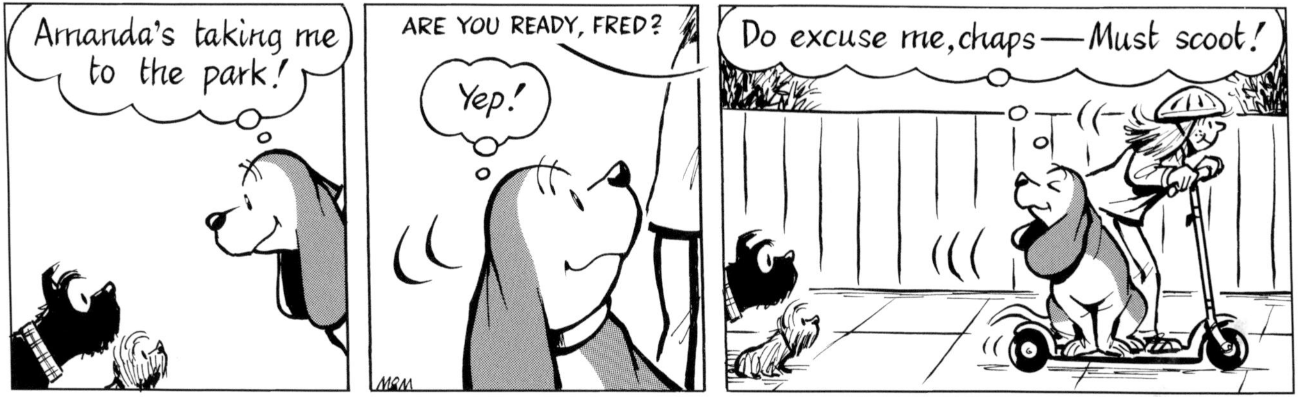
Amanda's taking me to the park!
ARE YOU READY, FRED?
Yep!
M&M
Do excuse me, chaps — Must scoot!

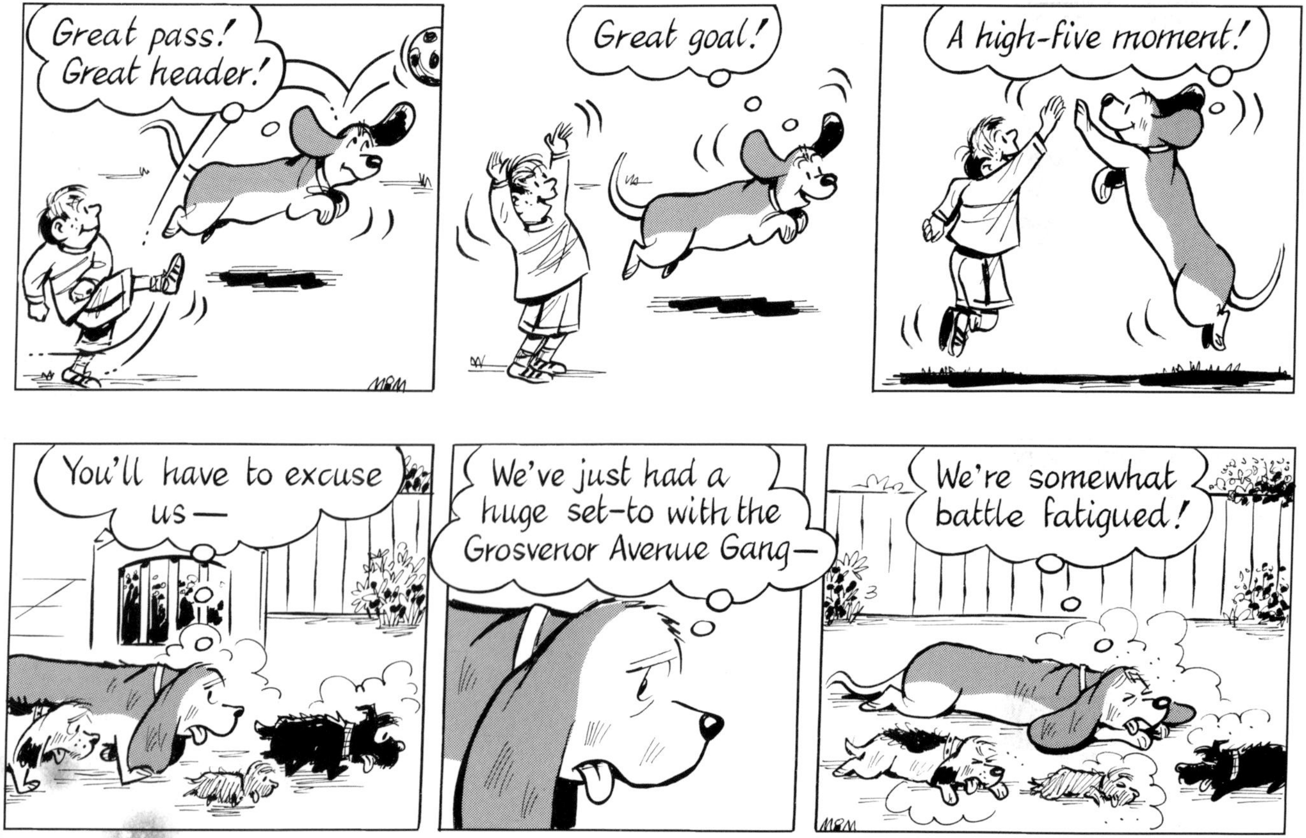
Great pass! Great header!
Great goal!
A high-five moment!
You'll have to excuse us—
We've just had a huge set-to with the Grosvenor Avenue Gang—
We're somewhat battle fatigued!

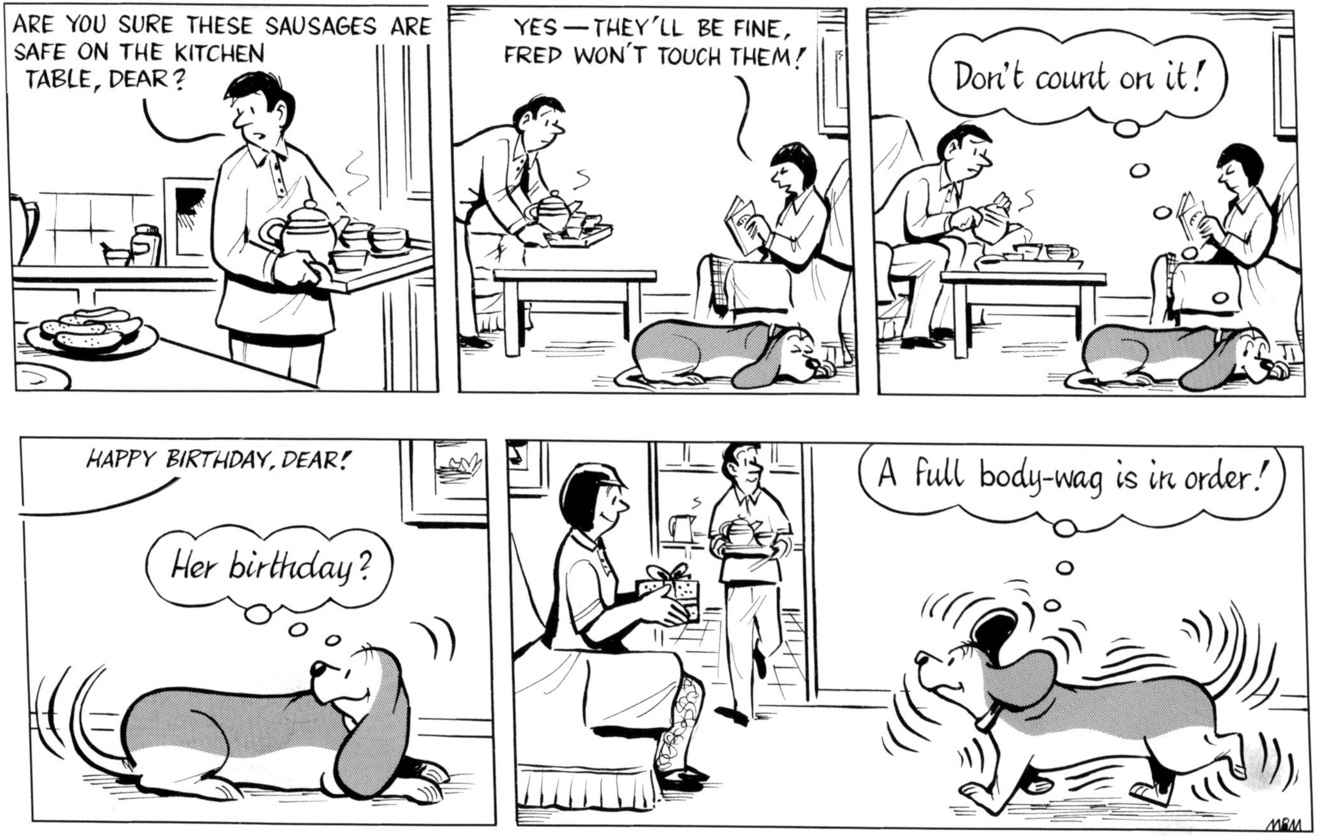
ARE YOU SURE THESE SAUSAGES ARE SAFE ON THE KITCHEN TABLE, DEAR?
YES — THEY'LL BE FINE, FRED WON'T TOUCH THEM!
Don't count on it!
HAPPY BIRTHDAY, DEAR!
Her birthday?
A full body-wag is in order!
MBM

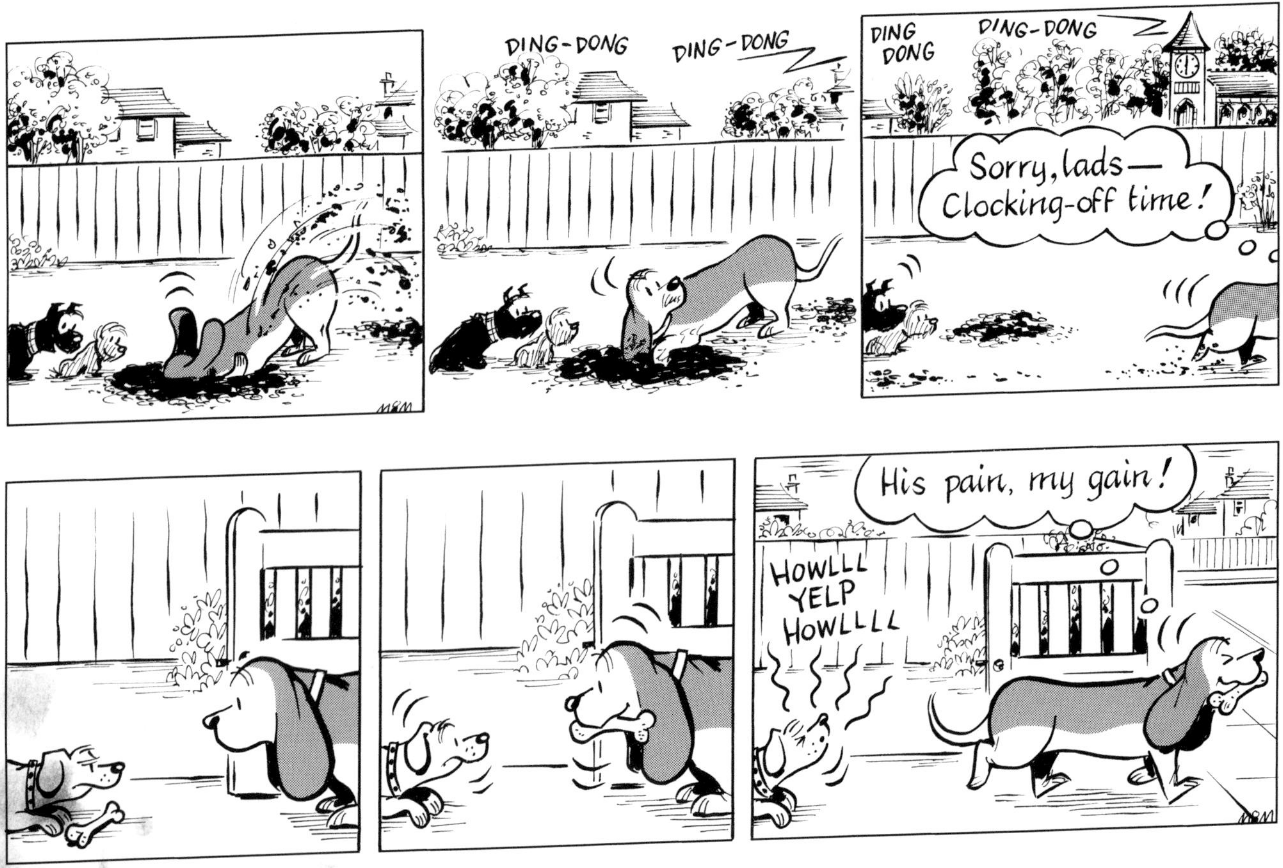
DING-DONG
DING-DONG
DING
DONG
DING-DONG
Sorry, lads—
Clocking-off time!
HOWLLL
YELP
HOWLLLL
His pain, my gain!

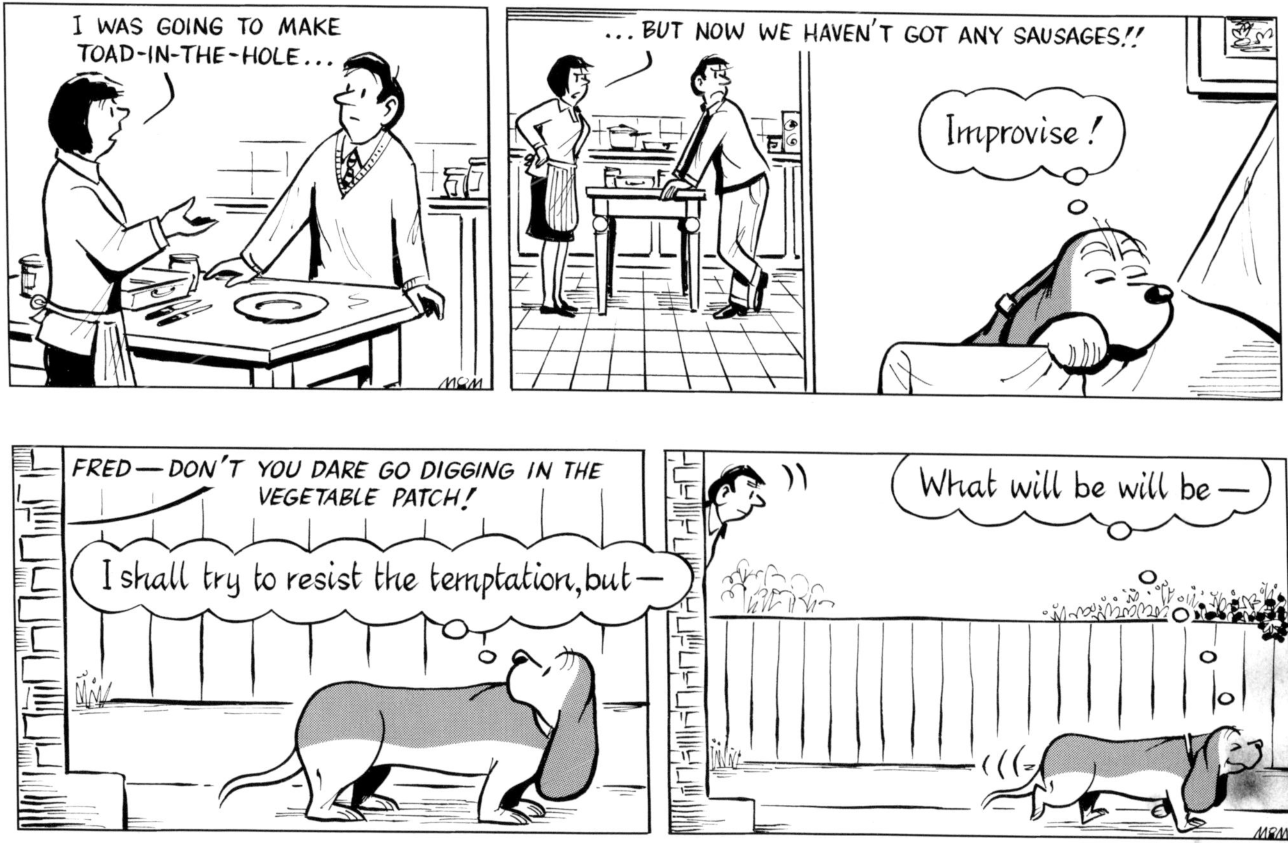

I WAS GOING TO MAKE TOAD-IN-THE-HOLE...
... BUT NOW WE HAVEN'T GOT ANY SAUSAGES!!
Improvise!
FRED — DON'T YOU DARE GO DIGGING IN THE VEGETABLE PATCH!
I shall try to resist the temptation, but —
What will be will be —

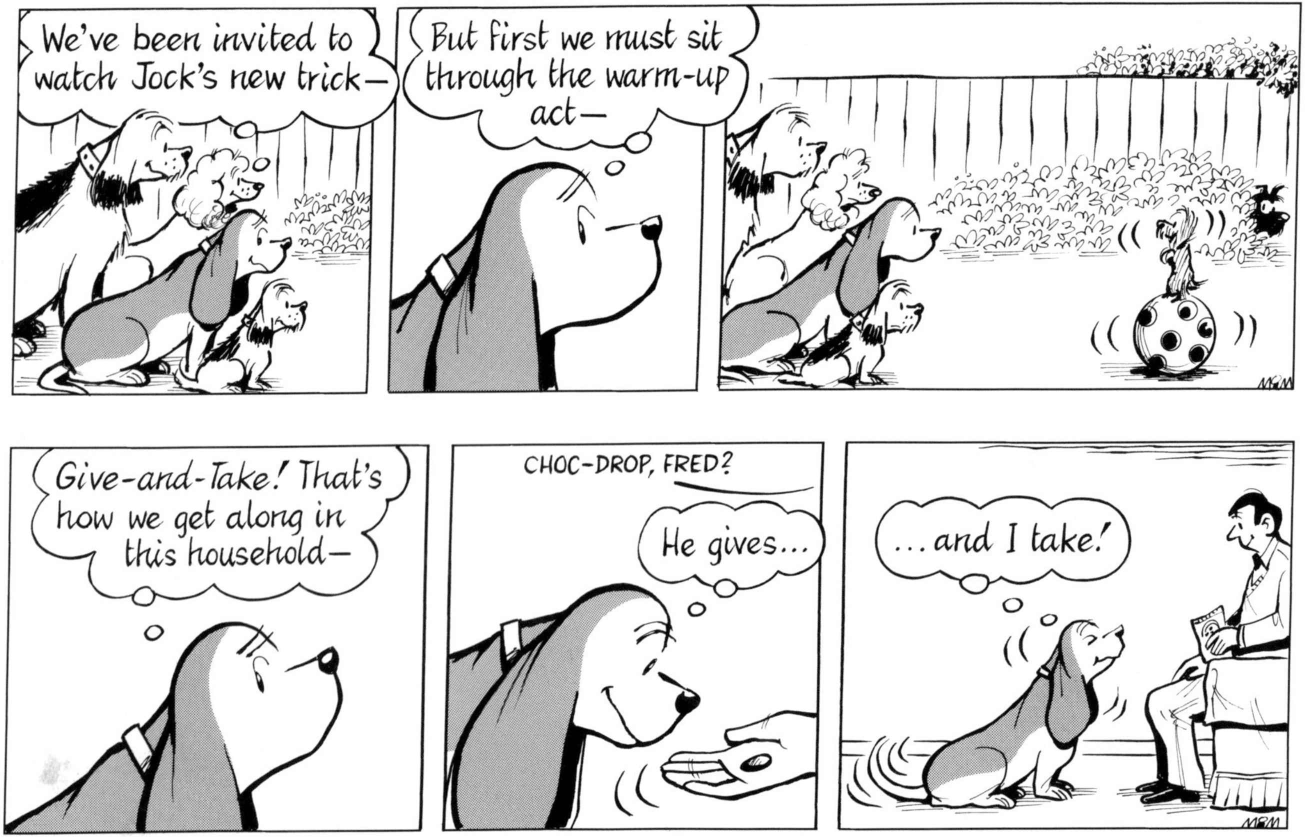

We've been invited to watch Jock's new trick—
But first we must sit through the warm-up act—
Give-and-Take! That's how we get along in this household—
CHOC-DROP, FRED?
He gives...
...and I take!

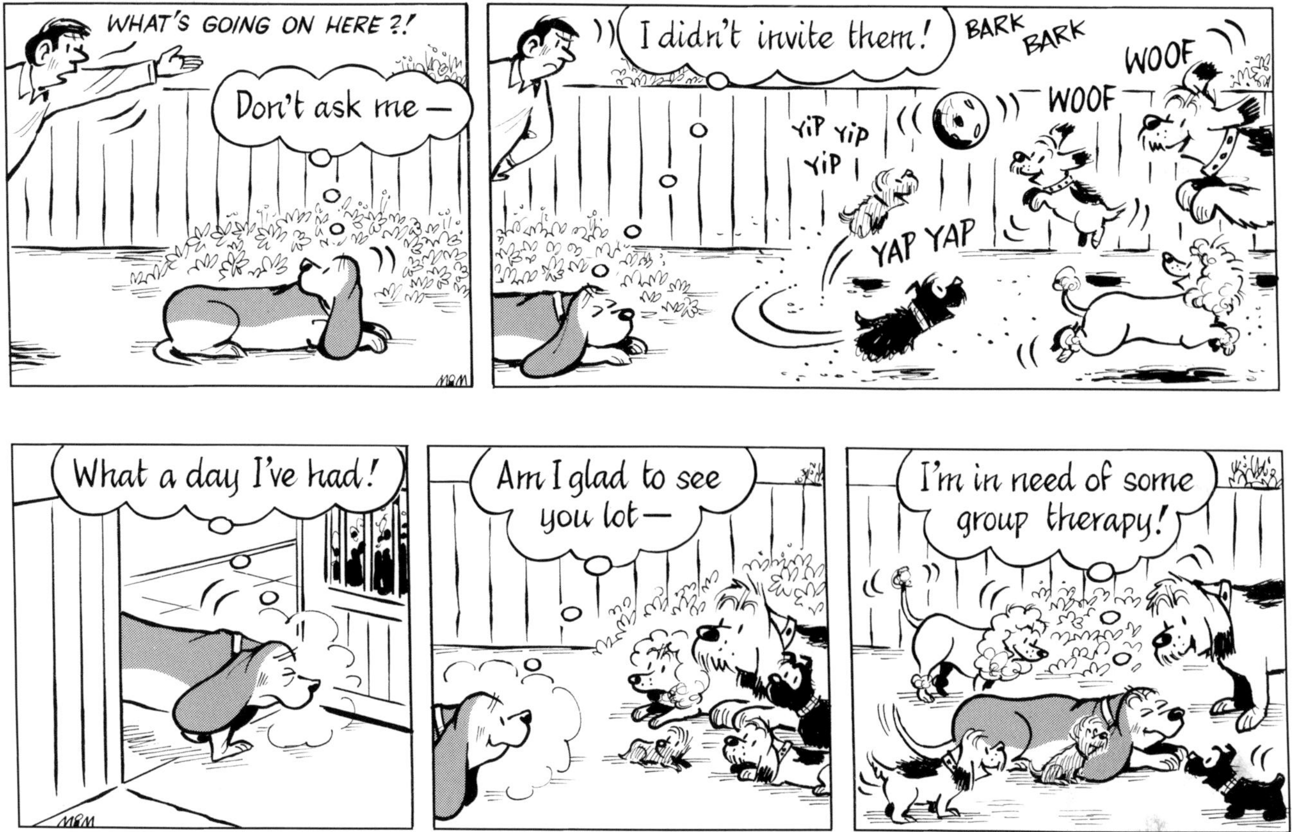
WHAT'S GOING ON HERE?!
Don't ask me —
I didn't invite them!
BARK BARK
WOOF
WOOF
YIP YIP
YIP
YAP YAP
What a day I've had!
Am I glad to see you lot —
I'm in need of some group therapy!

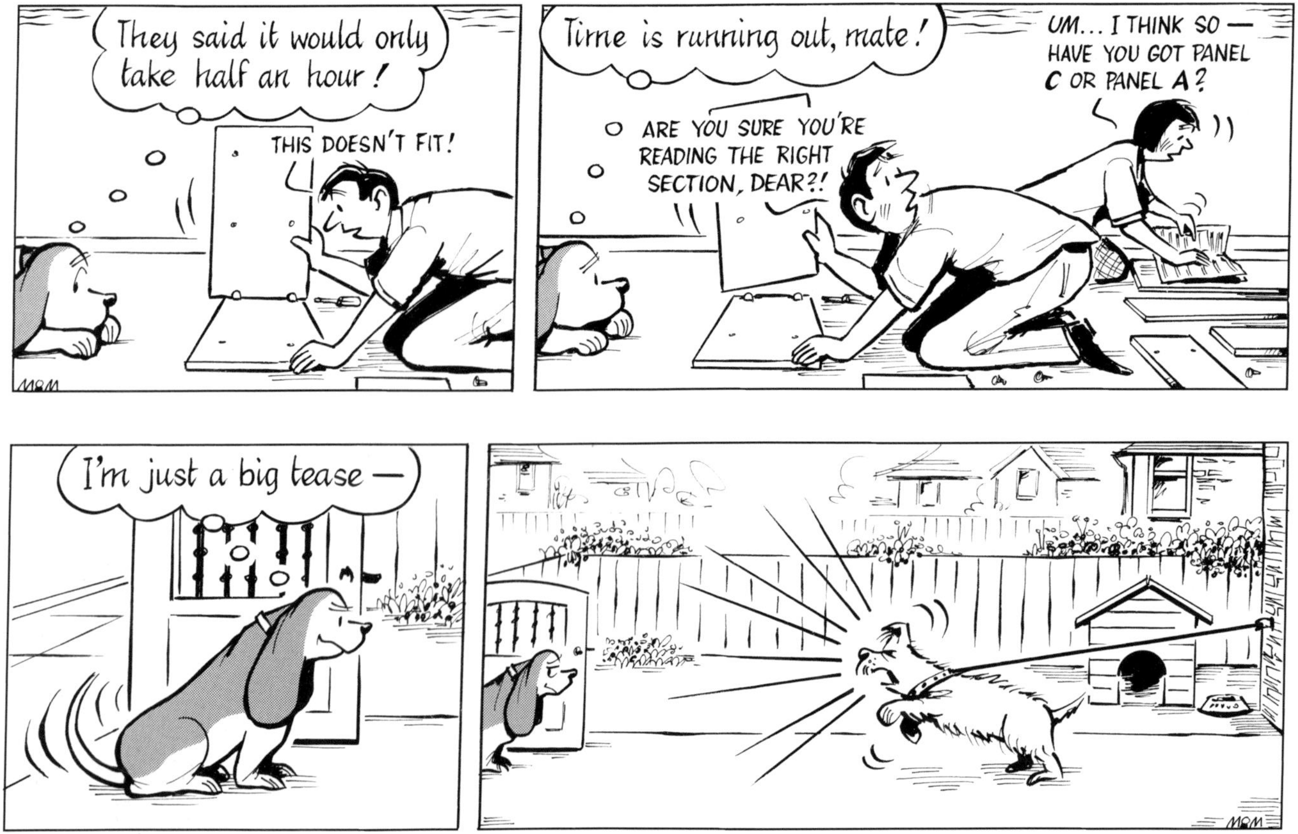
They said it would only take half an hour!
THIS DOESN'T FIT!
Time is running out, mate!
ARE YOU SURE YOU'RE READING THE RIGHT SECTION, DEAR?!
UM... I THINK SO — HAVE YOU GOT PANEL C OR PANEL A?
I'm just a big tease —
MGM
MGM

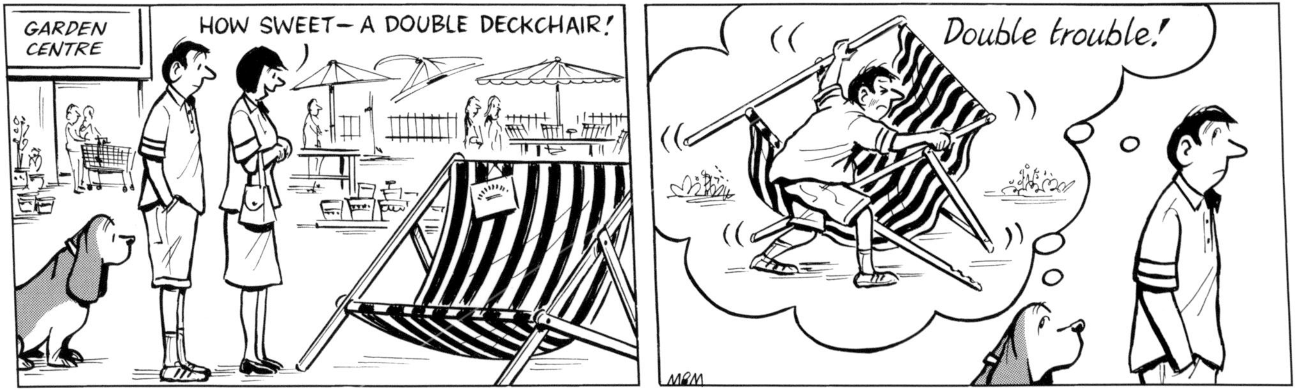
GARDEN CENTRE
HOW SWEET– A DOUBLE DECKCHAIR!
Double trouble!

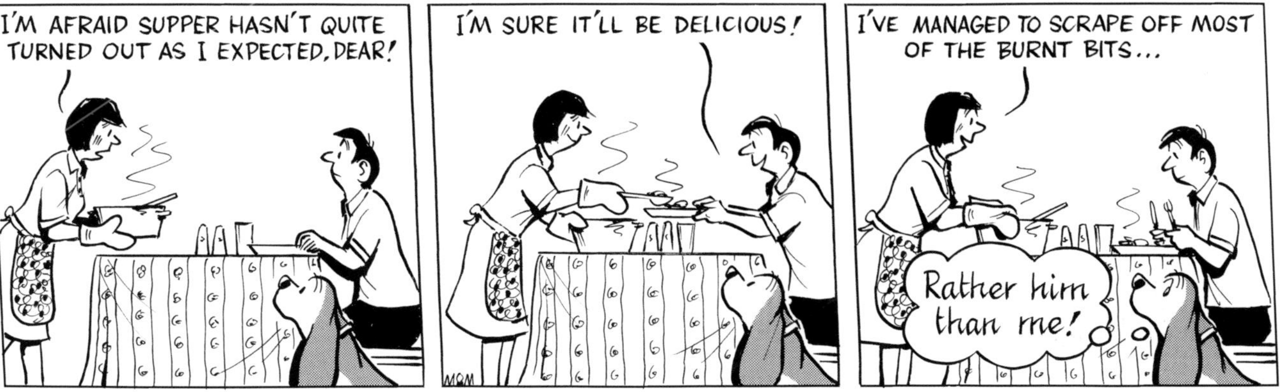
I'M AFRAID SUPPER HASN'T QUITE TURNED OUT AS I EXPECTED, DEAR!
I'M SURE IT'LL BE DELICIOUS!
I'VE MANAGED TO SCRAPE OFF MOST OF THE BURNT BITS...
Rather him than me!

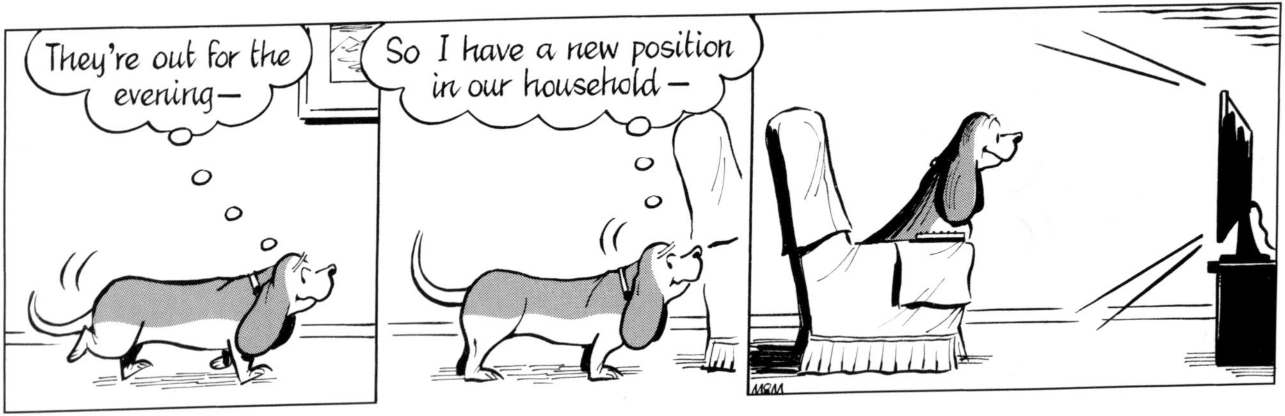
They're out for the evening—
So I have a new position in our household—

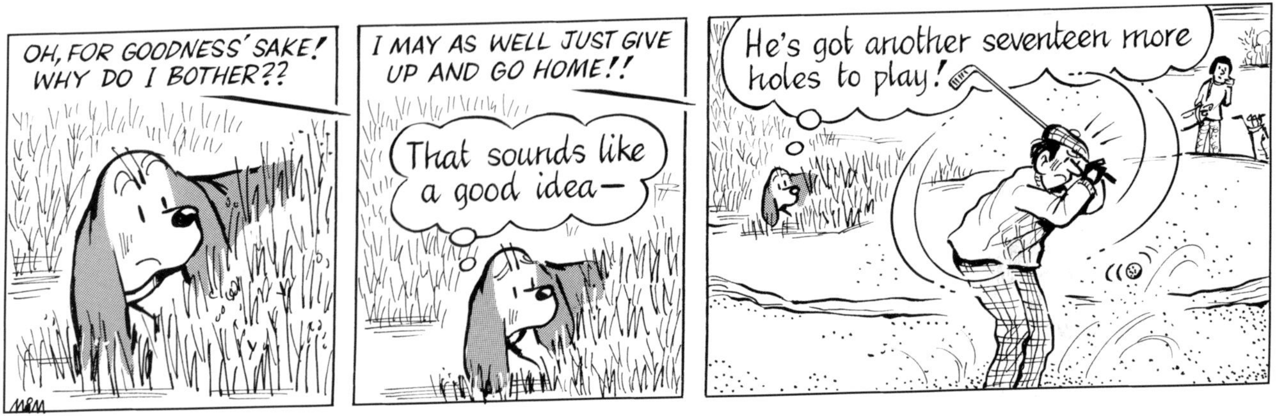
OH, FOR GOODNESS' SAKE! WHY DO I BOTHER??
I MAY AS WELL JUST GIVE UP AND GO HOME!!
That sounds like a good idea—
He's got another seventeen more holes to play!

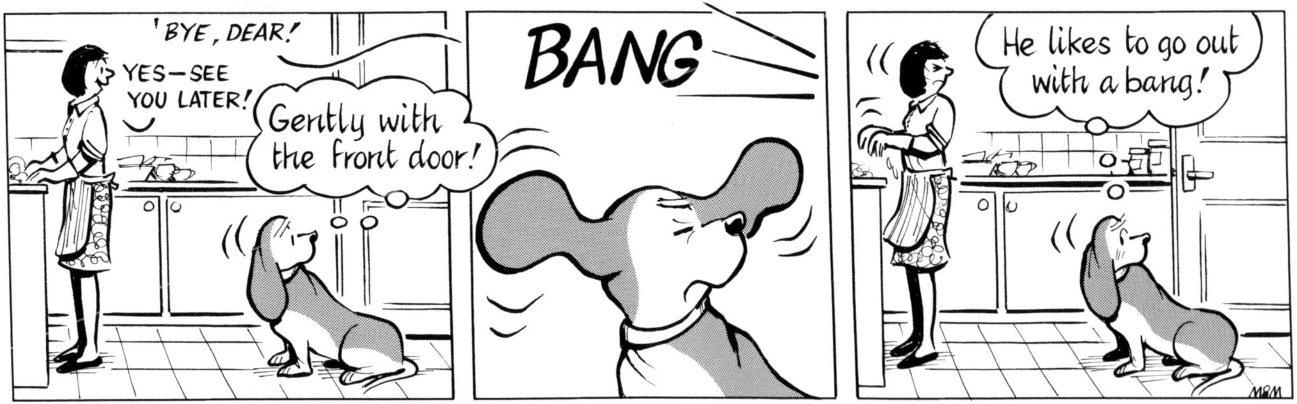
'BYE, DEAR!
YES—SEE YOU LATER!
Gently with the front door!
BANG
He likes to go out with a bang!

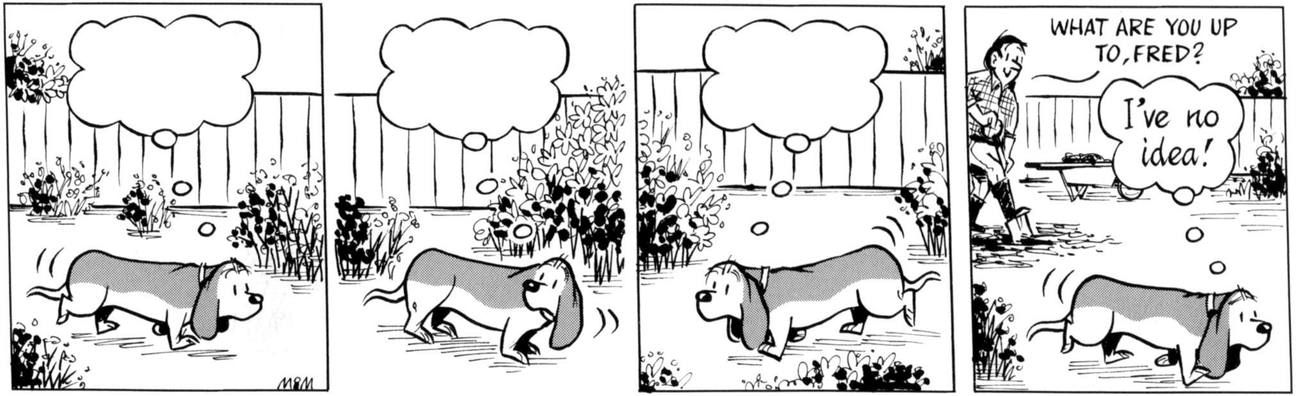
WHAT ARE YOU UP TO, FRED?
I've no idea!

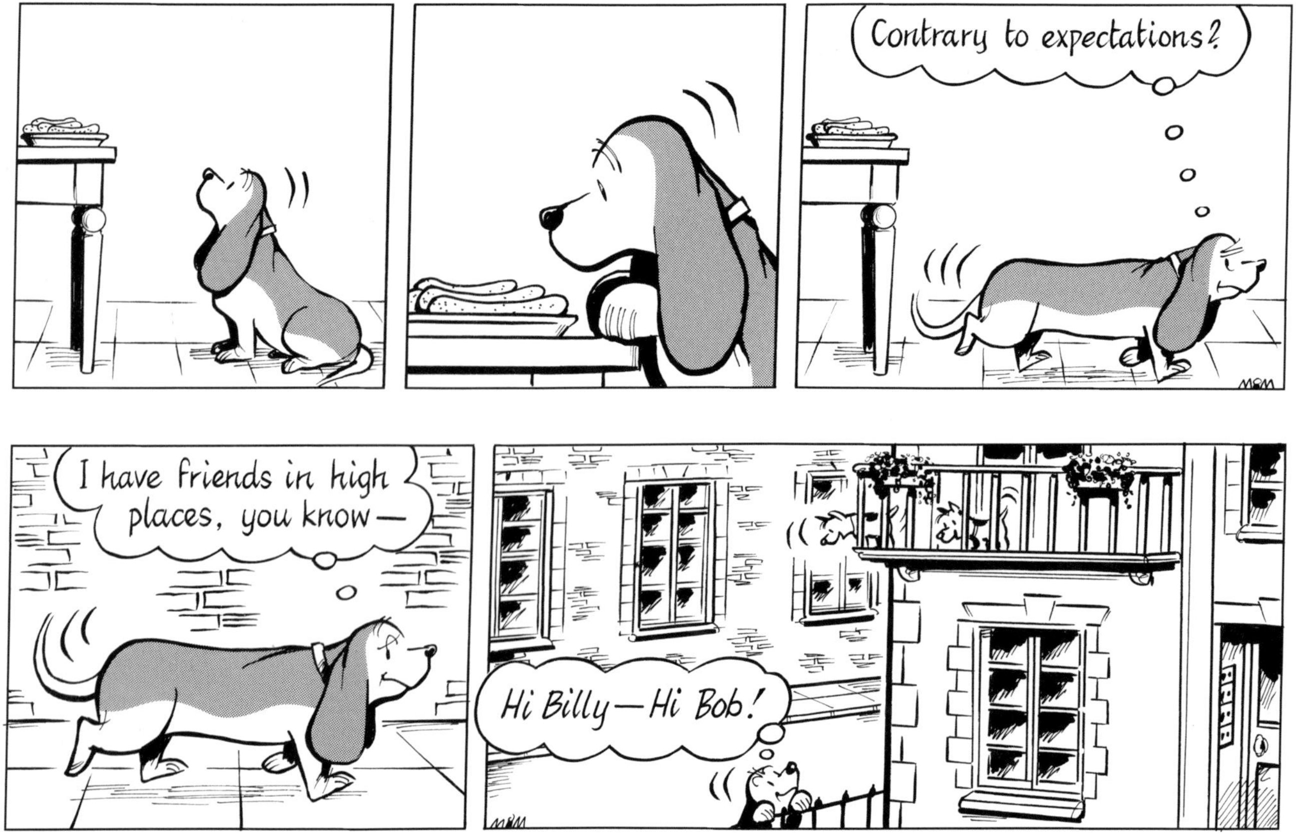
Contrary to expectations?
MGM
I have friends in high places, you know—
Hi Billy—Hi Bob!
MGM

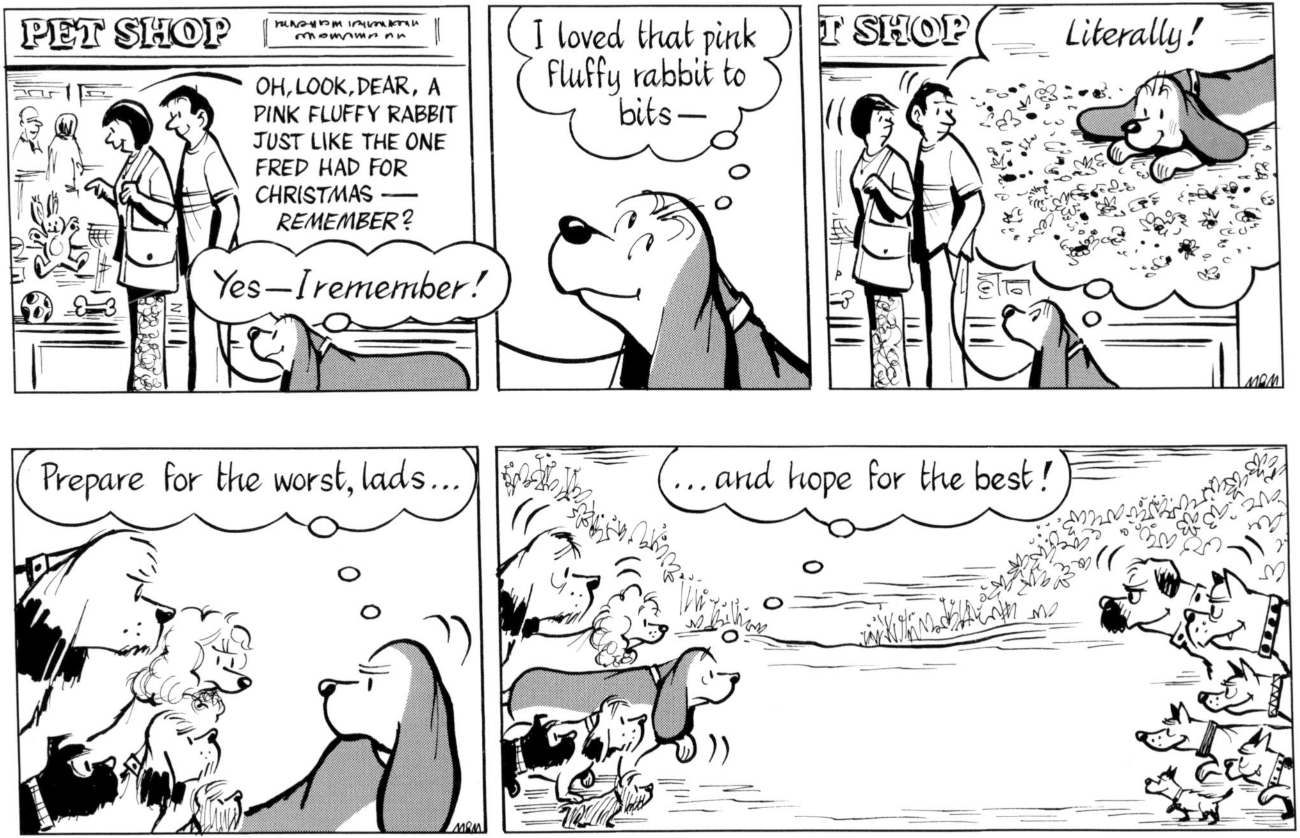
PET SHOP
OH, LOOK, DEAR, A PINK FLUFFY RABBIT JUST LIKE THE ONE FRED HAD FOR CHRISTMAS — REMEMBER?
Yes—I remember!
I loved that pink fluffy rabbit to bits—
T SHOP
Literally!
Prepare for the worst, lads...
...and hope for the best!

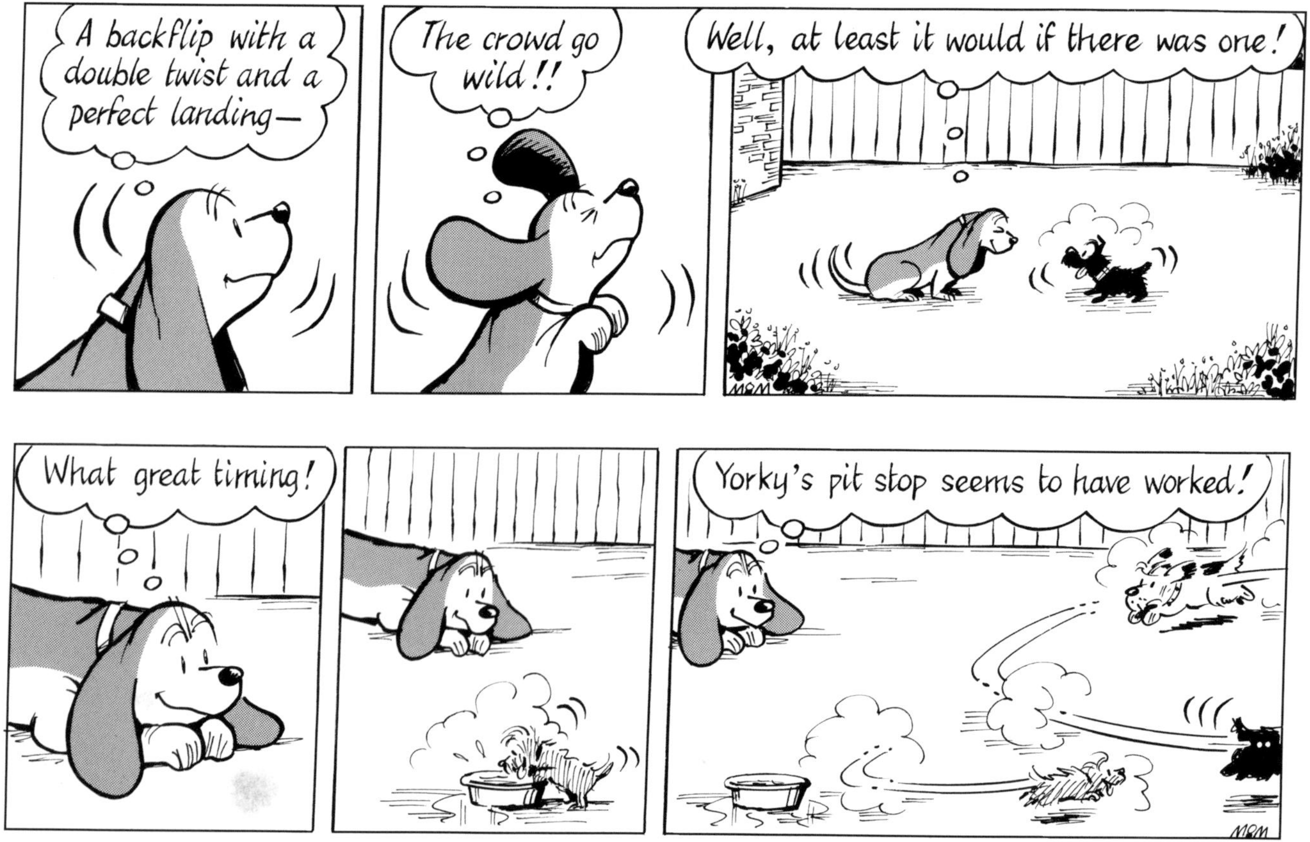
A backflip with a double twist and a perfect landing—
The crowd go wild!!
Well, at least it would if there was one!
MGM
What great timing!
Yorky's pit stop seems to have worked!
MGM

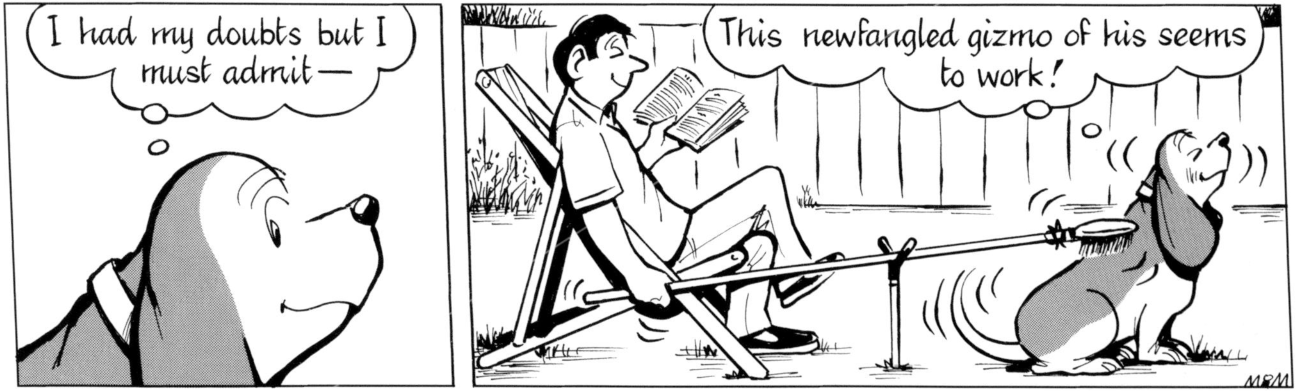
I had my doubts but I must admit—
This newfangled gizmo of his seems to work!

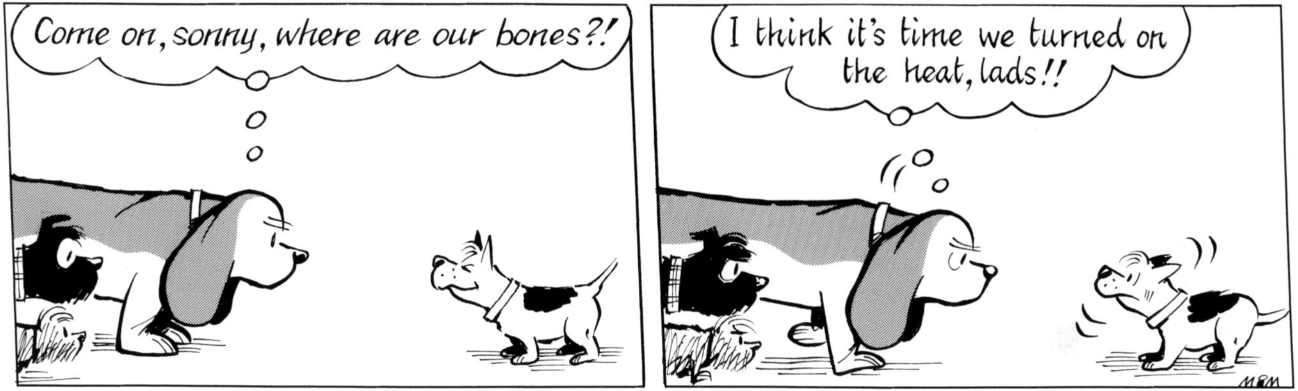
Come on, sonny, where are our bones?!
I think it's time we turned on the heat, lads!!

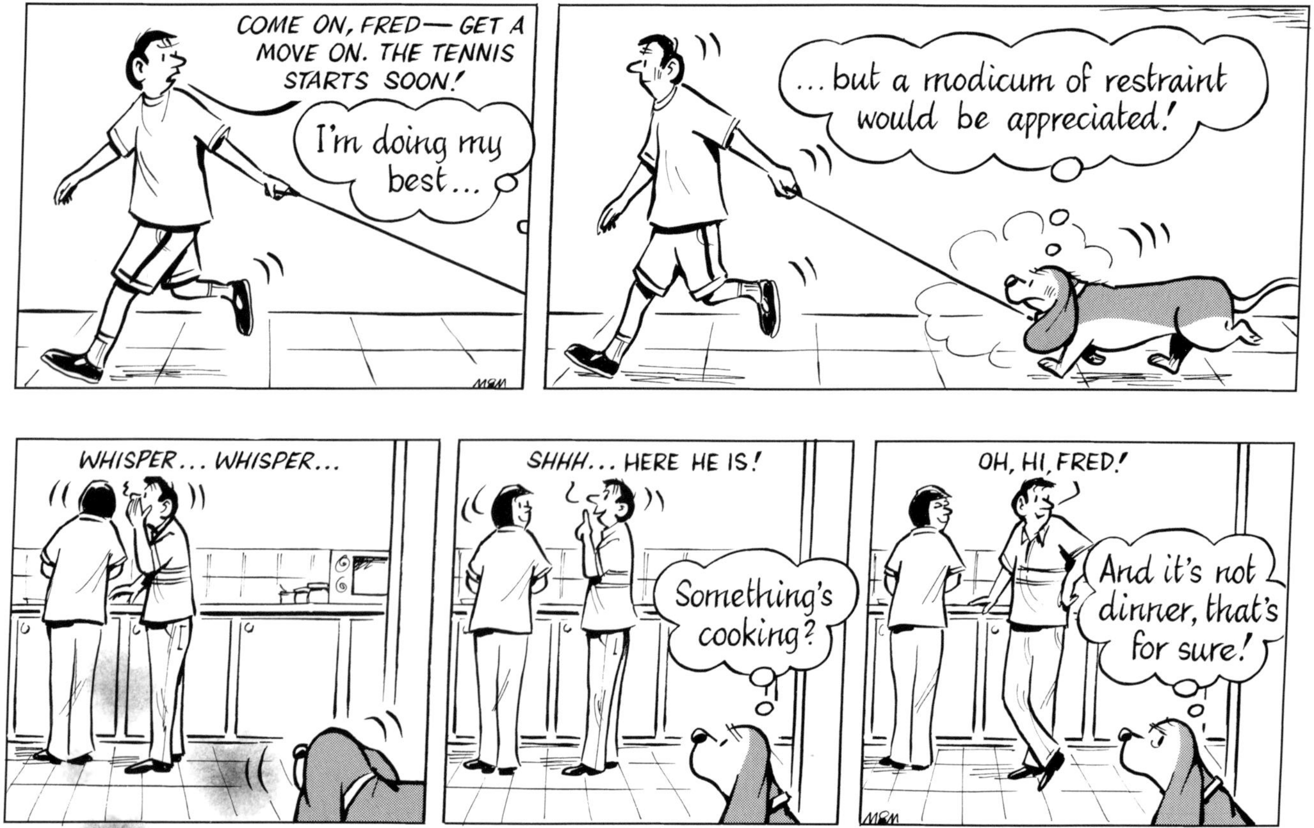
COME ON, FRED— GET A MOVE ON. THE TENNIS STARTS SOON!
I'm doing my best...
MSM
...but a modicum of restraint would be appreciated!
WHISPER... WHISPER...
SHHH... HERE HE IS!
Something's cooking?
OH, HI, FRED!
And it's not dinner, that's for sure!
MSM

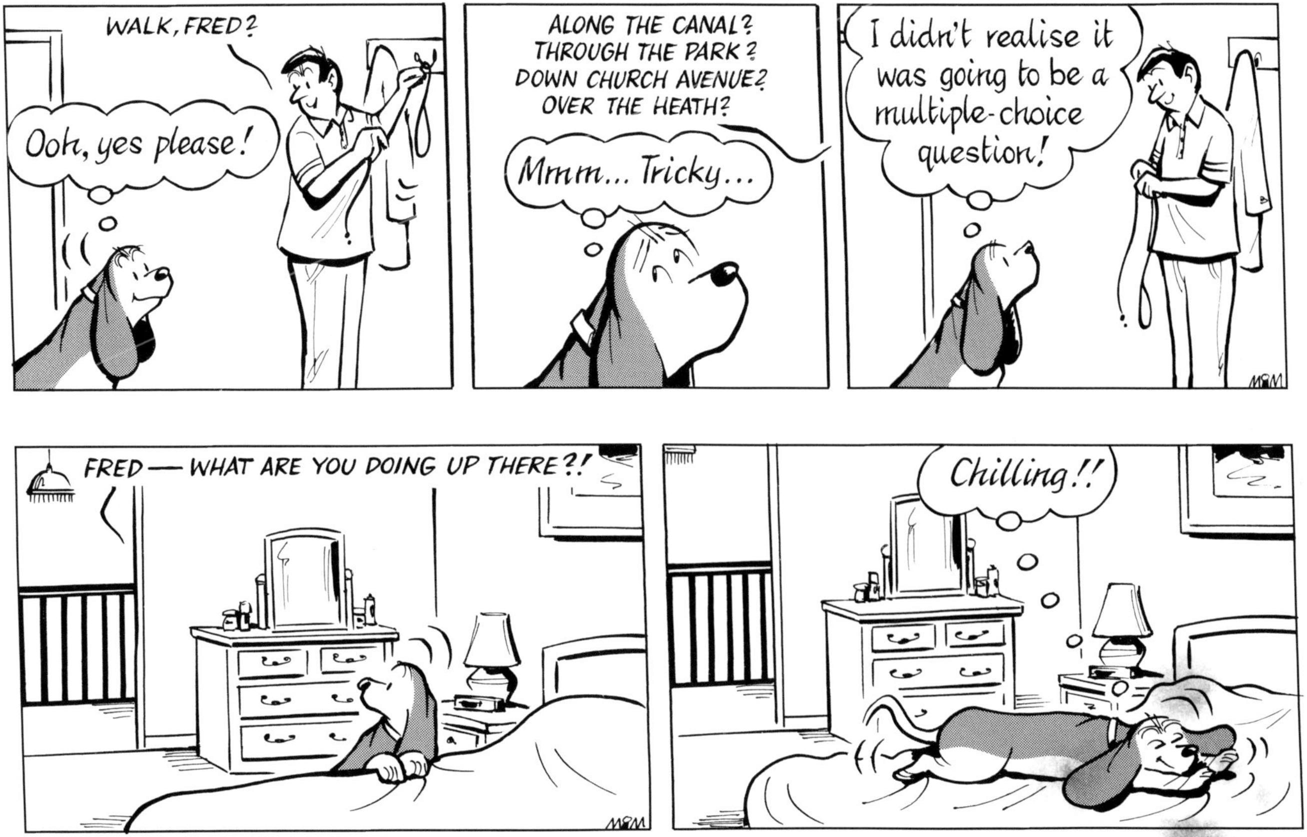
WALK, FRED?
Ooh, yes please!
ALONG THE CANAL? THROUGH THE PARK? DOWN CHURCH AVENUE? OVER THE HEATH?
Mmm... Tricky...
I didn't realise it was going to be a multiple-choice question!
MSM
FRED — WHAT ARE YOU DOING UP THERE?!
MSM
Chilling!!

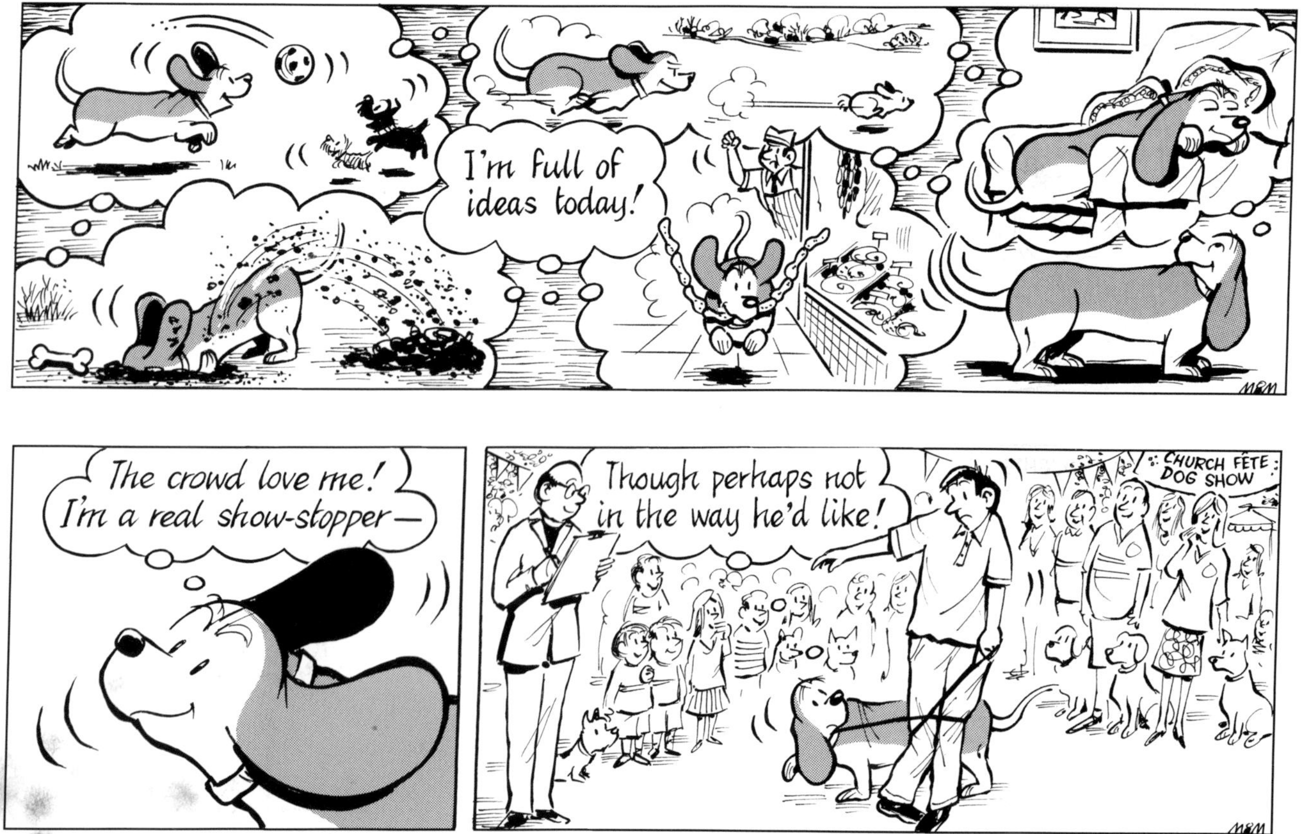
I'm full of ideas today!
M&M
The crowd love me! I'm a real show-stopper—
Though perhaps not in the way he'd like!
CHURCH FÊTE DOG SHOW
M&M

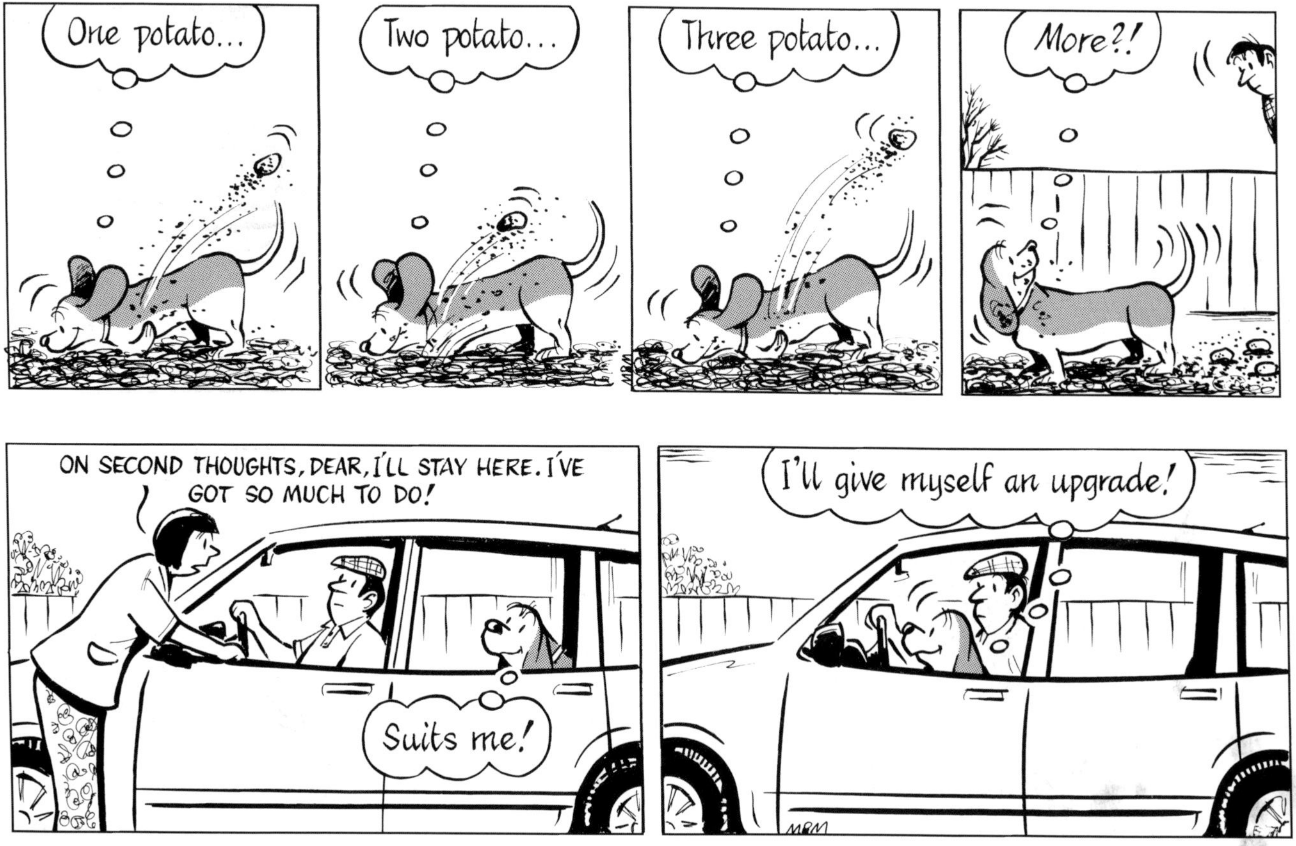

One potato...
Two potato...
Three potato...
More?!
ON SECOND THOUGHTS, DEAR, I'LL STAY HERE. I'VE GOT SO MUCH TO DO!
Suits me!
I'll give myself an upgrade!
MBM

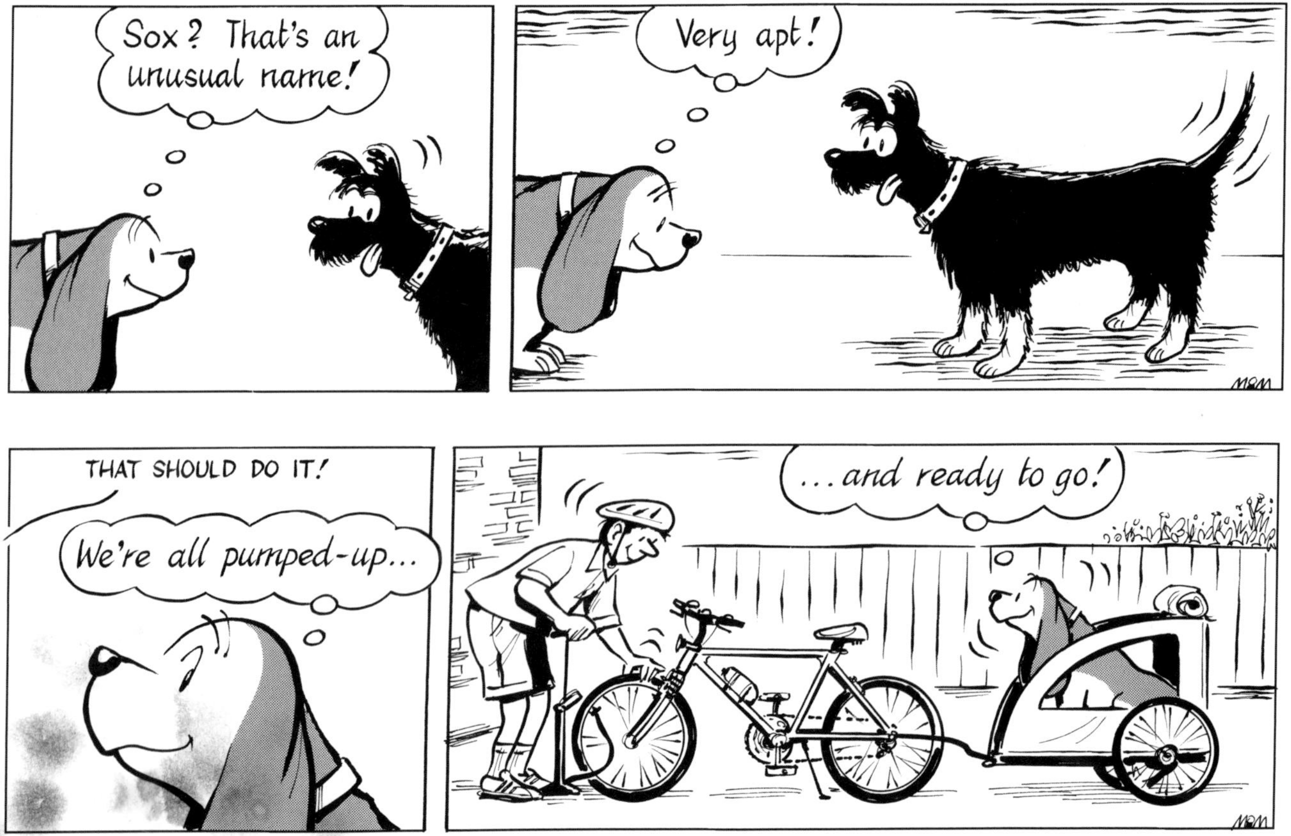
Sox? That's an unusual name!
Very apt!
THAT SHOULD DO IT!
We're all pumped-up...
...and ready to go!

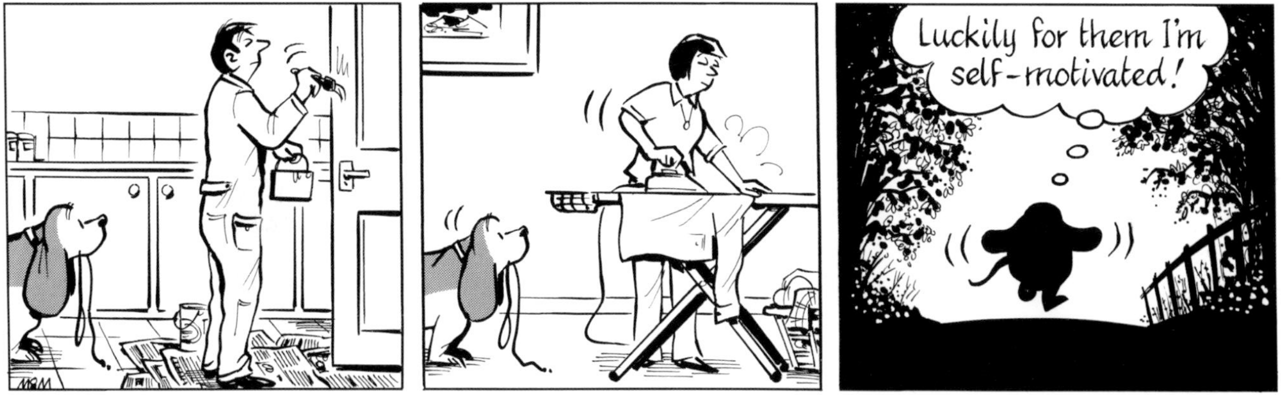
Luckily for them I'm self-motivated!

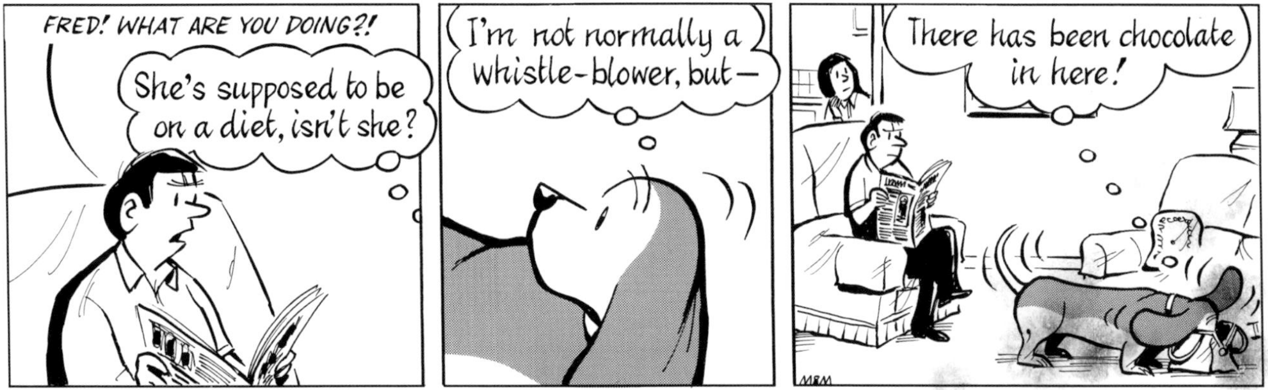
FRED! WHAT ARE YOU DOING?!
She's supposed to be on a diet, isn't she?
I'm not normally a whistle-blower, but—
There has been chocolate in here!

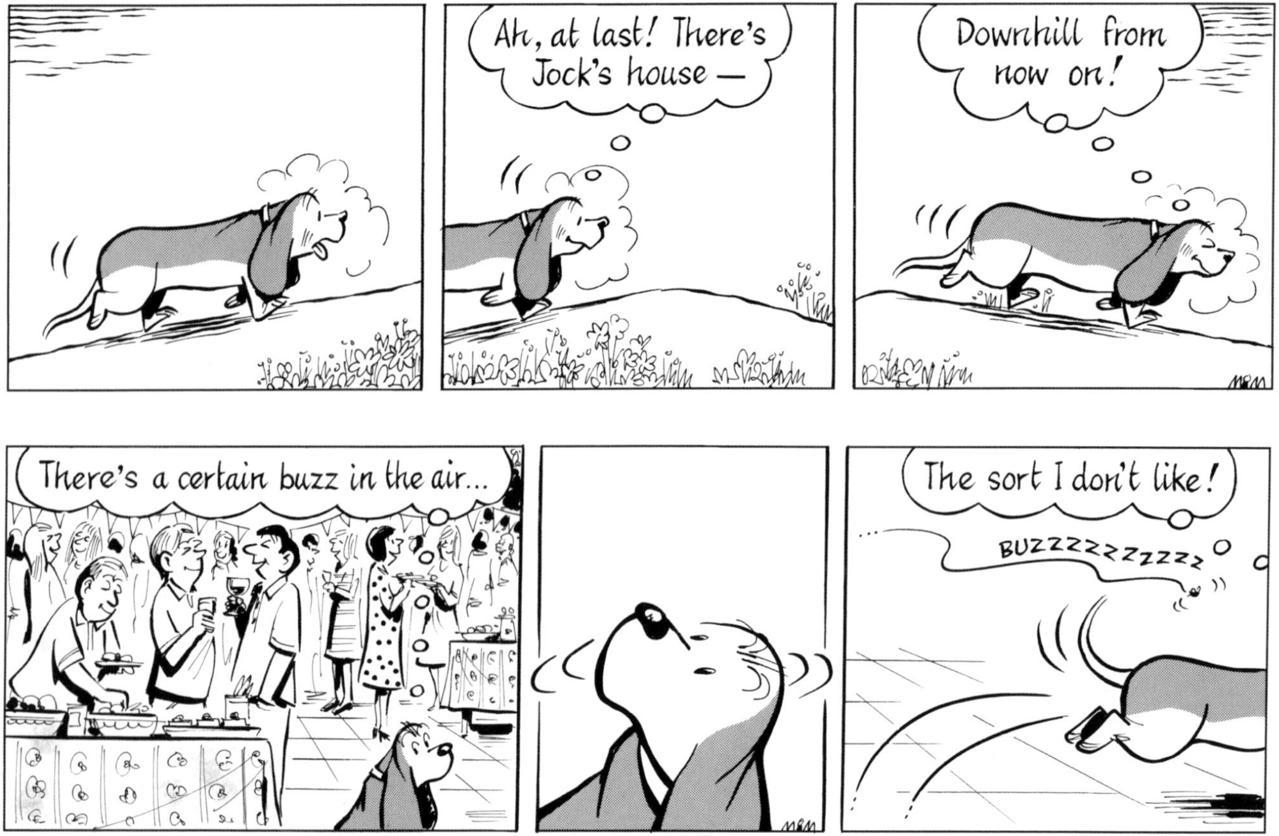
Ah, at last! There's Jock's house —
Downhill from now on!
There's a certain buzz in the air...
The sort I don't like!
BUZZZZZZZZZZZ

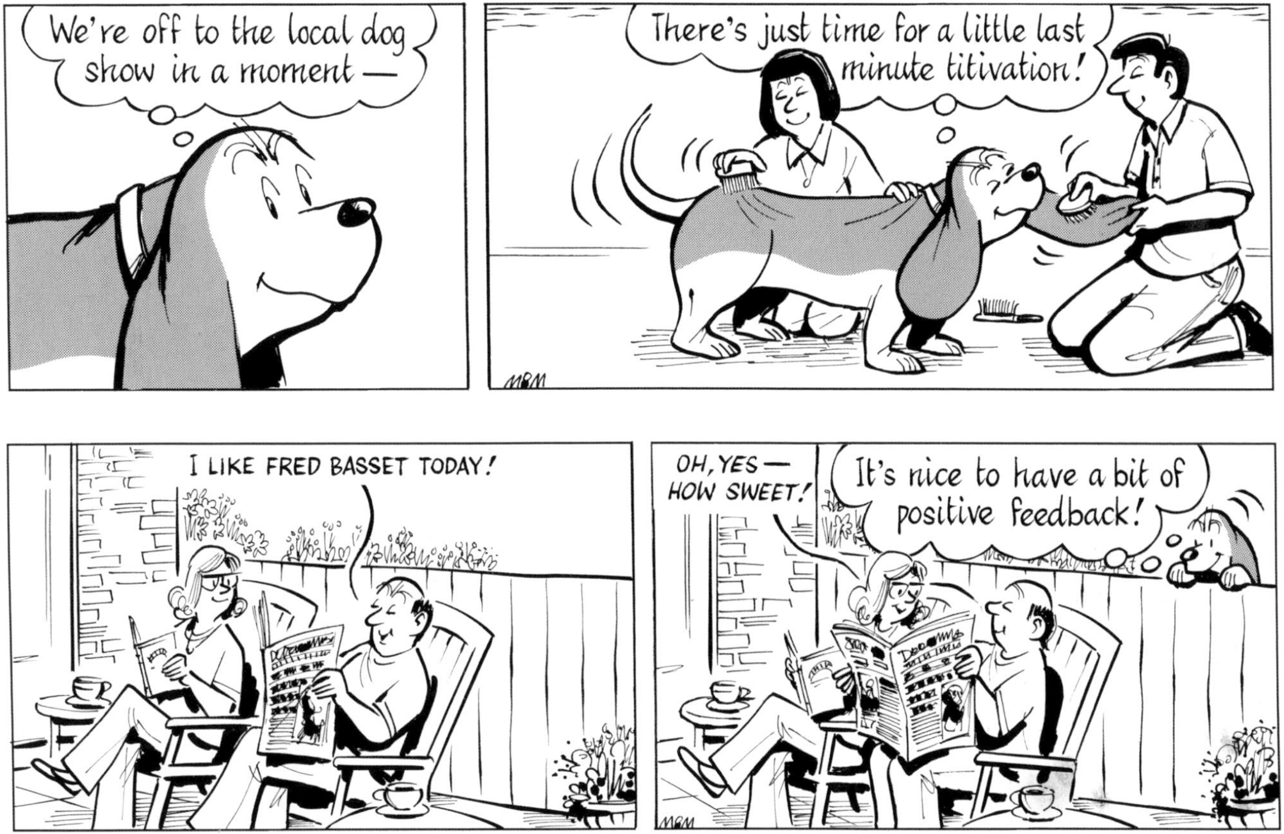
We're off to the local dog show in a moment —
There's just time for a little last minute titivation!
MBM
I LIKE FRED BASSET TODAY!
OH, YES — HOW SWEET!
It's nice to have a bit of positive feedback!
MBM

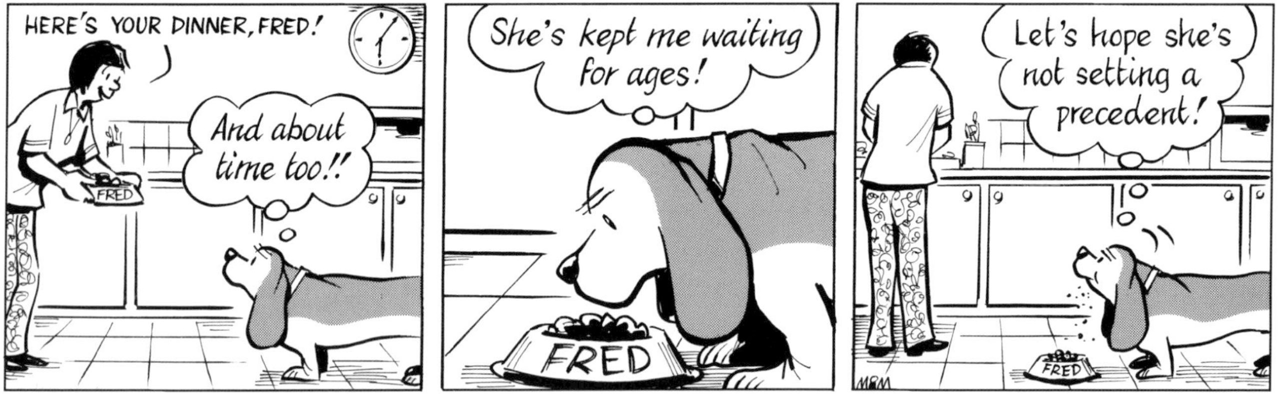
HERE'S YOUR DINNER, FRED!
And about time too!!
FRED
She's kept me waiting for ages!
FRED
Let's hope she's not setting a precedent!
FRED
M&M

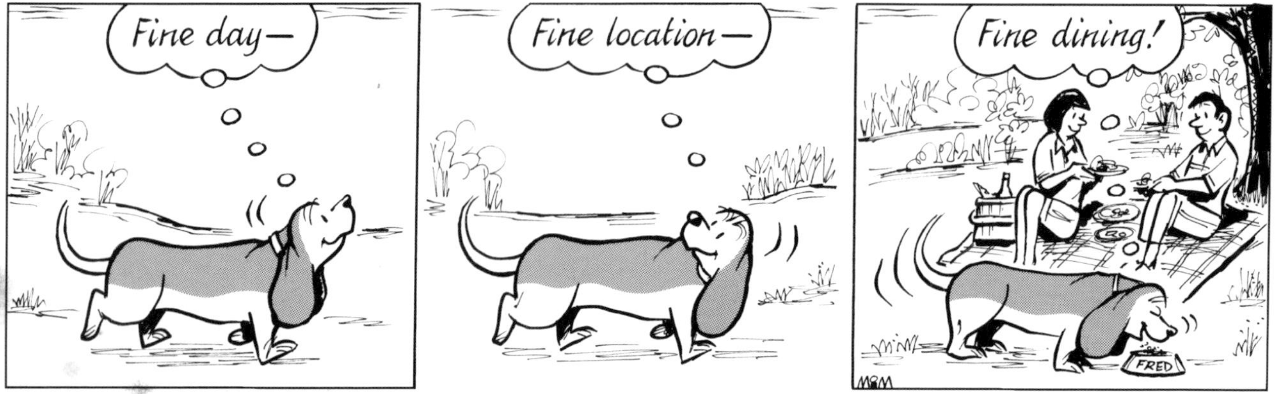
Fine day—
Fine location—
Fine dining!
FRED
M&M

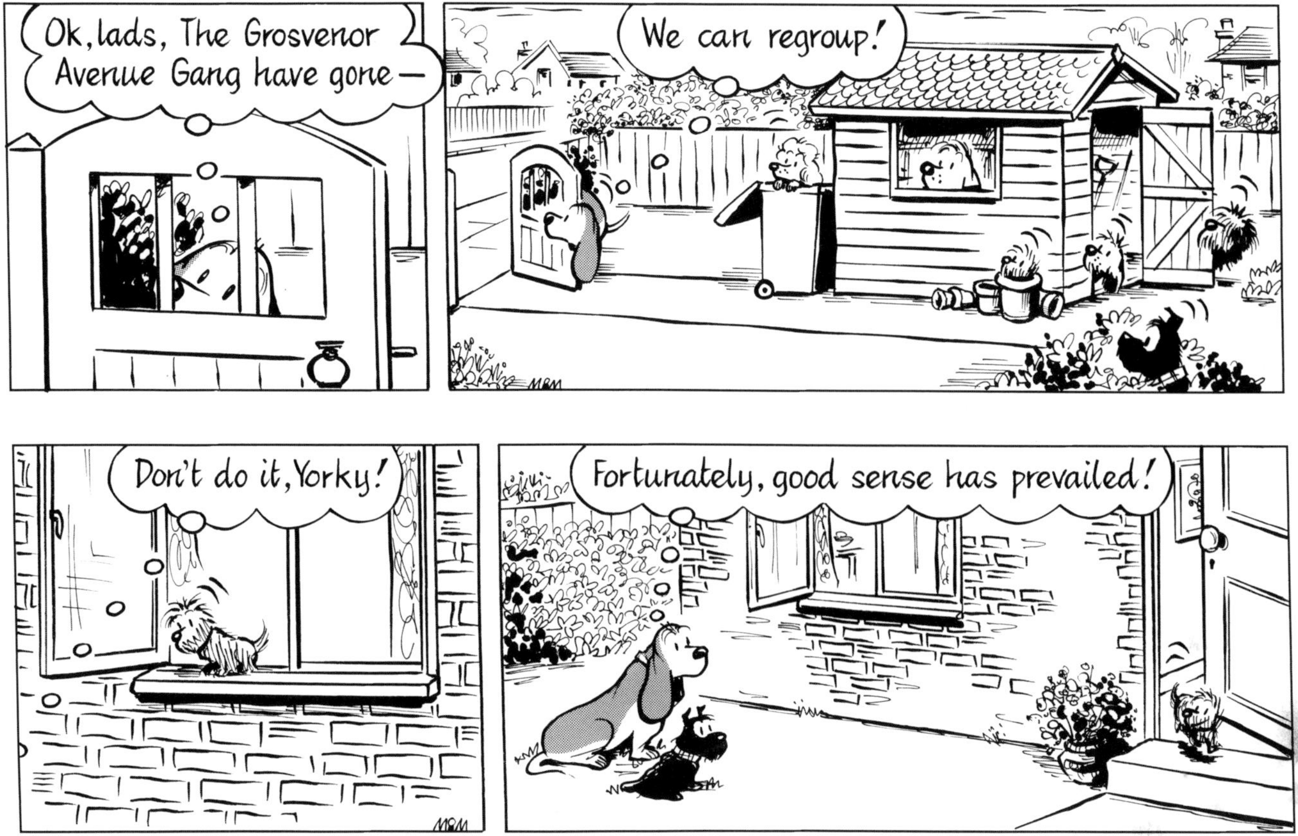
Ok, lads, The Grosvenor Avenue Gang have gone —
We can regroup!
Don't do it, Yorky!
Fortunately, good sense has prevailed!

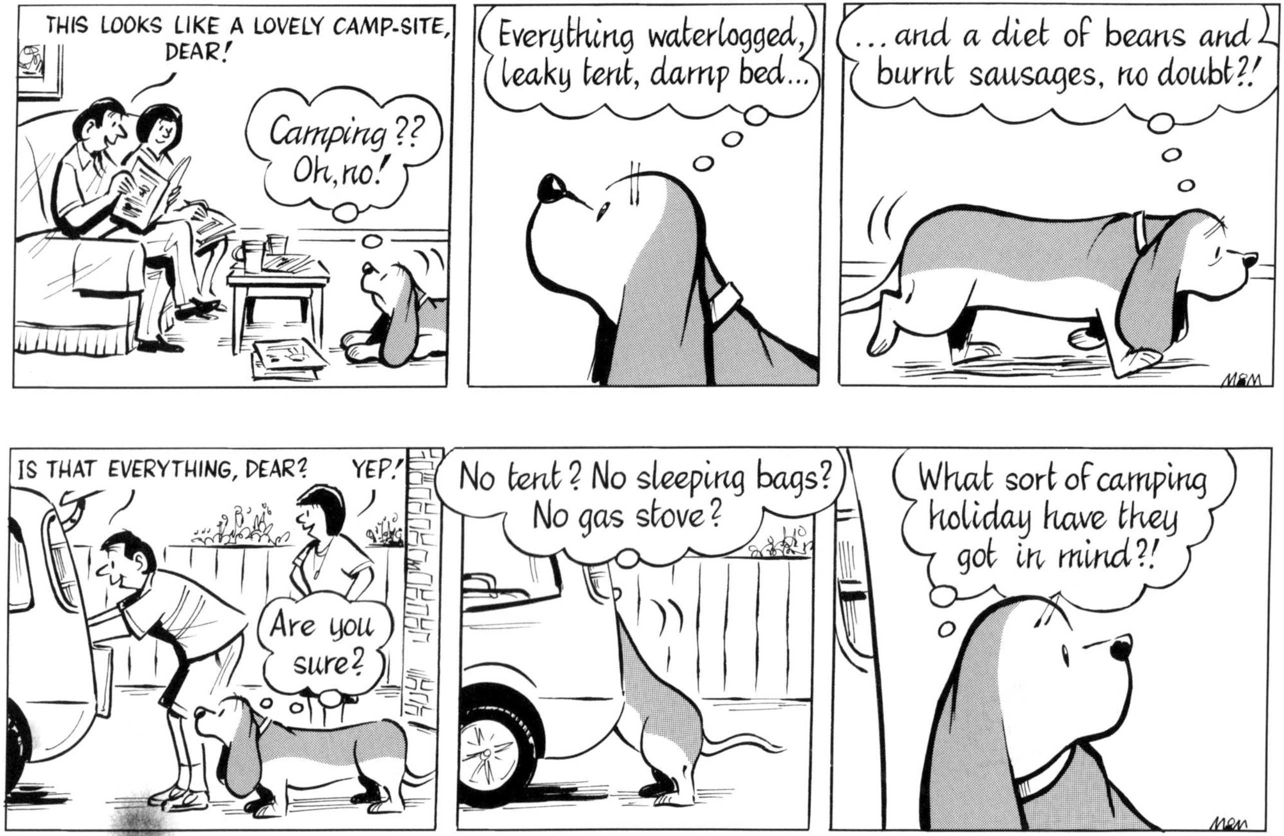
THIS LOOKS LIKE A LOVELY CAMP-SITE, DEAR!
Camping?? Oh, no!
Everything waterlogged, leaky tent, damp bed...
... and a diet of beans and burnt sausages, no doubt?!
IS THAT EVERYTHING, DEAR?
YEP!
Are you sure?
No tent? No sleeping bags? No gas stove?
What sort of camping holiday have they got in mind?!

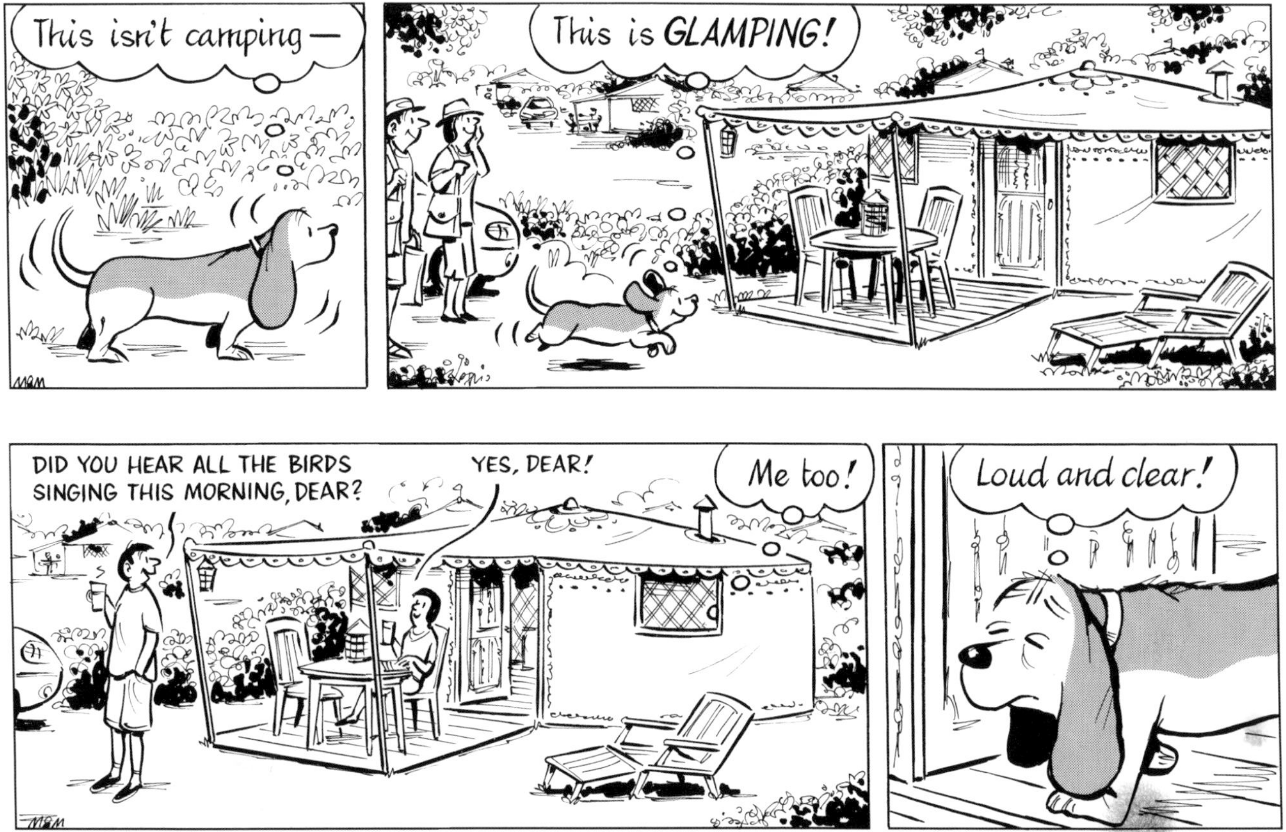
This isn't camping—
This is GLAMPING!
DID YOU HEAR ALL THE BIRDS SINGING THIS MORNING, DEAR?
YES, DEAR!
Me too!
Loud and clear!

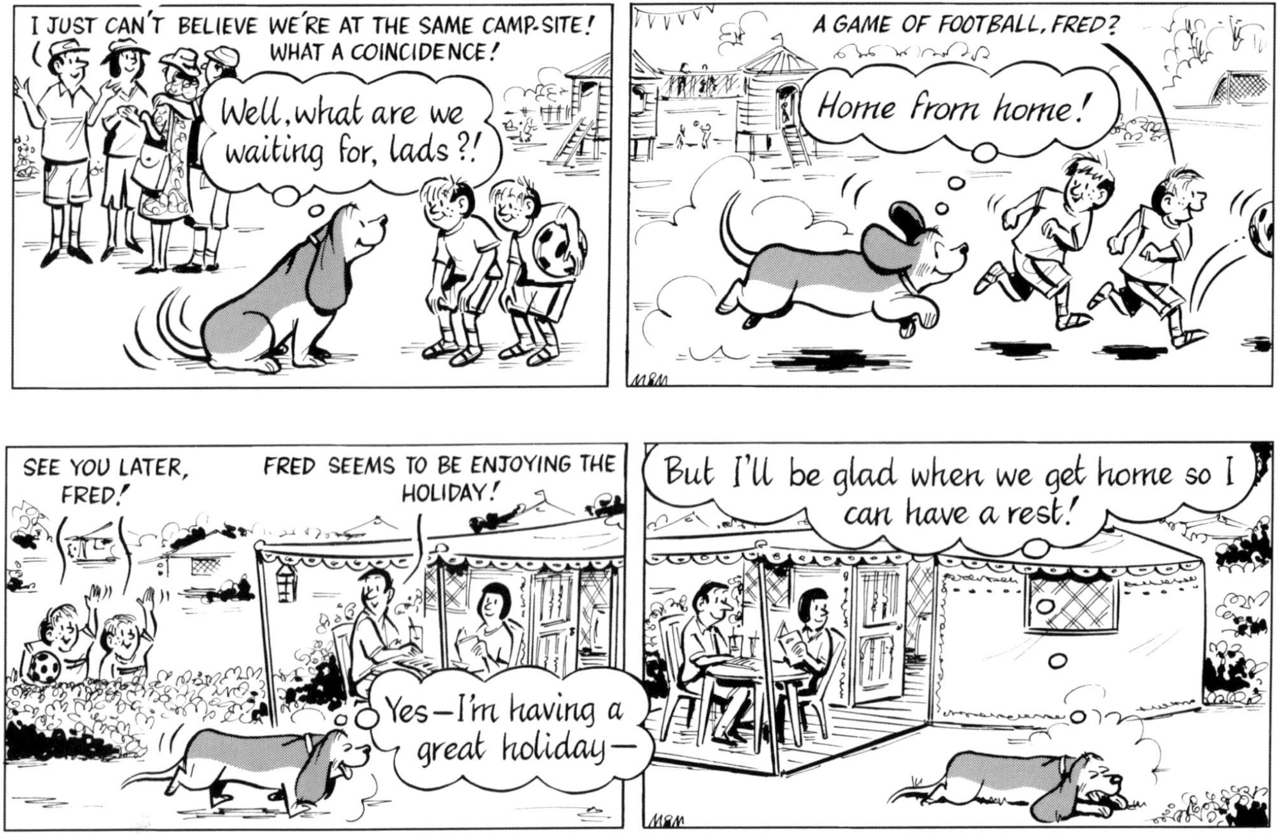
I JUST CAN'T BELIEVE WE'RE AT THE SAME CAMP-SITE! WHAT A COINCIDENCE!
Well, what are we waiting for, lads?!
A GAME OF FOOTBALL, FRED?
Home from home!
SEE YOU LATER, FRED!
FRED SEEMS TO BE ENJOYING THE HOLIDAY!
Yes—I'm having a great holiday—
But I'll be glad when we get home so I can have a rest!

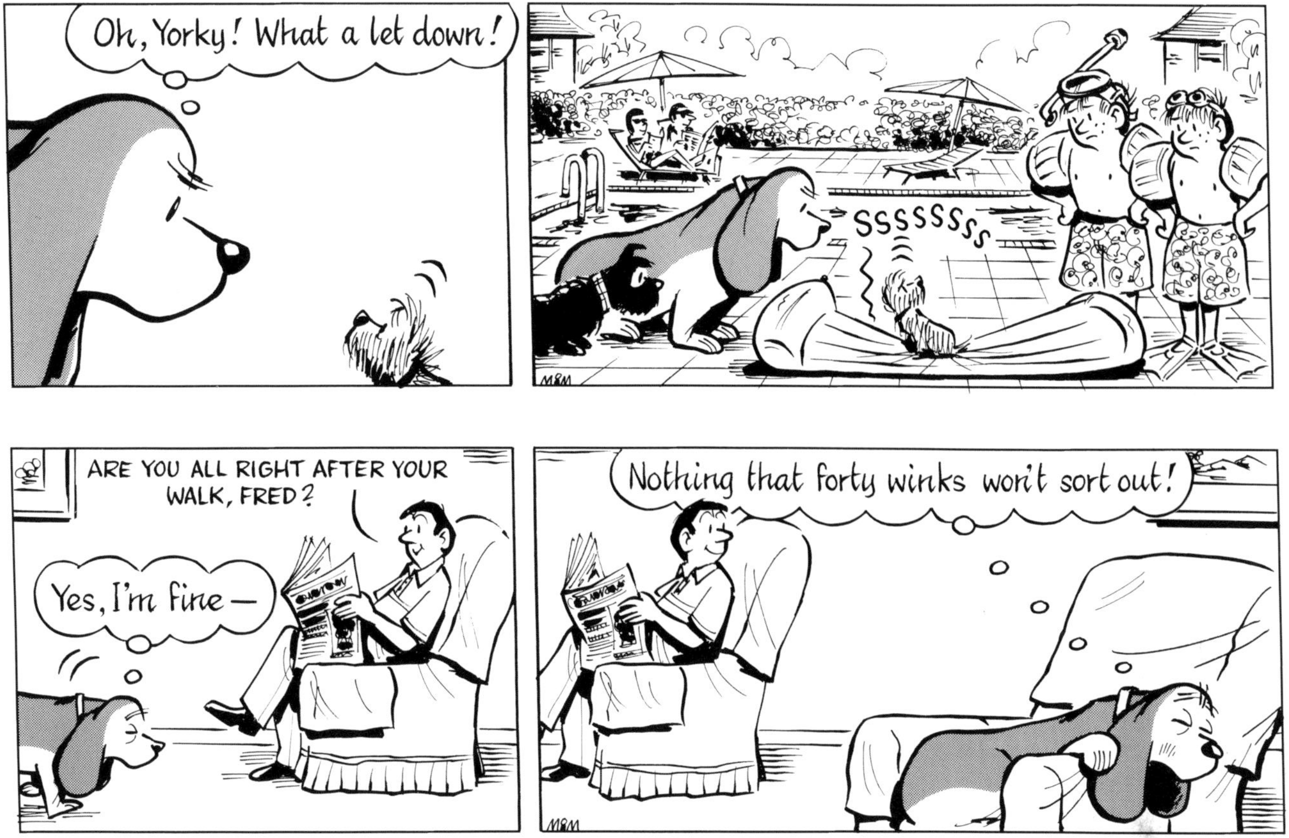

Oh, Yorky! What a let down!
SSSSSSSss
M&M
ARE YOU ALL RIGHT AFTER YOUR WALK, FRED?
Yes, I'm fine –
Nothing that forty winks won't sort out!
M&M

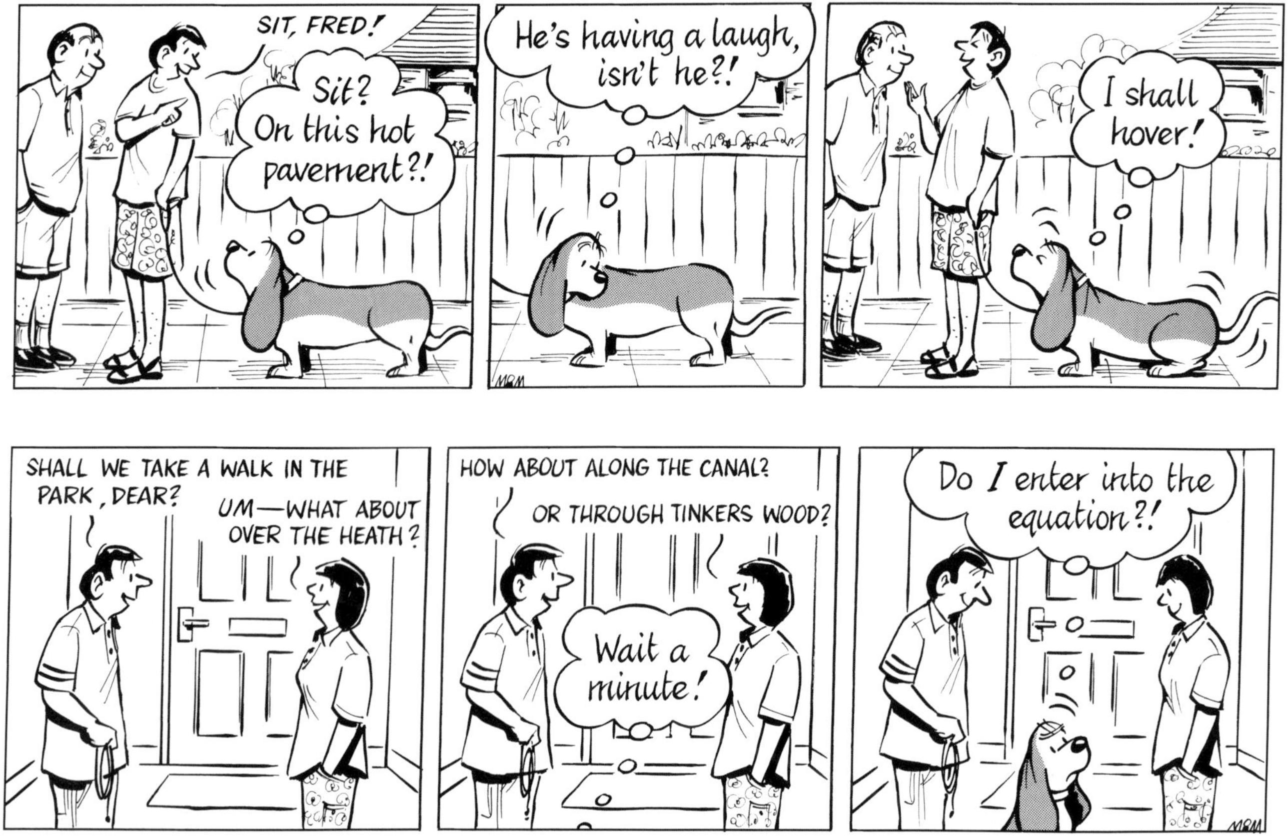
SIT, FRED!
Sit? On this hot pavement?!
He's having a laugh, isn't he?!
MRM
I shall hover!
SHALL WE TAKE A WALK IN THE PARK, DEAR?
UM—WHAT ABOUT OVER THE HEATH?
HOW ABOUT ALONG THE CANAL?
OR THROUGH TINKERS WOOD?
Wait a minute!
Do I enter into the equation?!
MRM

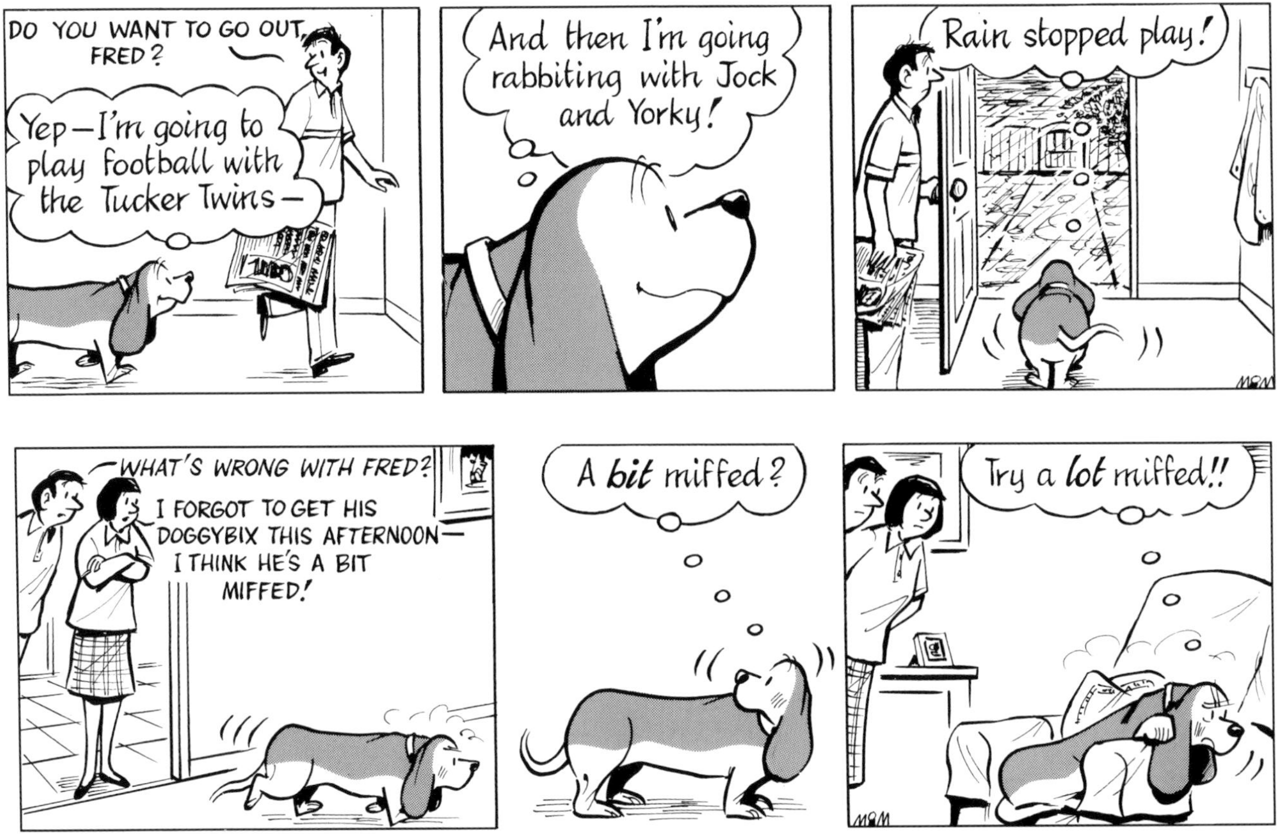
DO YOU WANT TO GO OUT, FRED?
Yep—I'm going to play football with the Tucker Twins—
And then I'm going rabbiting with Jock and Yorky!
Rain stopped play!
WHAT'S WRONG WITH FRED?
I FORGOT TO GET HIS DOGGYBIX THIS AFTERNOON— I THINK HE'S A BIT MIFFED!
A **bit** miffed?
Try a **lot** miffed!!
M&M

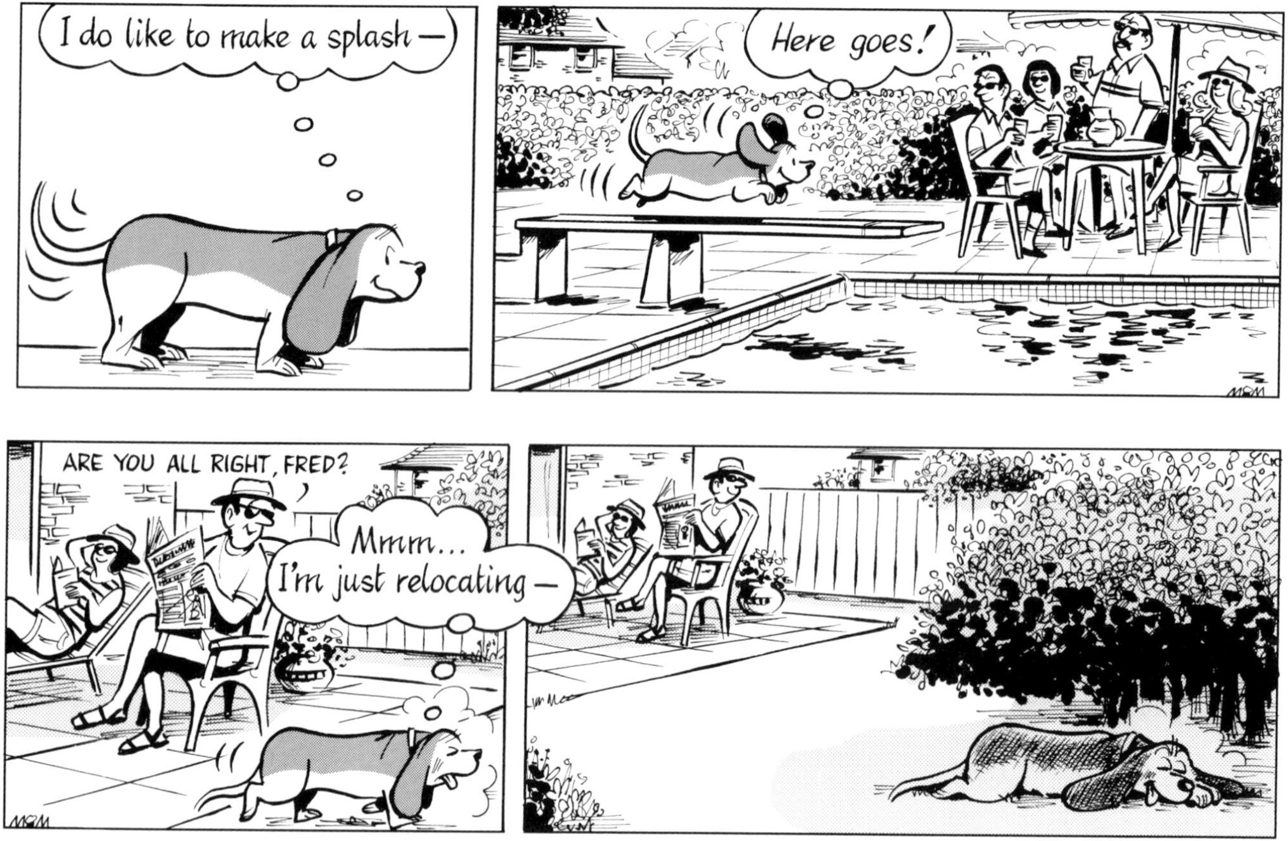
I do like to make a splash –
Here goes!
ARE YOU ALL RIGHT, FRED?
Mmm...
I'm just relocating –

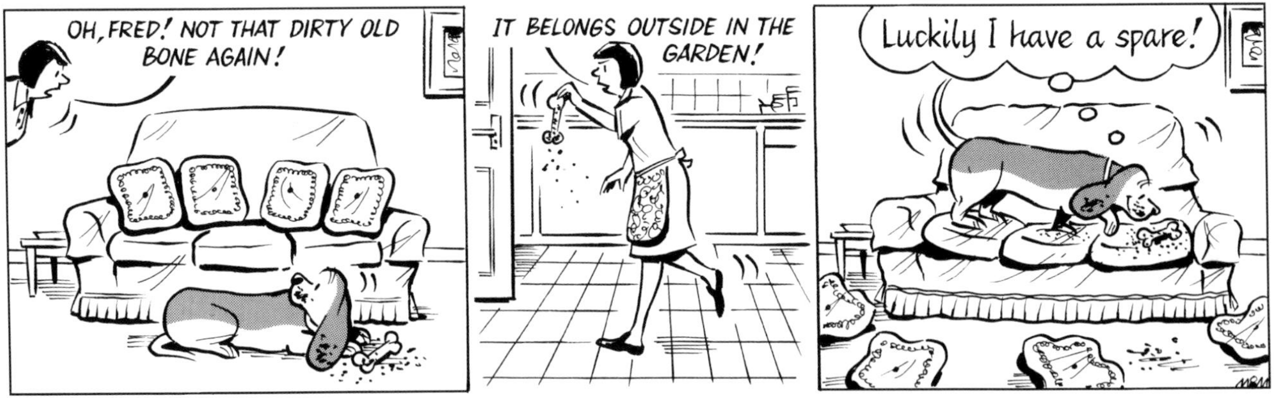
OH, FRED! NOT THAT DIRTY OLD BONE AGAIN!
IT BELONGS OUTSIDE IN THE GARDEN!
Luckily I have a spare!

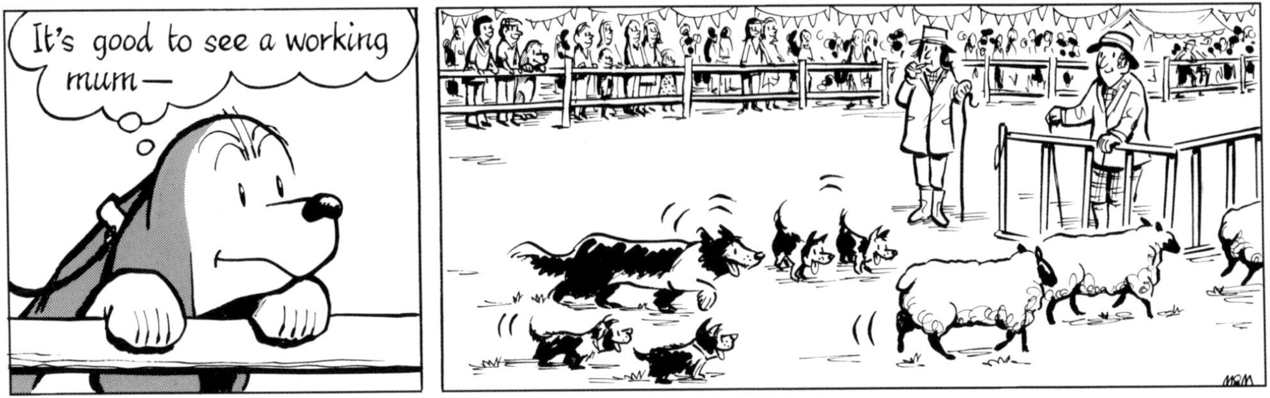
It's good to see a working mum—

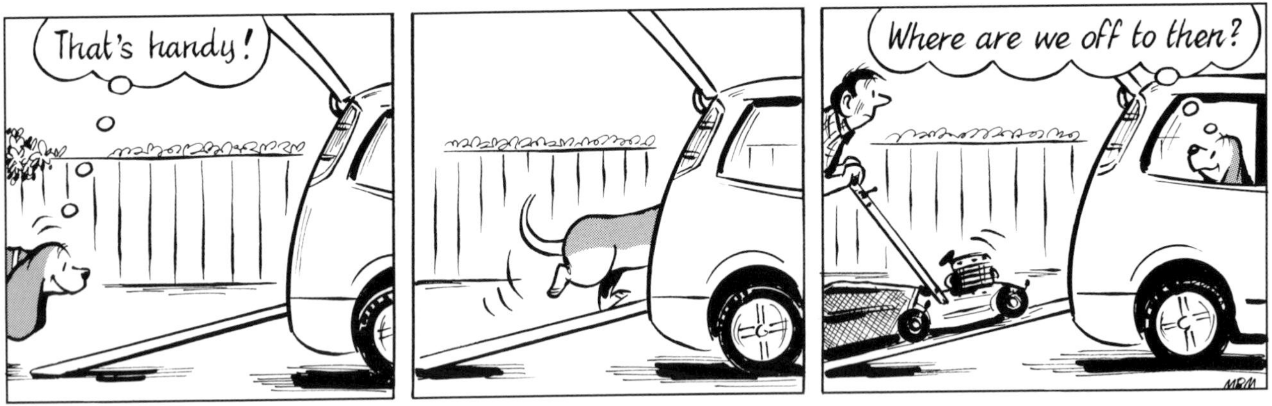
That's handy!
Where are we off to then?

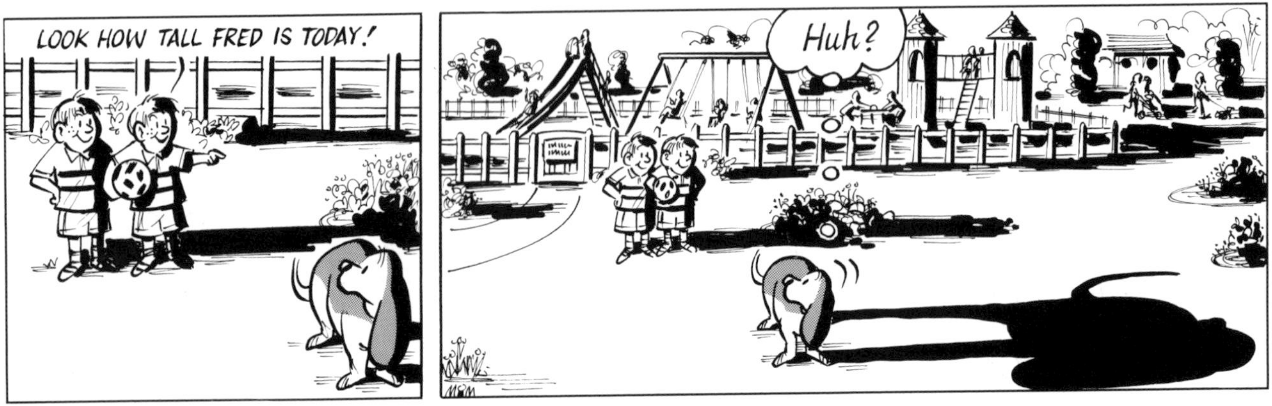
LOOK HOW TALL FRED IS TODAY!
Huh?

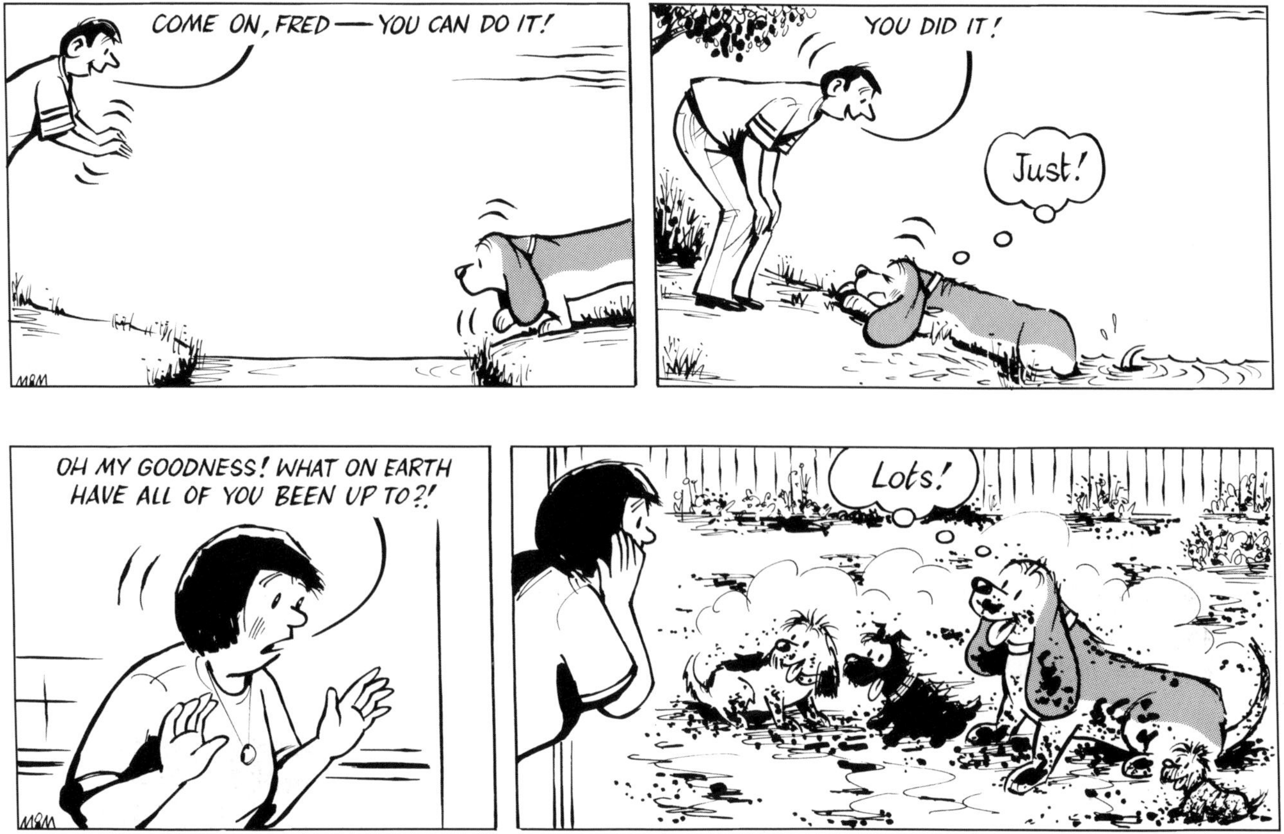
COME ON, FRED — YOU CAN DO IT!
M&M
YOU DID IT!
Just!
OH MY GOODNESS! WHAT ON EARTH HAVE ALL OF YOU BEEN UP TO?!
M&M
Lots!

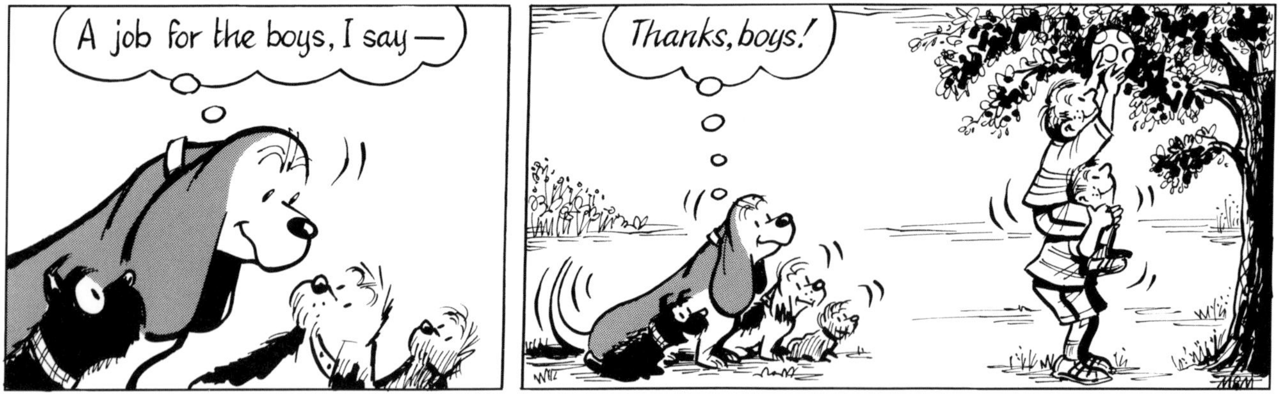
A job for the boys, I say—
Thanks, boys!

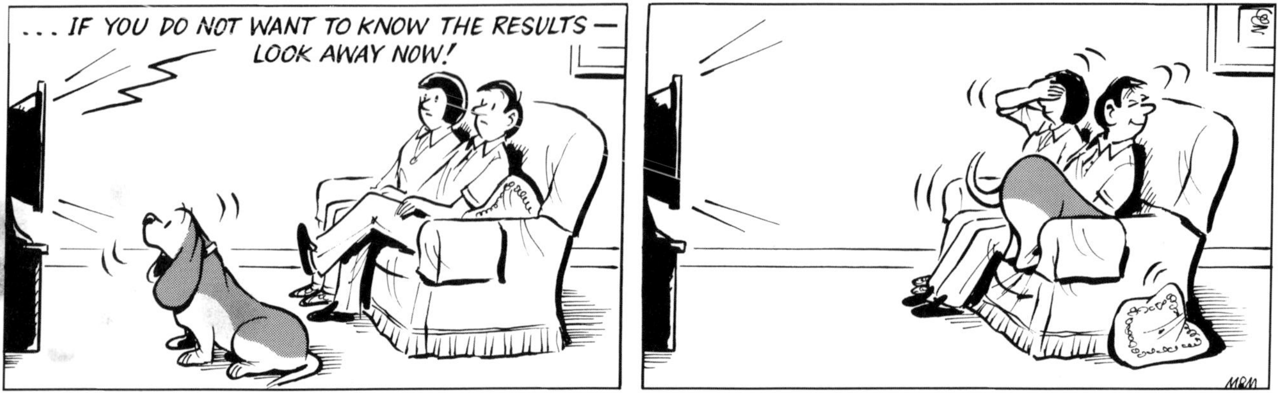
. . . IF YOU DO NOT WANT TO KNOW THE RESULTS — LOOK AWAY NOW!

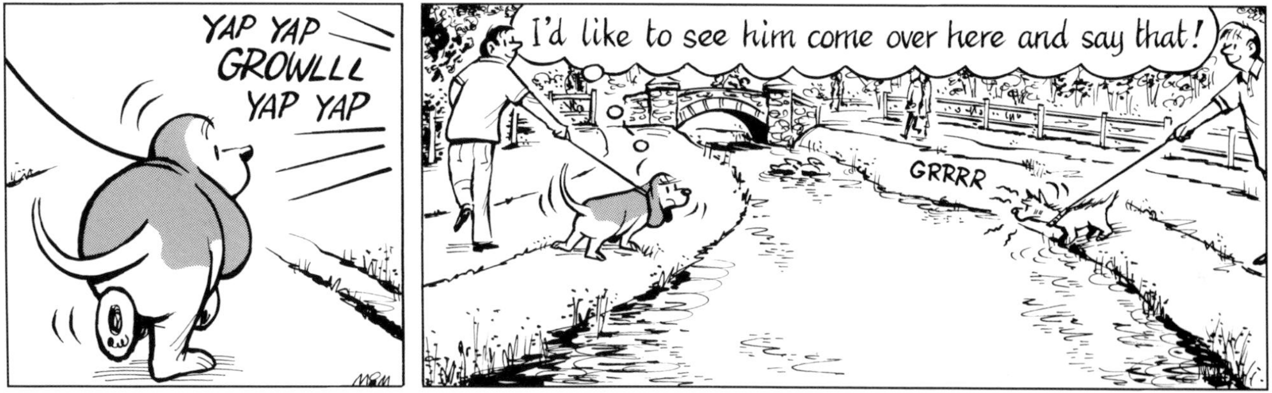
YAP YAP
GROWLLL
YAP YAP
MGM
I'd like to see him come over here and say that!
GRRRR

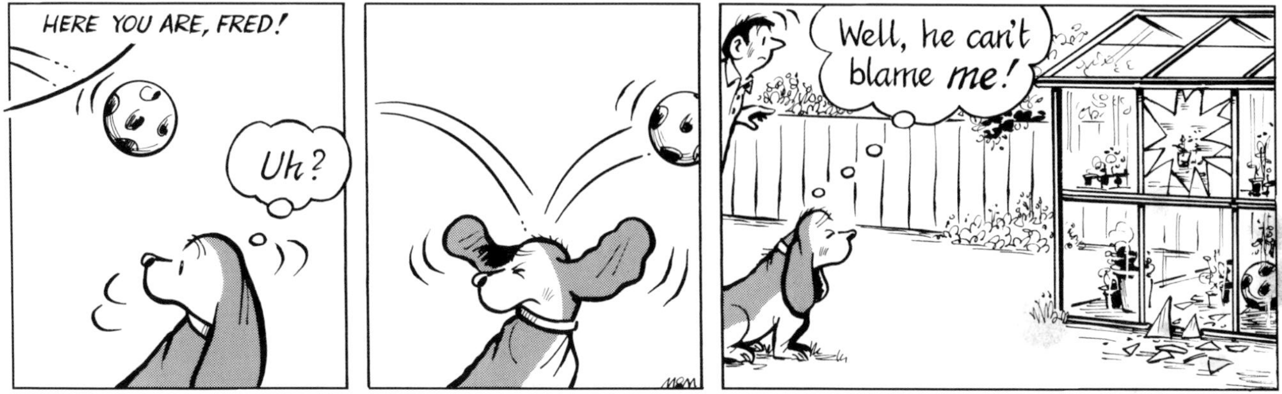
HERE YOU ARE, FRED!
Uh?
MGM
Well, he can't blame *me*!

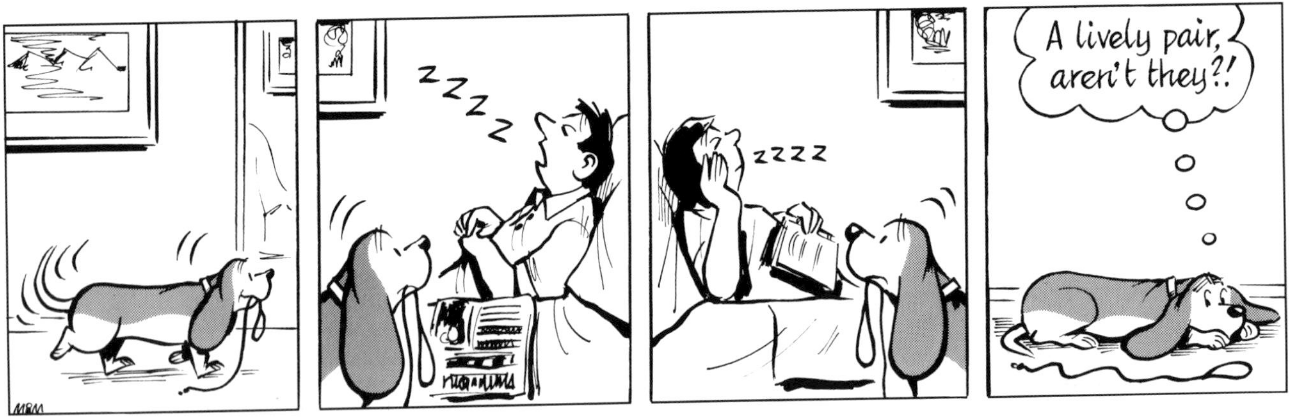
ZZZZ
ZZZZ
A lively pair, aren't they?!

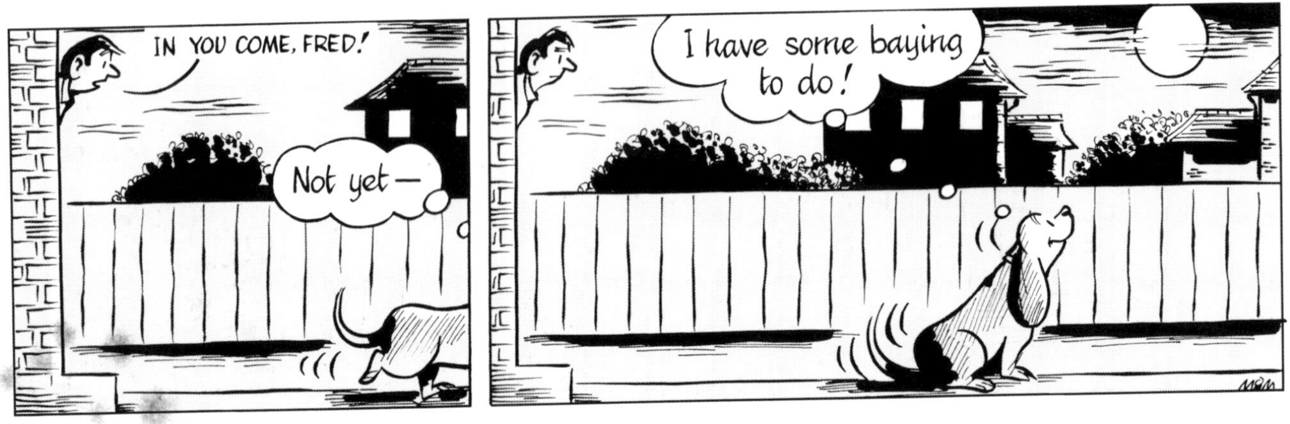
IN YOU COME, FRED!
Not yet—
I have some baying to do!

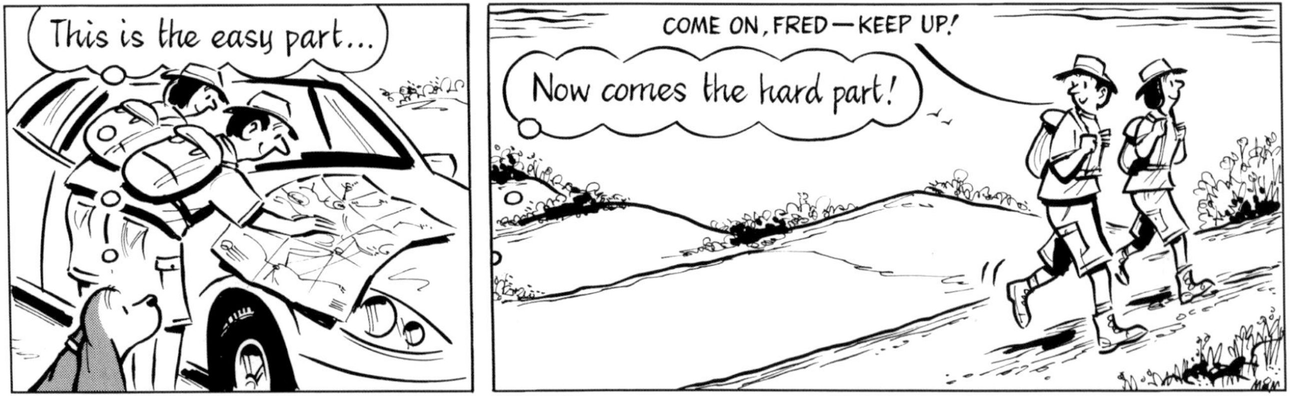
This is the easy part...
COME ON, FRED—KEEP UP!
Now comes the hard part!

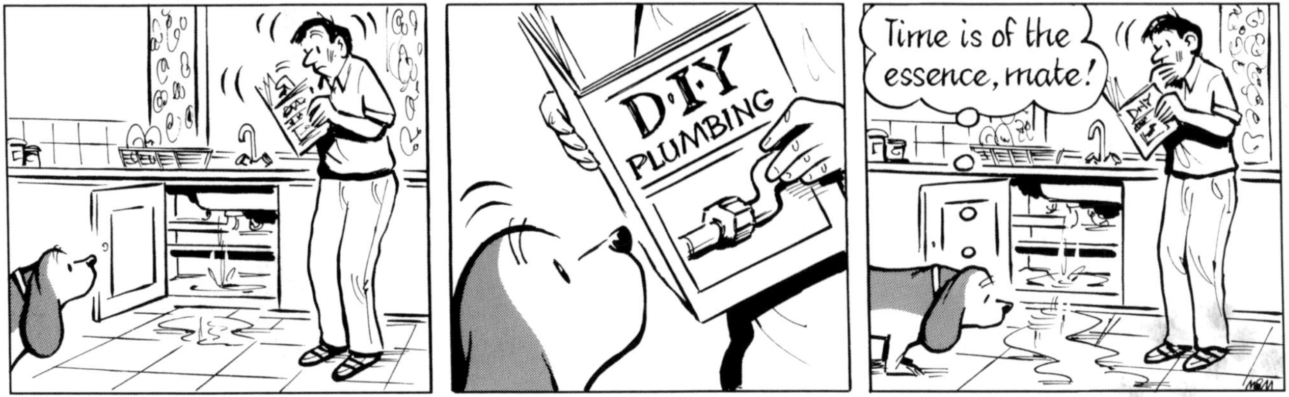
D·I·Y
PLUMBING
Time is of the essence, mate!

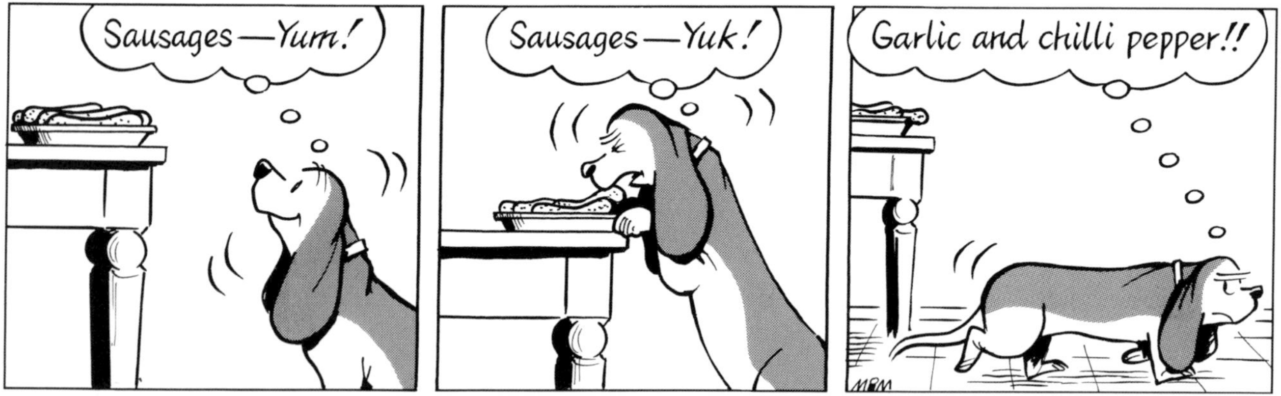
Sausages—Yum!
Sausages—Yuk!
Garlic and chilli pepper!!

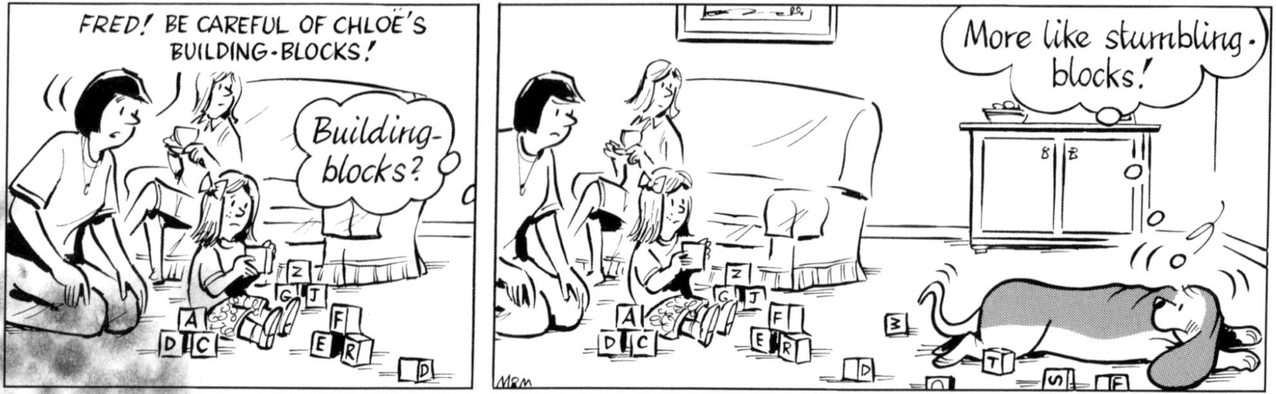
FRED! BE CAREFUL OF CHLOË'S BUILDING-BLOCKS!
Building-blocks?
More like stumbling-blocks!

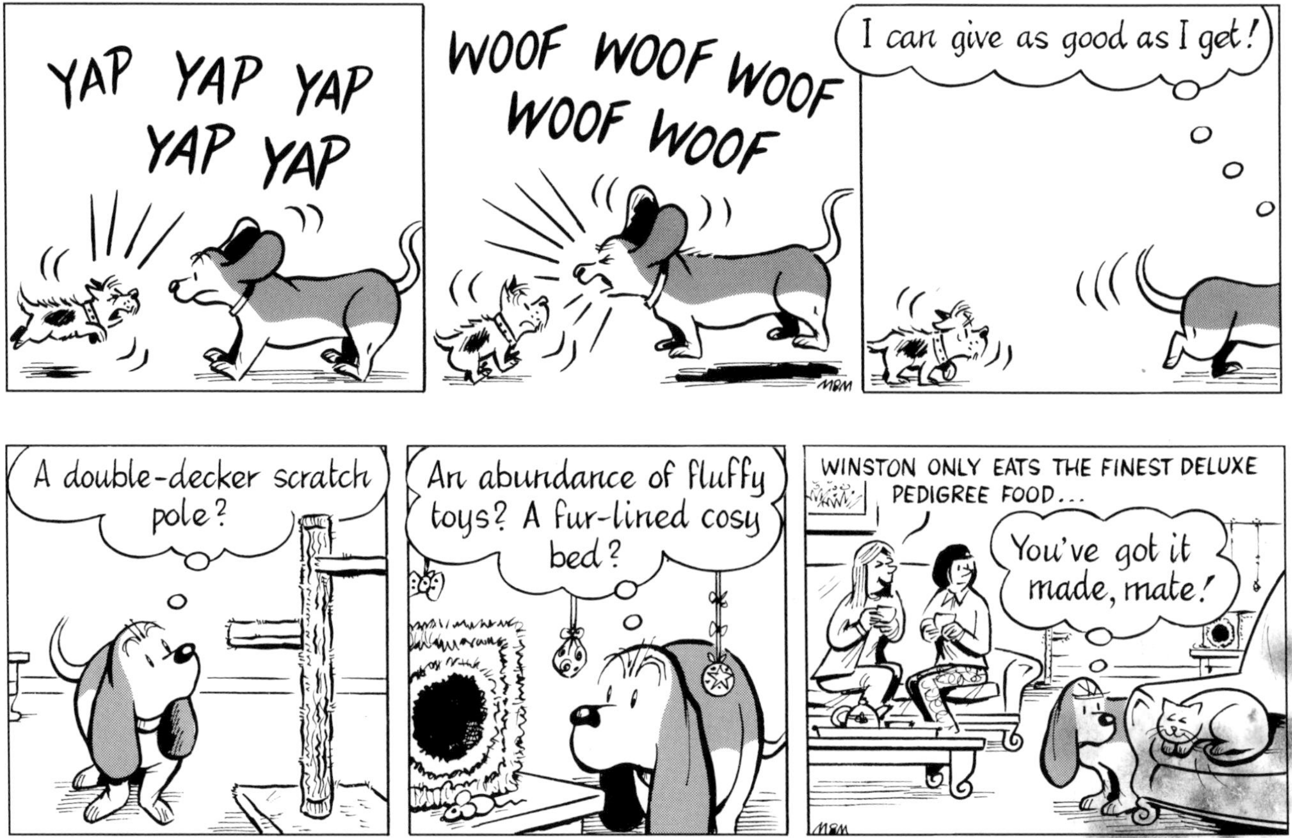
YAP YAP YAP
YAP YAP
WOOF WOOF WOOF
WOOF WOOF
MBM
I can give as good as I get!
A double-decker scratch pole?
An abundance of fluffy toys? A fur-lined cosy bed?
WINSTON ONLY EATS THE FINEST DELUXE PEDIGREE FOOD...
You've got it made, mate!
MBM

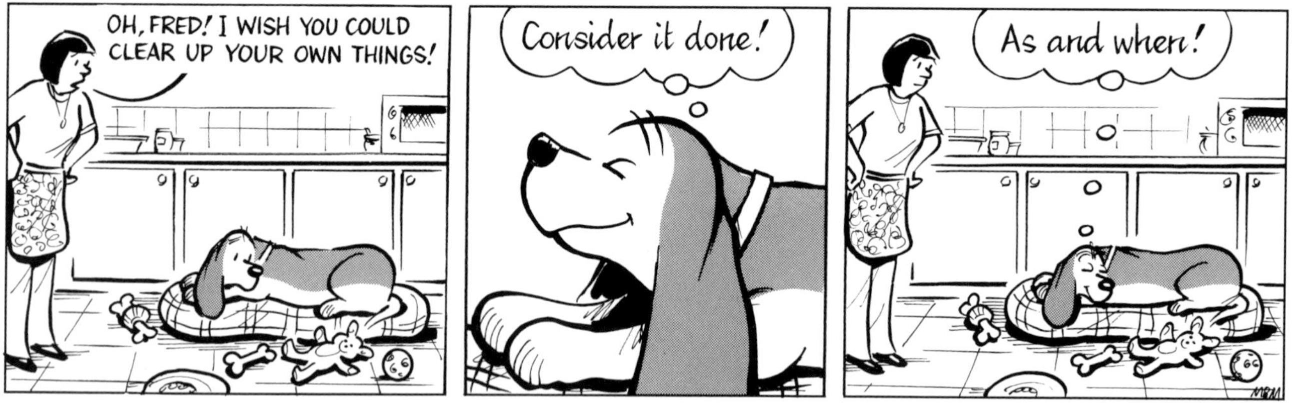
OH, FRED! I WISH YOU COULD CLEAR UP YOUR OWN THINGS!
Consider it done!
As and when!

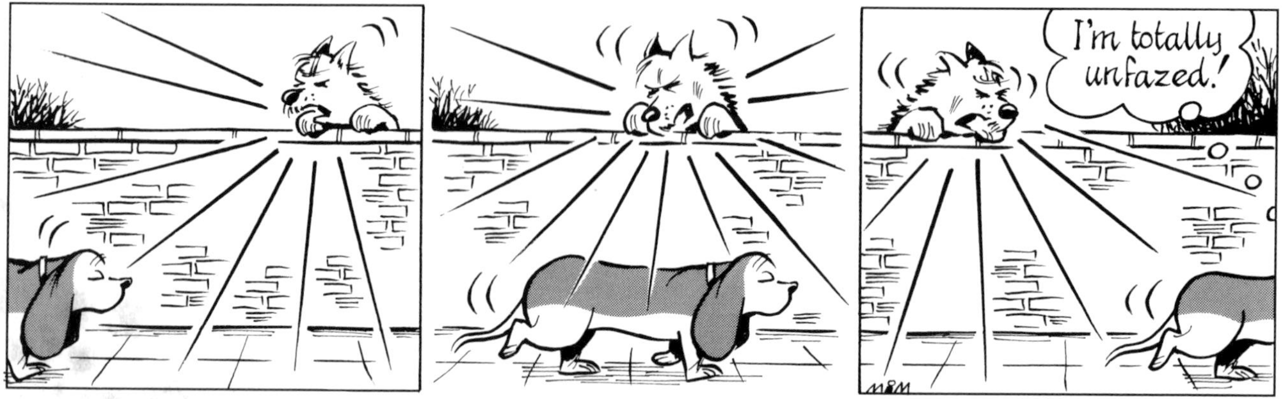
I'm totally unfazed!

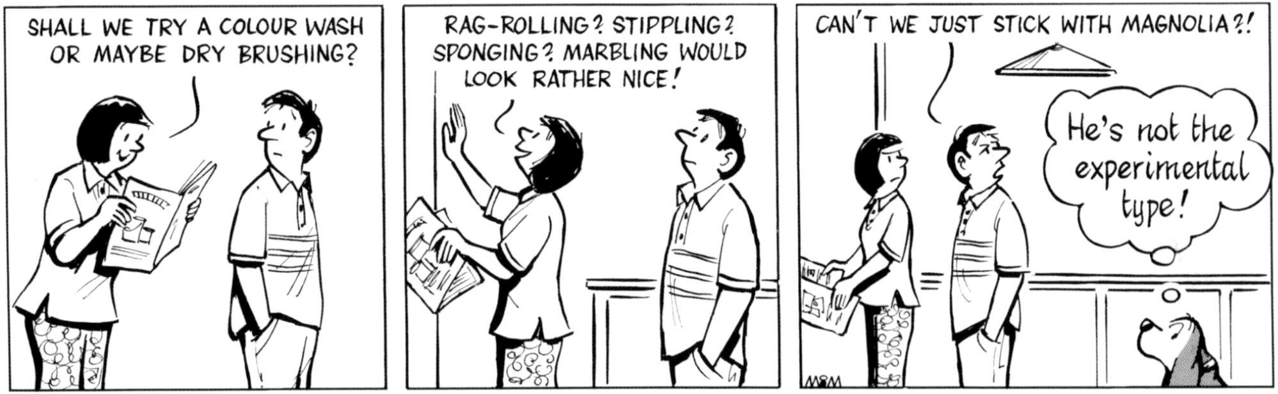
SHALL WE TRY A COLOUR WASH OR MAYBE DRY BRUSHING?
RAG-ROLLING? STIPPLING? SPONGING? MARBLING WOULD LOOK RATHER NICE!
CAN'T WE JUST STICK WITH MAGNOLIA?!
He's not the experimental type!
M&M

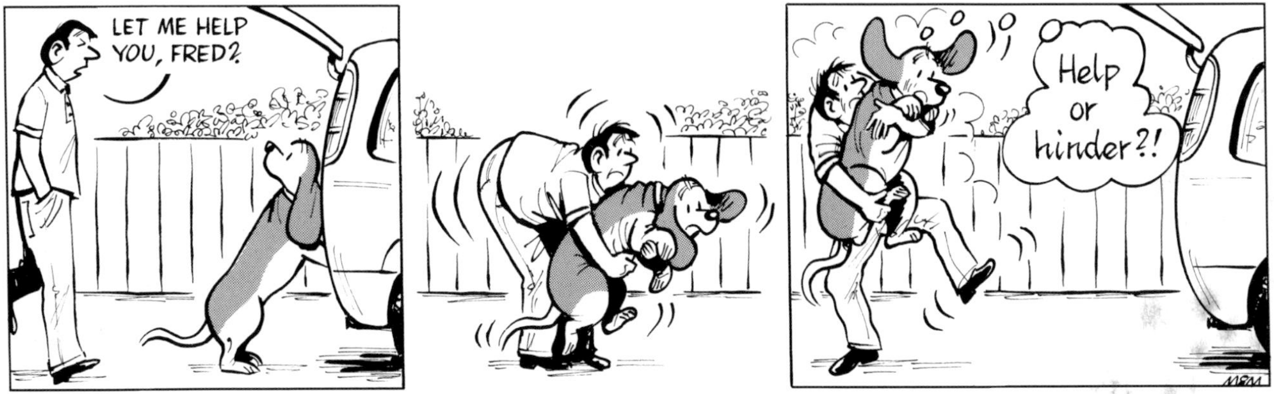
LET ME HELP YOU, FRED?
Help or hinder?!
M&M

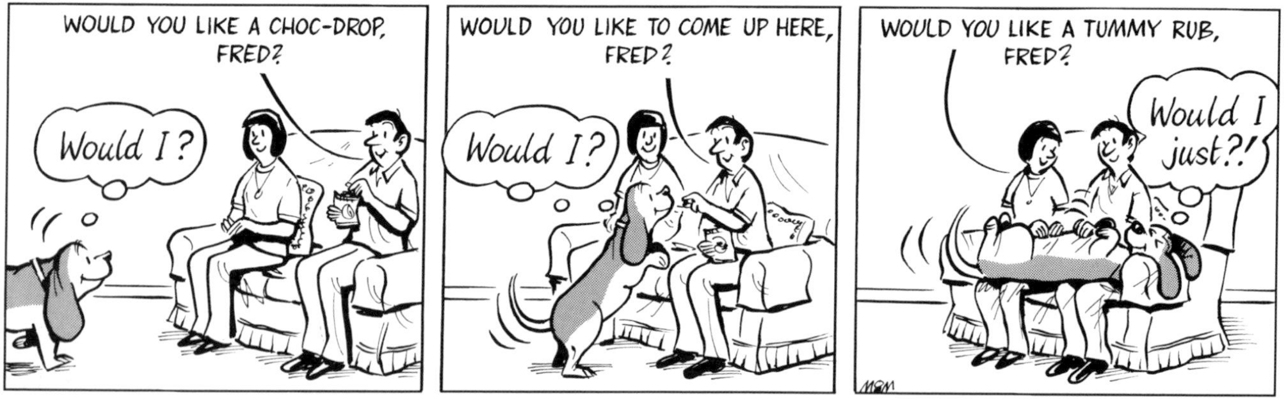
WOULD YOU LIKE A CHOC-DROP, FRED?
Would I?
WOULD YOU LIKE TO COME UP HERE, FRED?
Would I?
WOULD YOU LIKE A TUMMY RUB, FRED?
Would I just?!

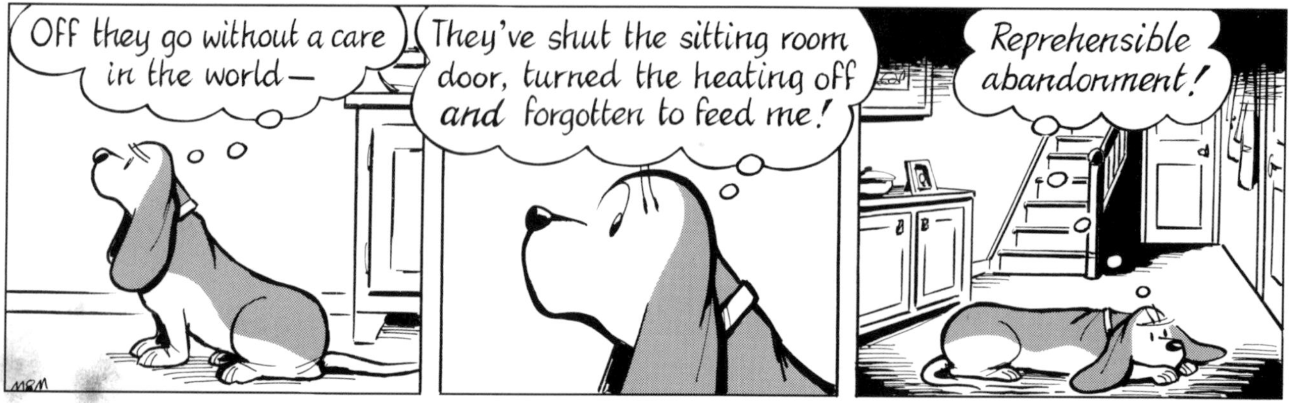
Off they go without a care in the world—
They've shut the sitting room door, turned the heating off and forgotten to feed me!
Reprehensible abandonment!

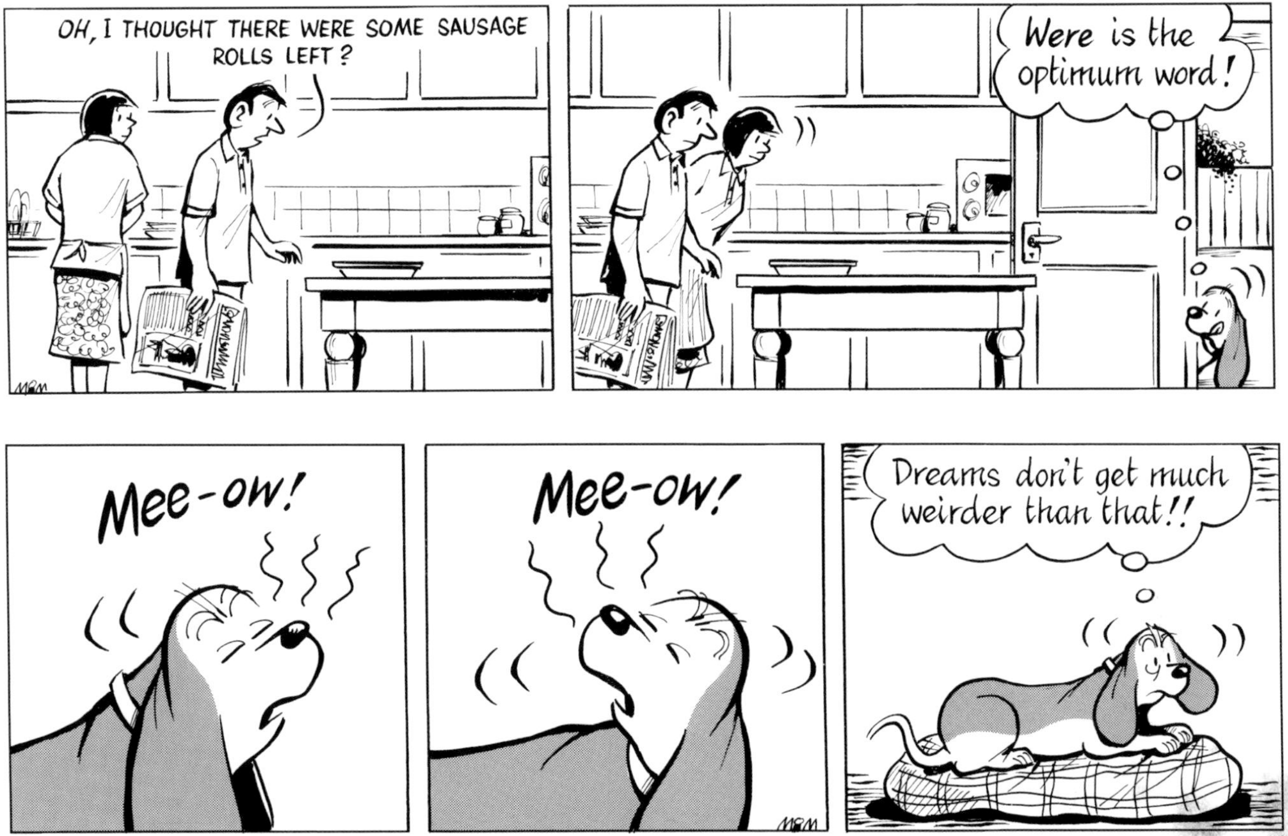
OH, I THOUGHT THERE WERE SOME SAUSAGE ROLLS LEFT?
Were is the optimum word!
Mee-ow!
Mee-ow!
Dreams don't get much weirder than that!!

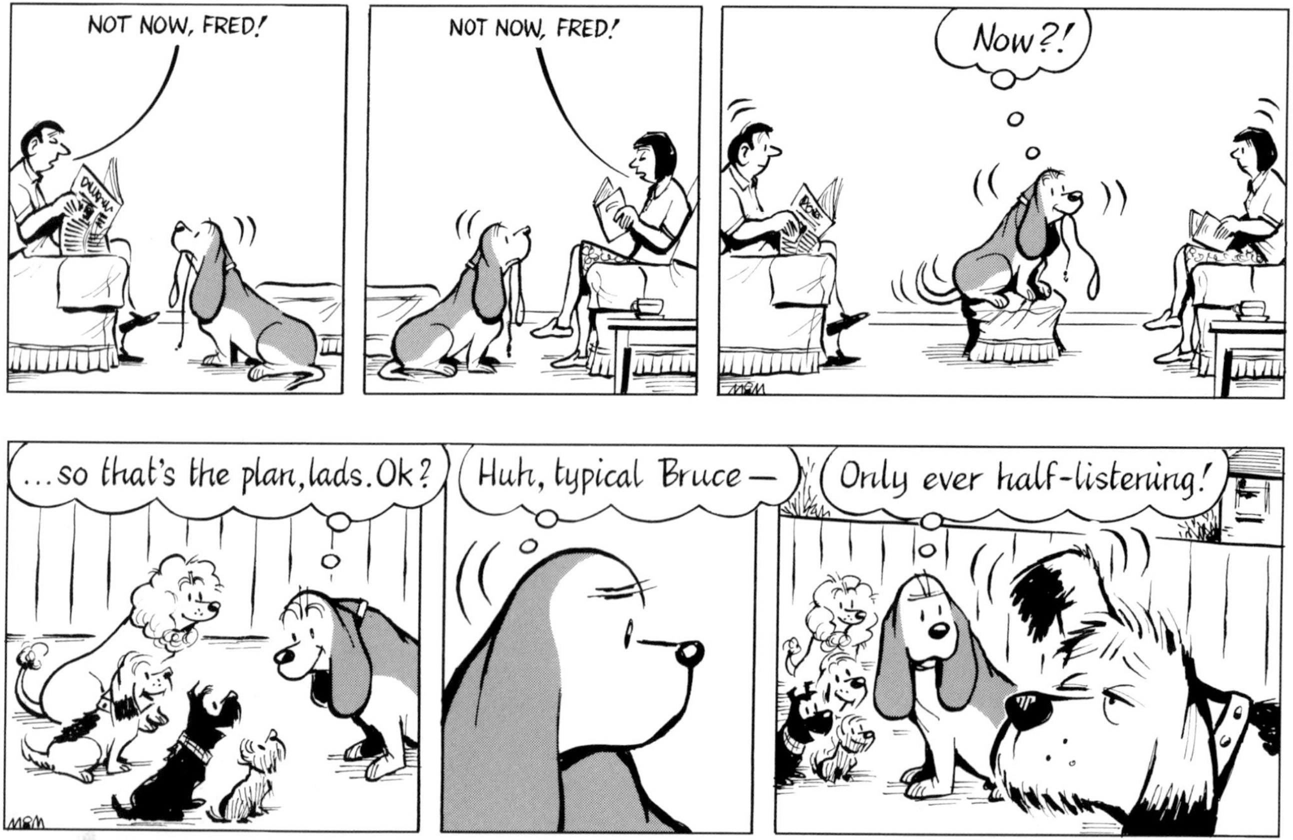
NOT NOW, FRED!
NOT NOW, FRED!
Now?!
...so that's the plan, lads. Ok?
Huh, typical Bruce—
Only ever half-listening!

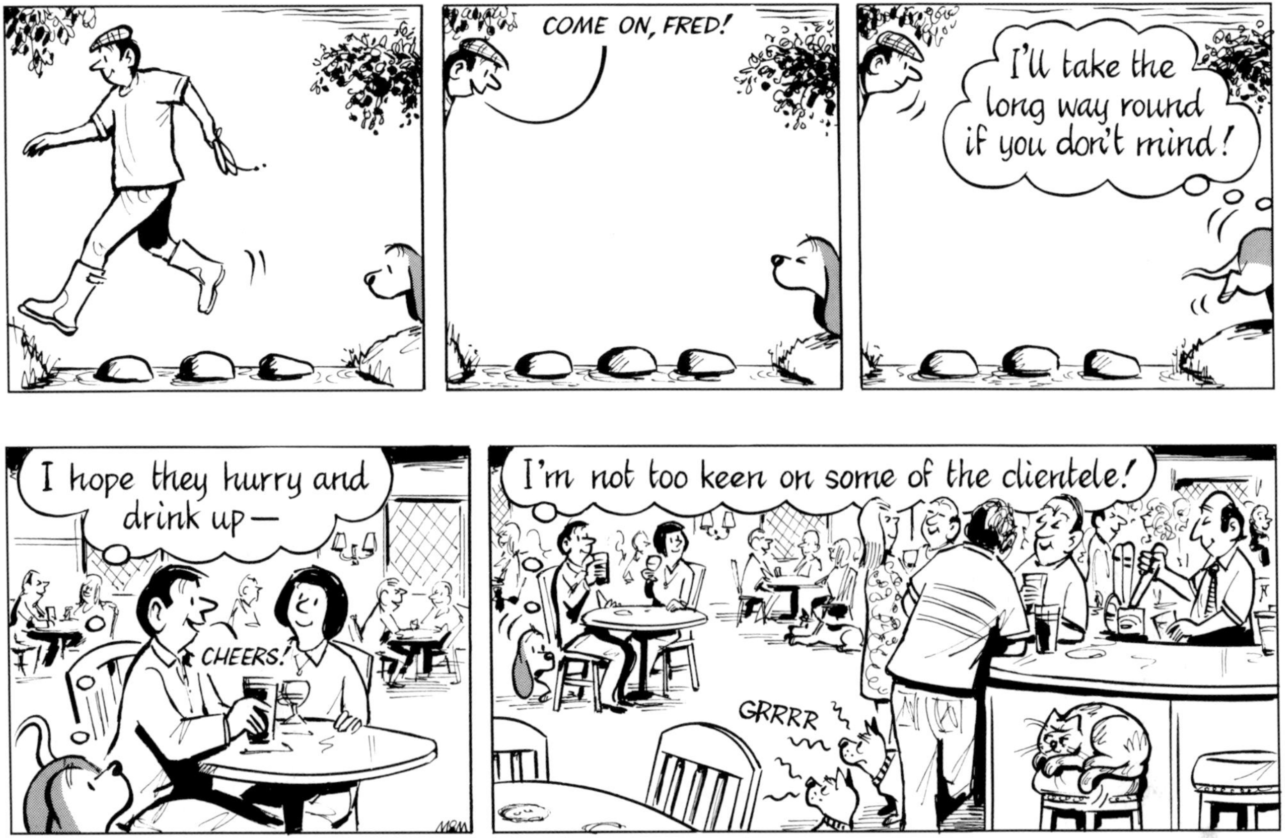
COME ON, FRED!
I'll take the long way round if you don't mind!
I hope they hurry and drink up —
CHEERS!
I'm not too keen on some of the clientele!
GRRRR

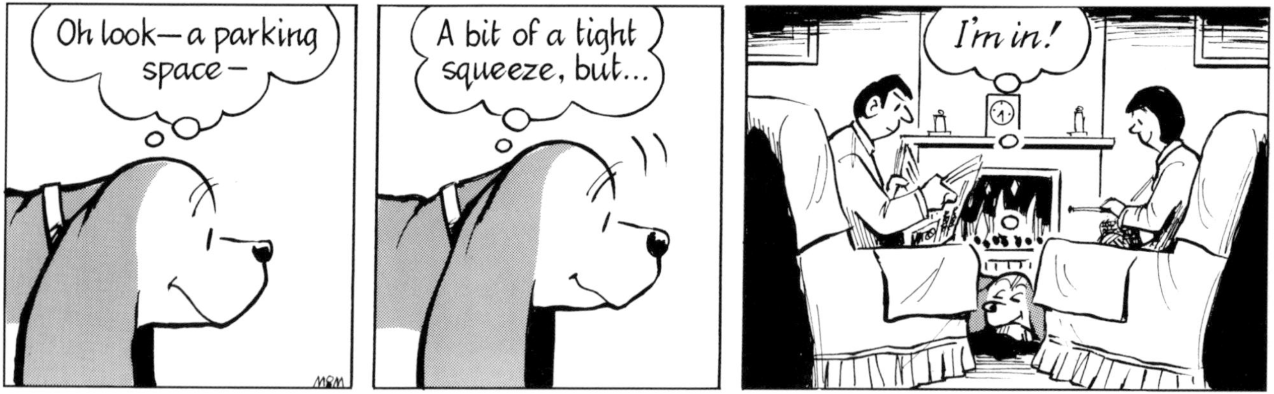
Oh look—a parking space—
A bit of a tight squeeze, but...
I'm in!

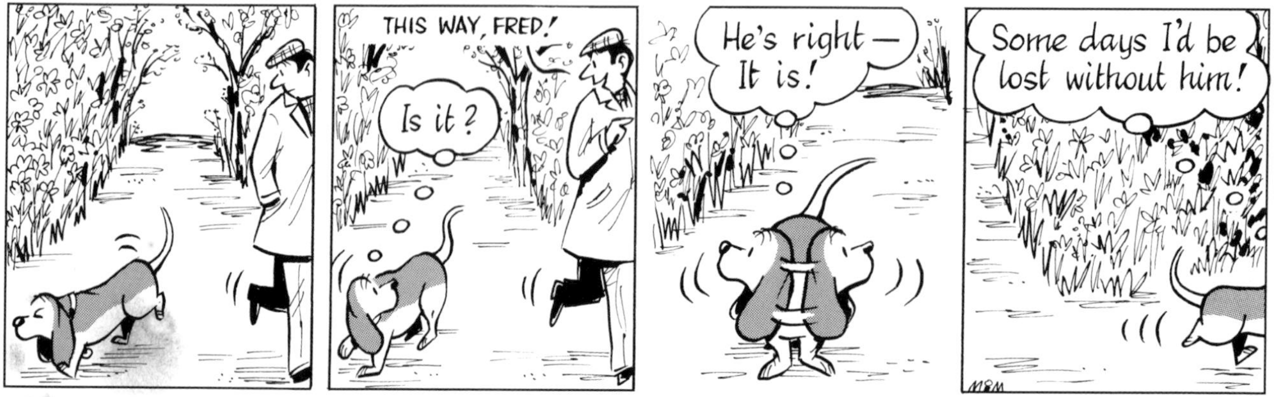
THIS WAY, FRED!
Is it?
He's right— It is!
Some days I'd be lost without him!

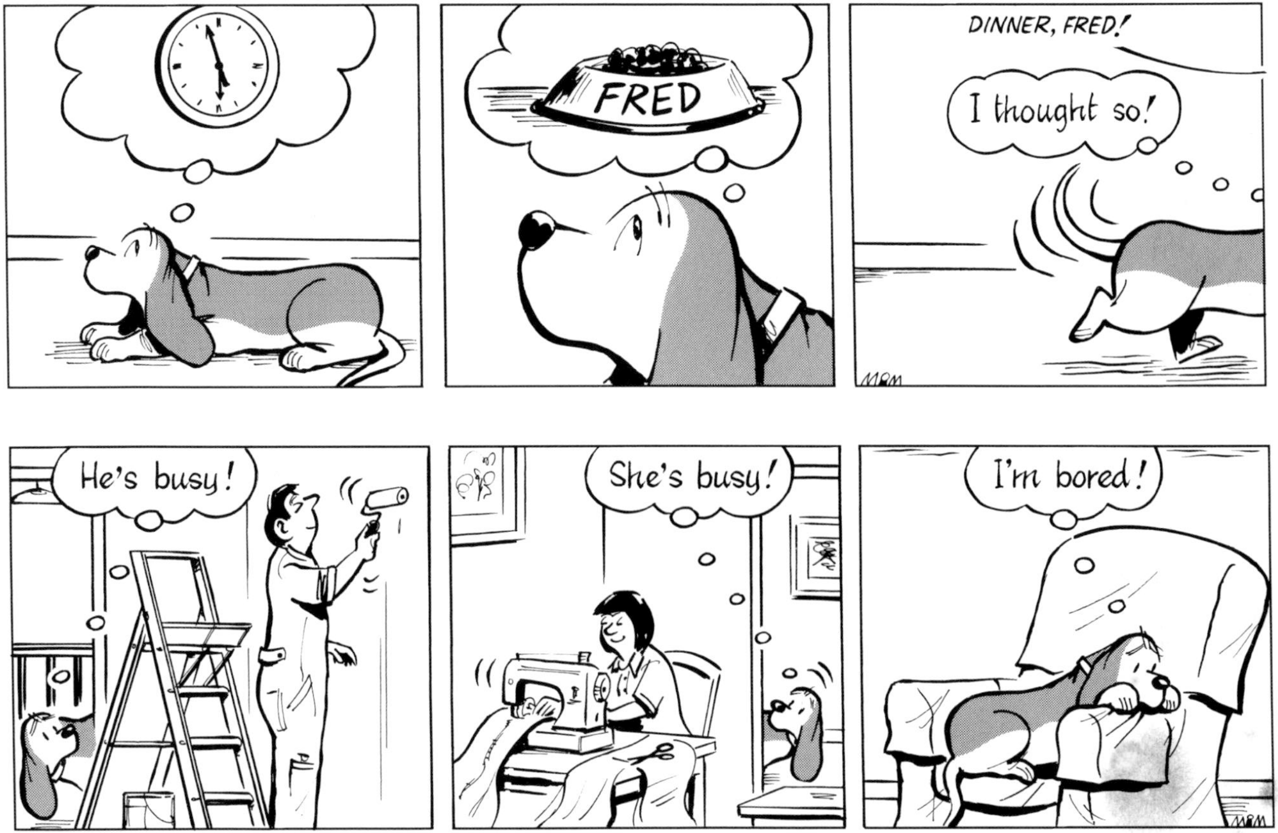

FRED
DINNER, FRED!
I thought so!
MBM
He's busy!
She's busy!
I'm bored!
MBM

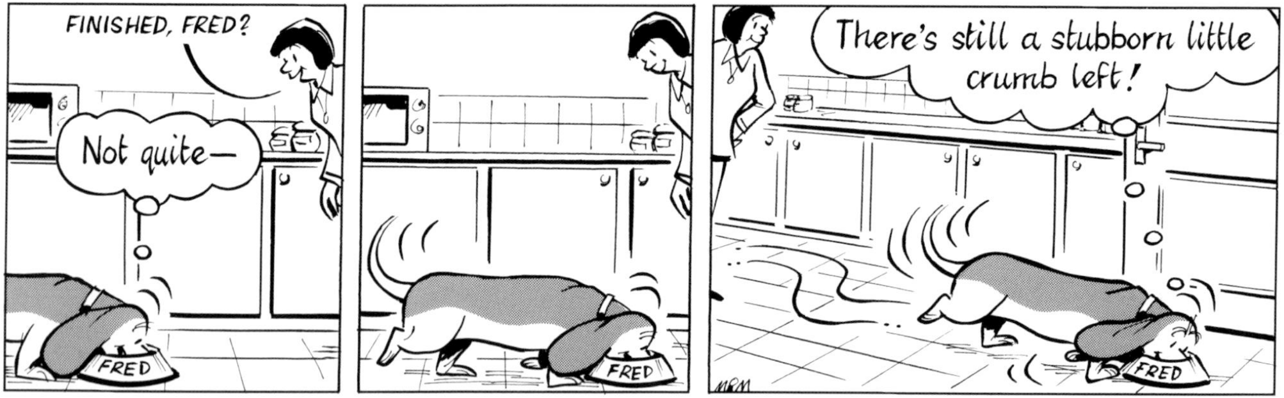
FINISHED, FRED?
Not quite—
FRED
FRED
There's still a stubborn little crumb left!
FRED

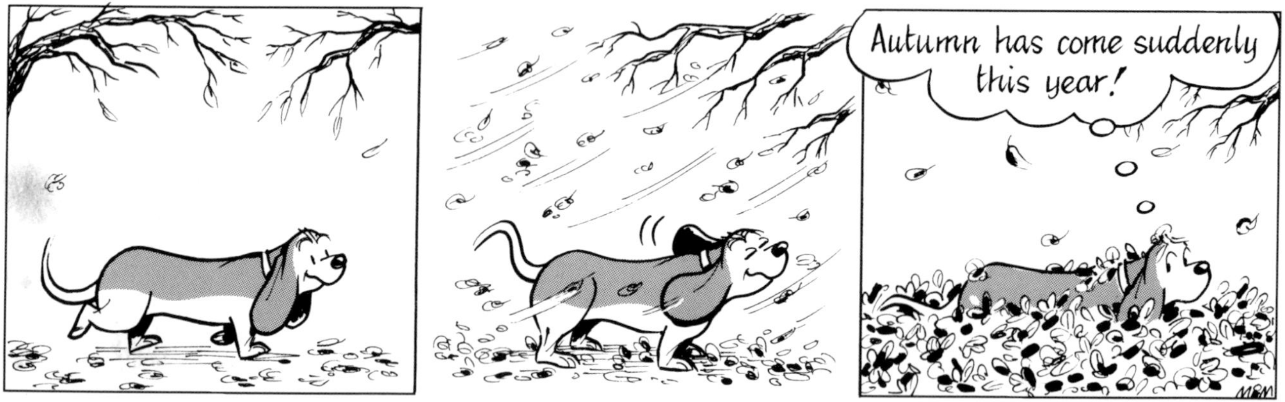
Autumn has come suddenly this year!

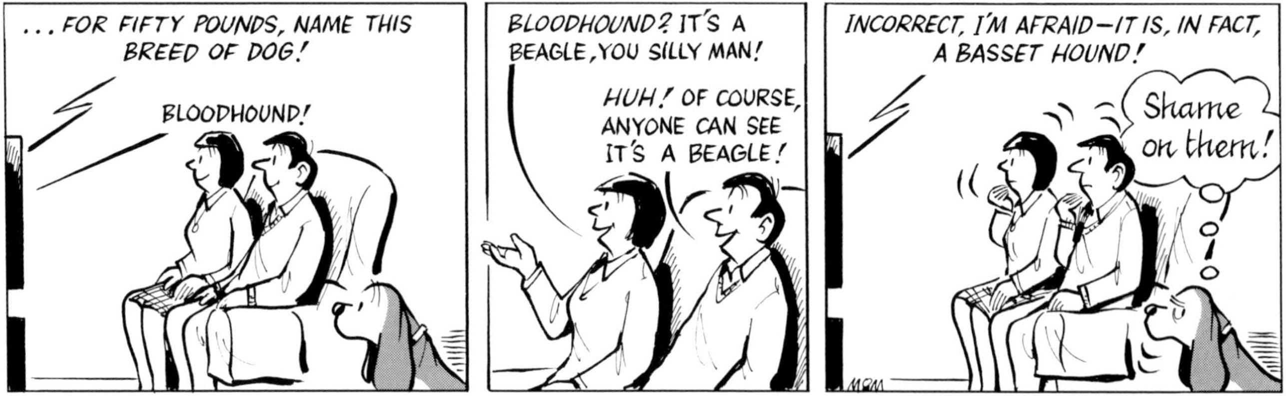
...FOR FIFTY POUNDS, NAME THIS BREED OF DOG!
BLOODHOUND!
BLOODHOUND? IT'S A BEAGLE, YOU SILLY MAN!
HUH! OF COURSE, ANYONE CAN SEE IT'S A BEAGLE!
INCORRECT, I'M AFRAID—IT IS, IN FACT, A BASSET HOUND!
Shame on them!

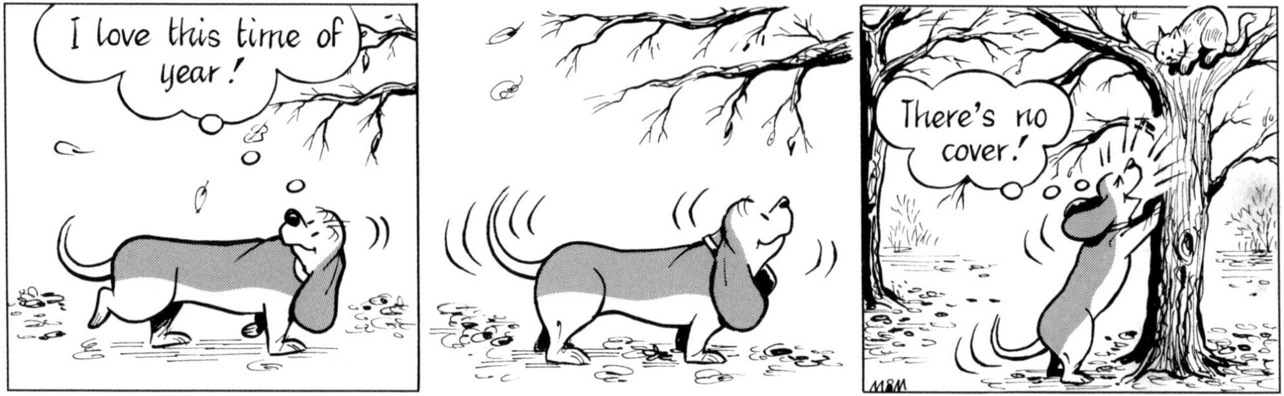
I love this time of year!
There's no cover!

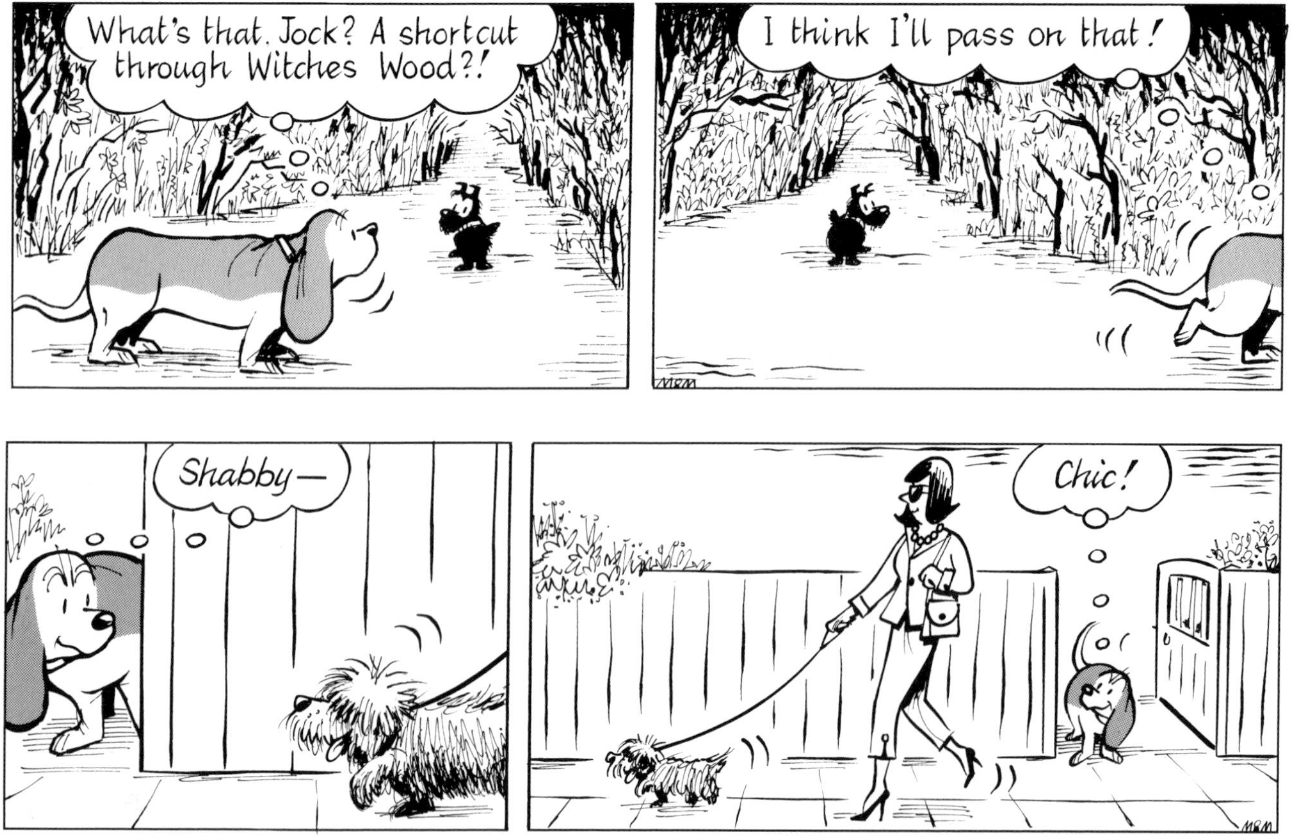
What's that, Jock? A shortcut through Witches Wood?!
I think I'll pass on that!
Shabby—
Chic!

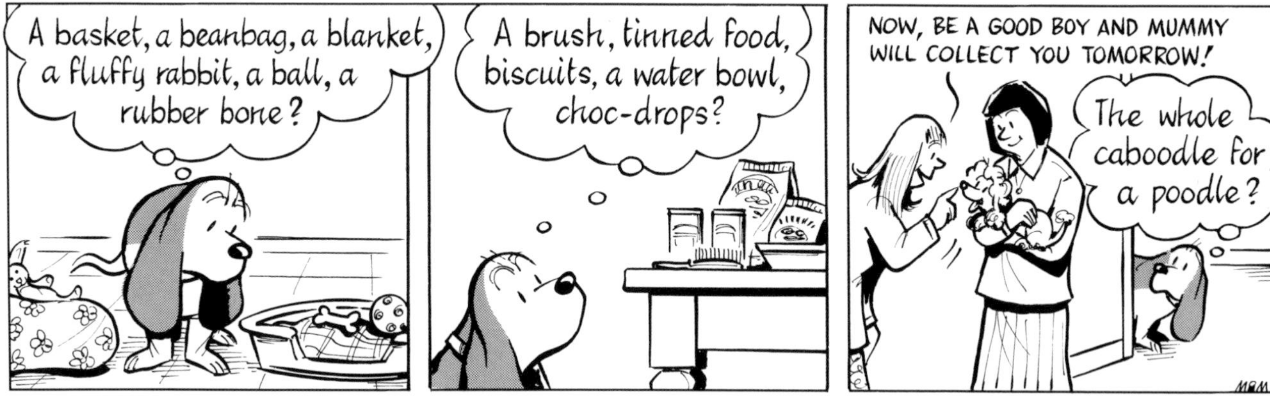
A basket, a beanbag, a blanket, a fluffy rabbit, a ball, a rubber bone?
A brush, tinned food, biscuits, a water bowl, choc-drops?
NOW, BE A GOOD BOY AND MUMMY WILL COLLECT YOU TOMORROW!
The whole caboodle for a poodle?

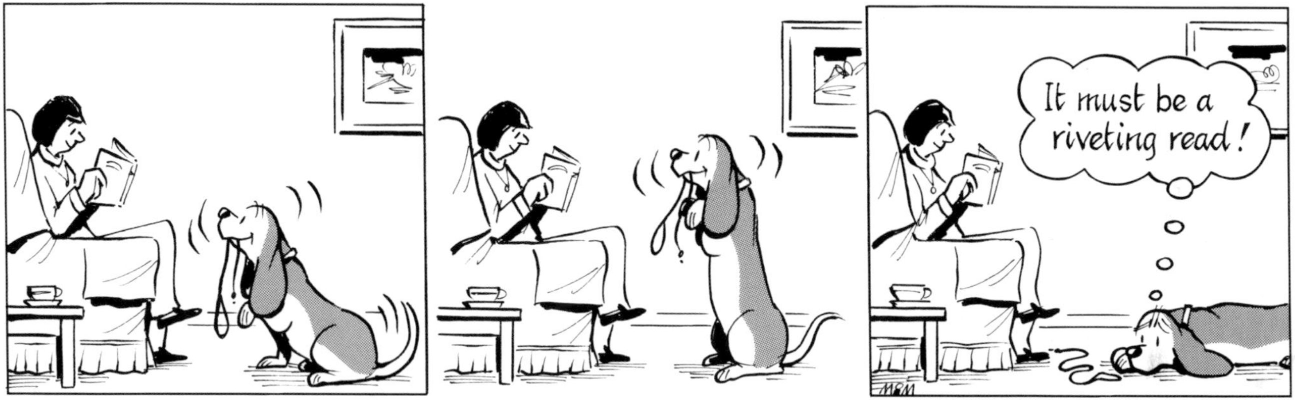
It must be a riveting read!

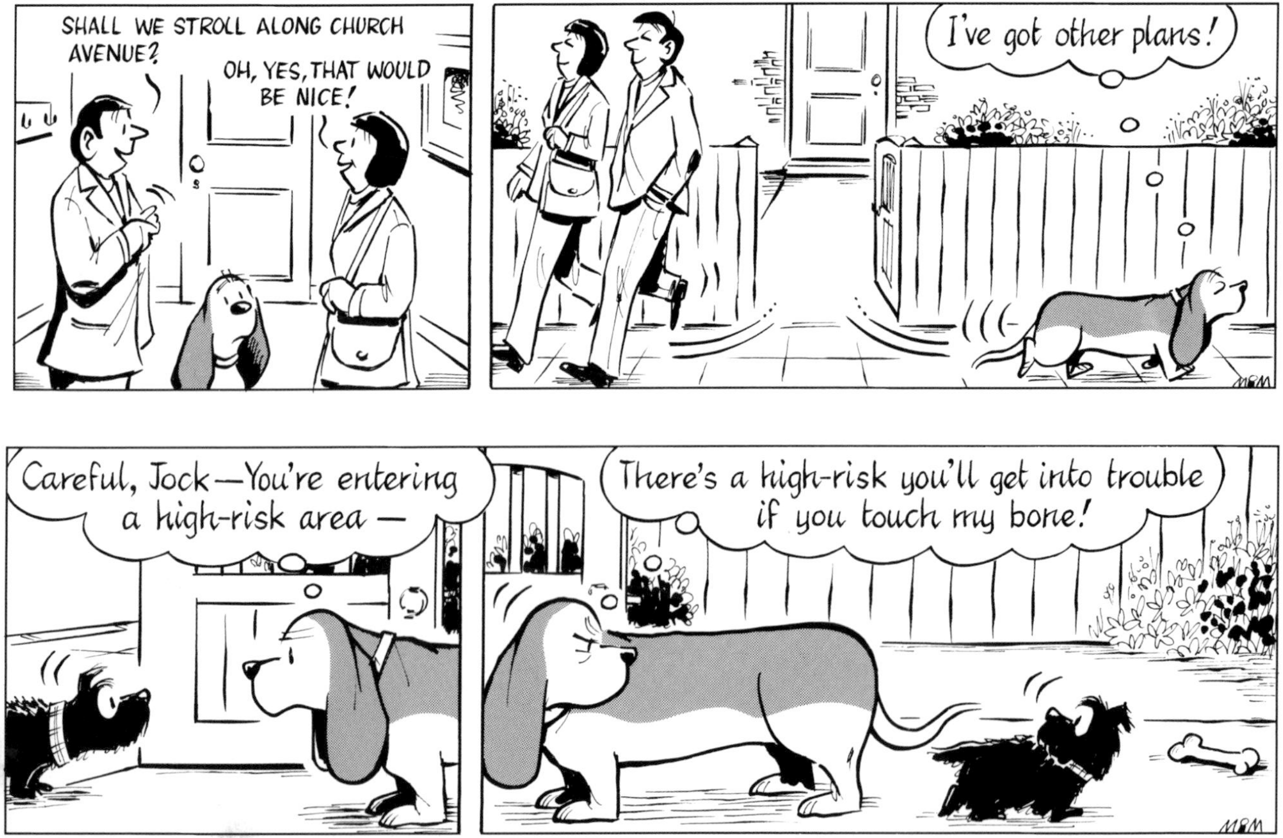
SHALL WE STROLL ALONG CHURCH AVENUE?
OH, YES, THAT WOULD BE NICE!
I've got other plans!
Careful, Jock—You're entering a high-risk area —
There's a high-risk you'll get into trouble if you touch my bone!
M&M
M&M

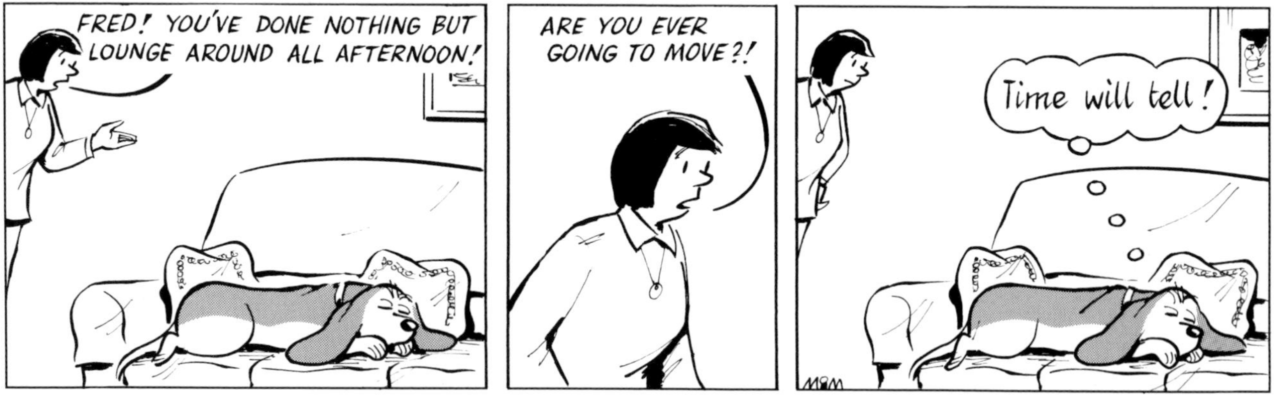
FRED! YOU'VE DONE NOTHING BUT LOUNGE AROUND ALL AFTERNOON!
ARE YOU EVER GOING TO MOVE?!
Time will tell!

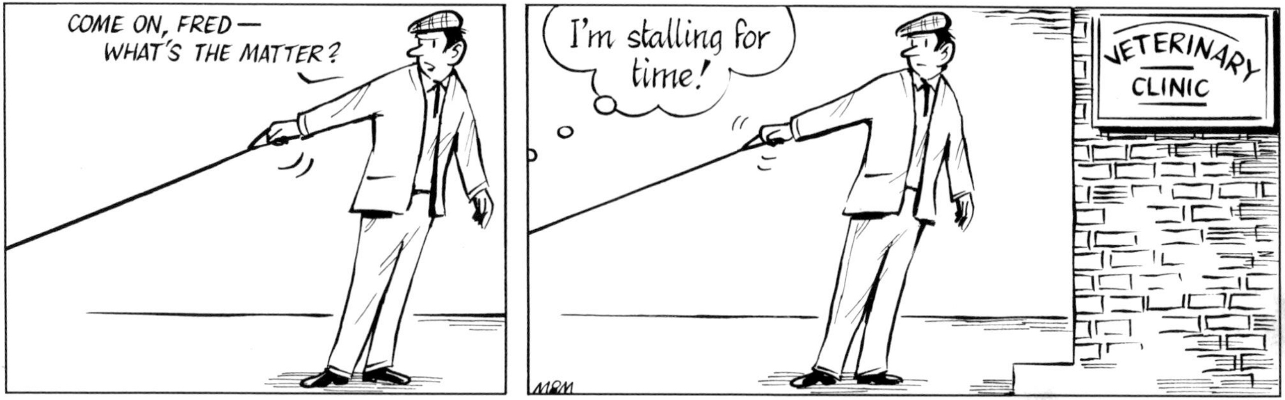
COME ON, FRED— WHAT'S THE MATTER?
I'm stalling for time!
VETERINARY CLINIC

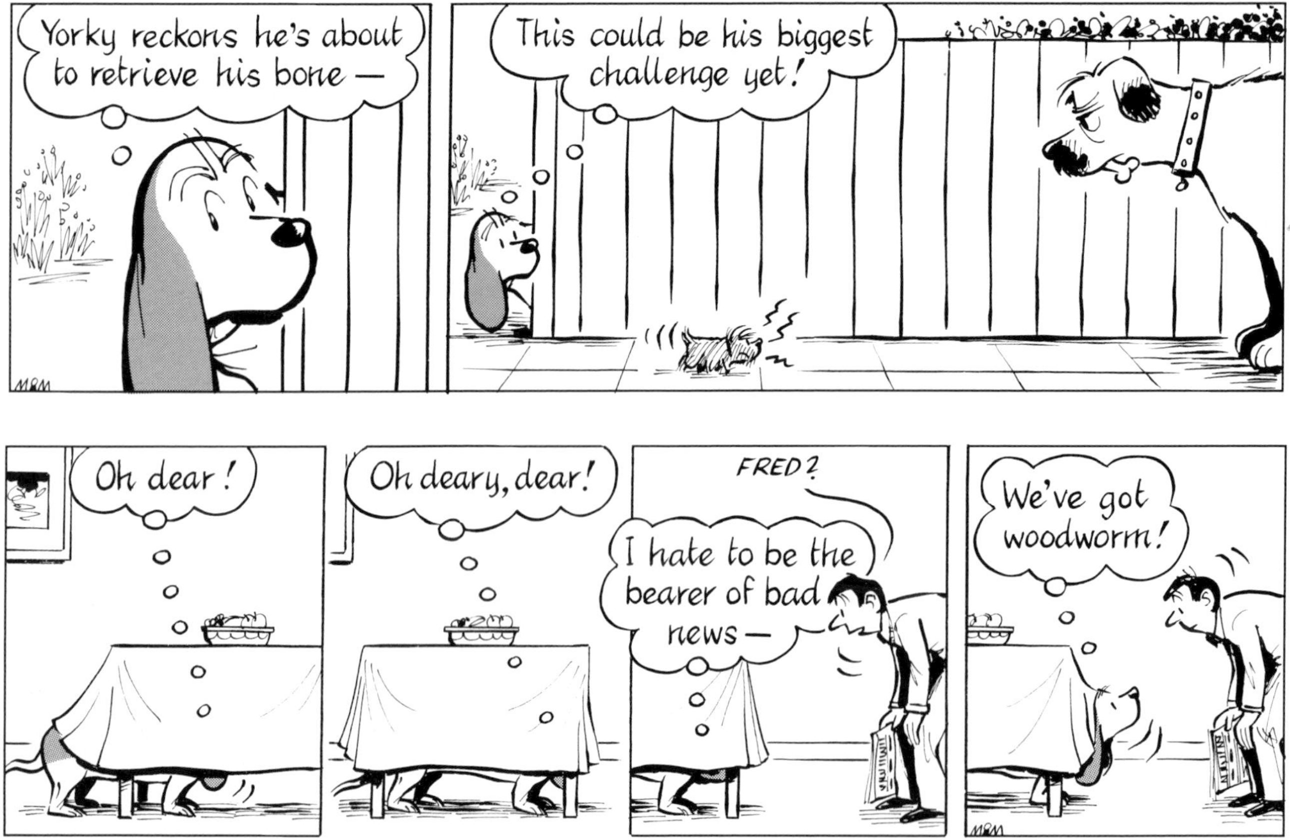
Yorky reckons he's about to retrieve his bone —
This could be his biggest challenge yet!
Oh dear!
Oh deary, dear!
FRED?
I hate to be the bearer of bad news —
We've got woodworm!

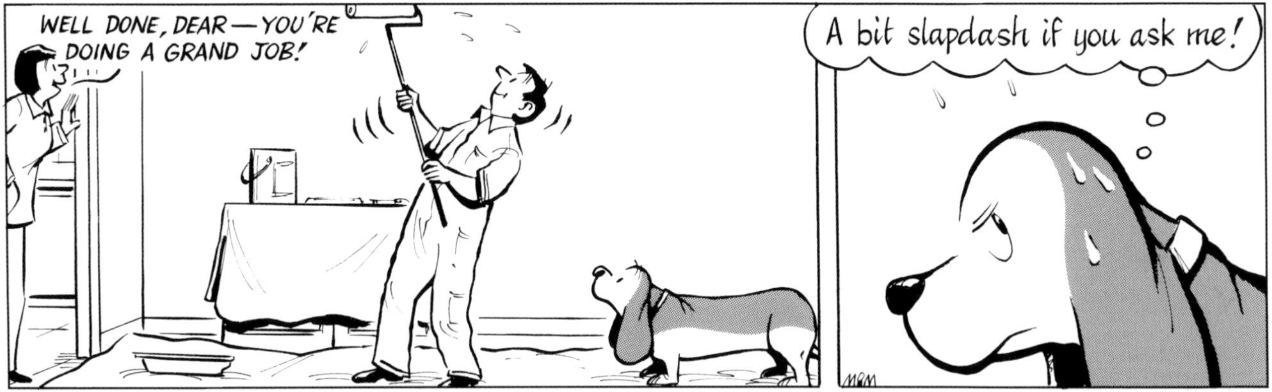
WELL DONE, DEAR — YOU'RE DOING A GRAND JOB!
A bit slapdash if you ask me!

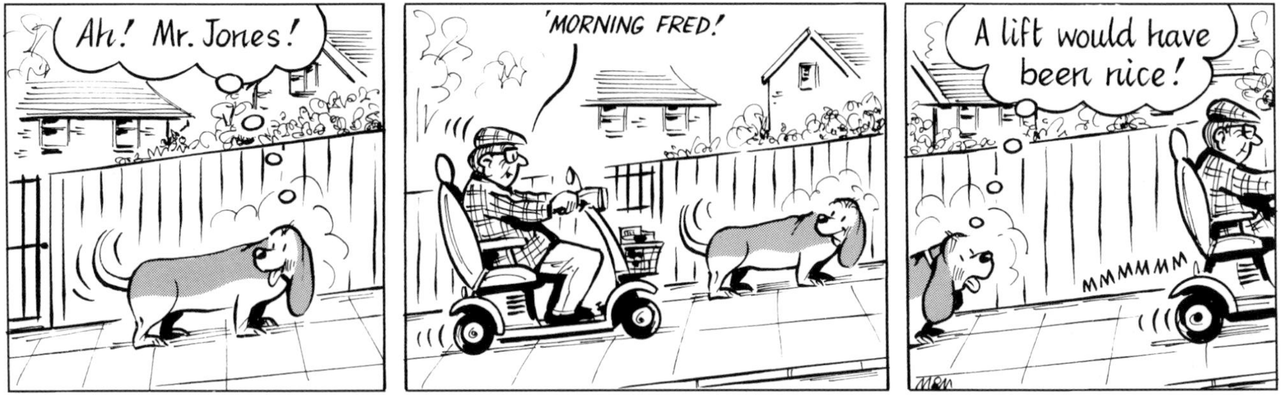
Ah! Mr. Jones!
'MORNING FRED!
A lift would have been nice!
MMMMMM

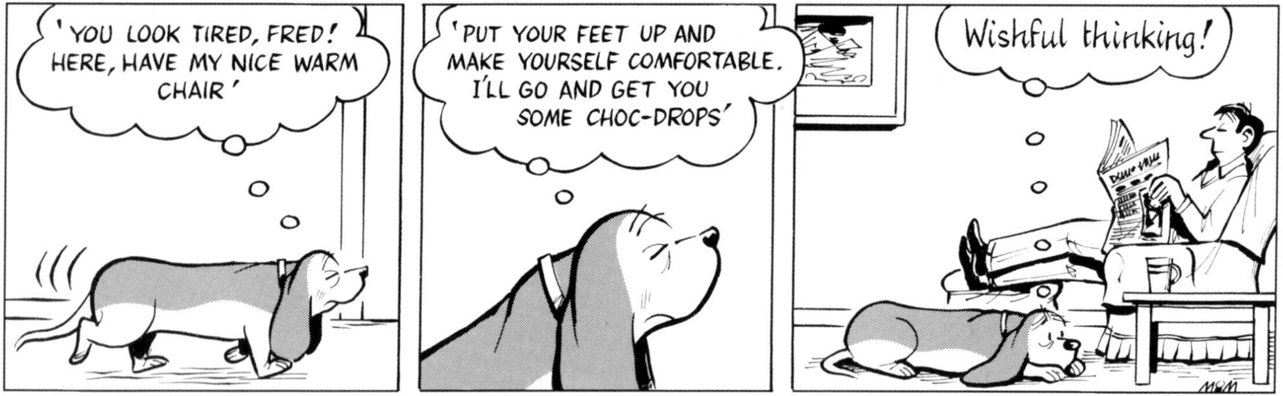
'YOU LOOK TIRED, FRED! HERE, HAVE MY NICE WARM CHAIR'
'PUT YOUR FEET UP AND MAKE YOURSELF COMFORTABLE. I'LL GO AND GET YOU SOME CHOC-DROPS'
Wishful thinking!

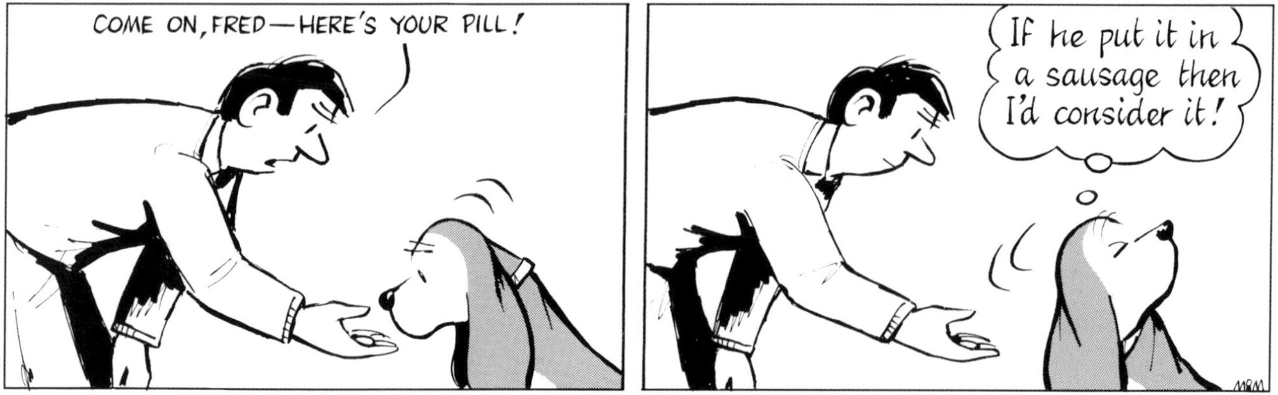
COME ON, FRED—HERE'S YOUR PILL!
If he put it in a sausage then I'd consider it!

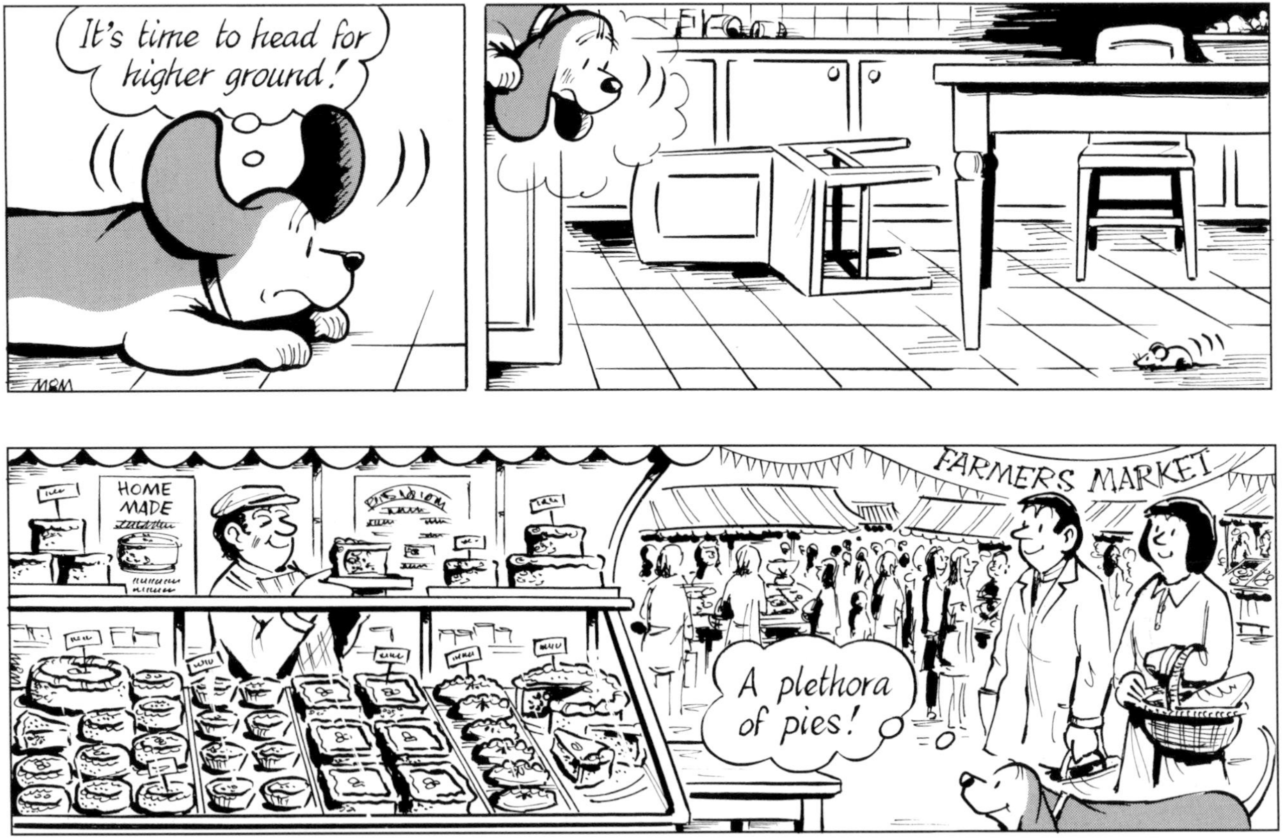
It's time to head for higher ground!
HOME MADE
FARMERS MARKET
A plethora of pies!

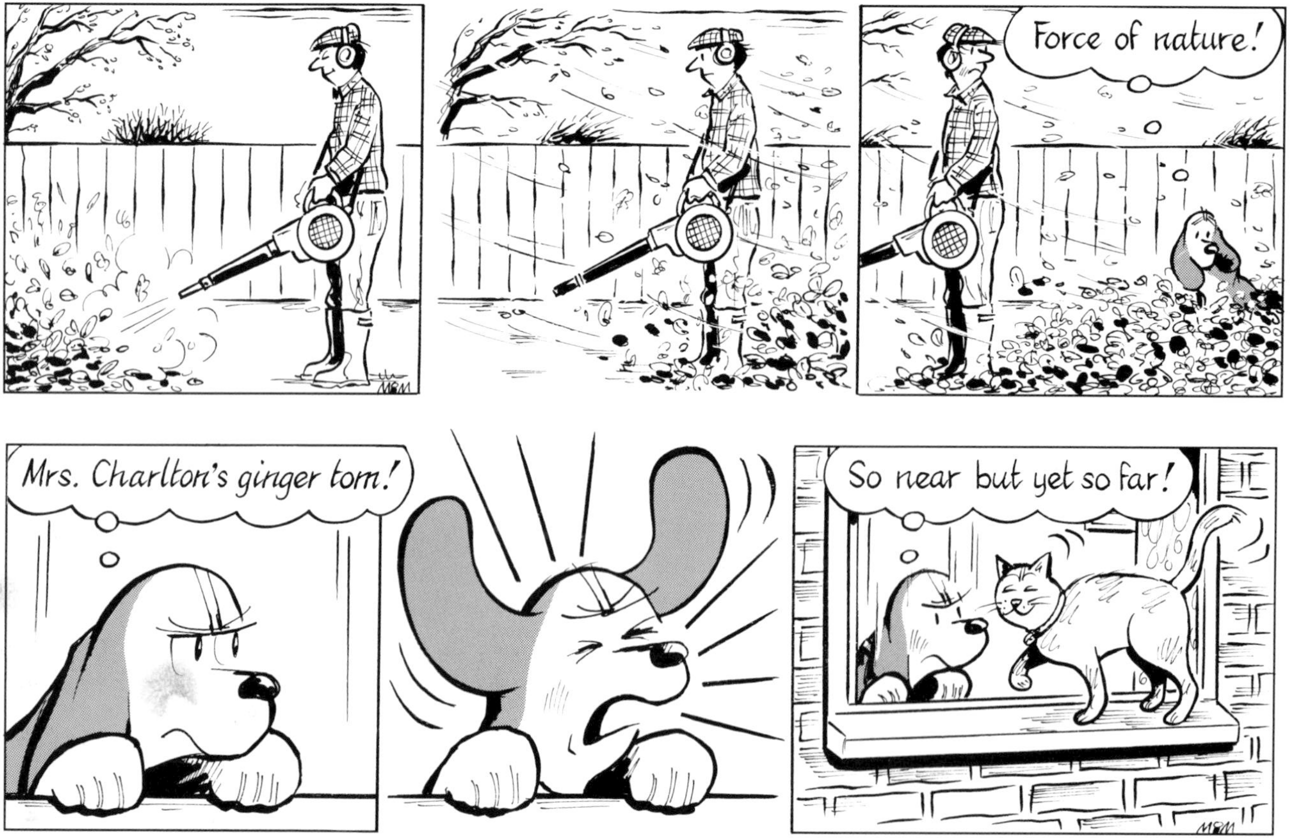
Force of nature!
Mrs. Charlton's ginger tom!
So near but yet so far!
MGM

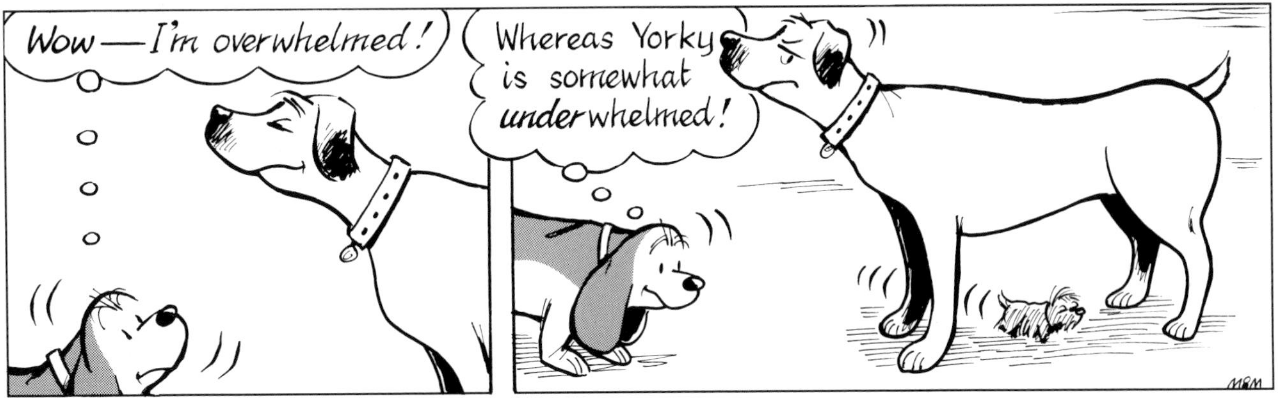
Wow — I'm overwhelmed!
Whereas Yorky is somewhat *under*whelmed!

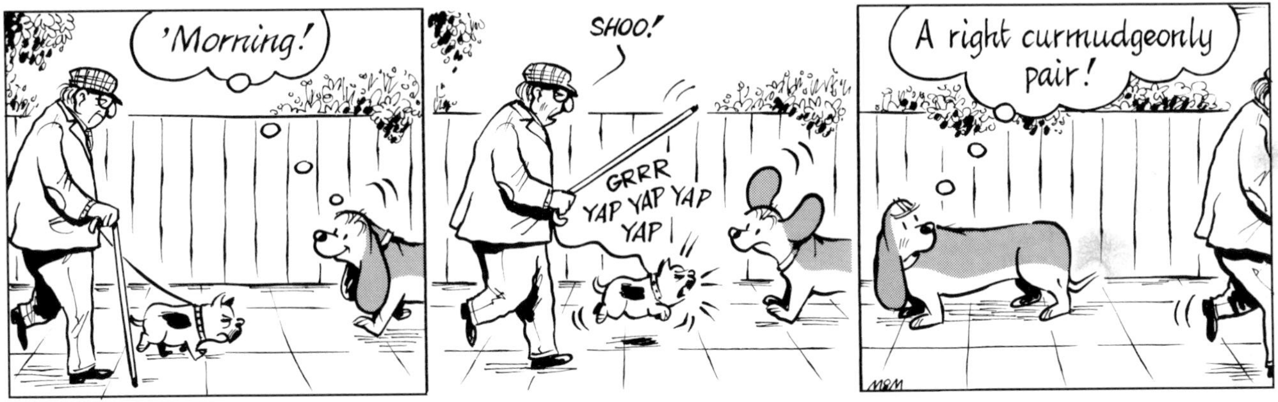
'Morning!
SHOO!
GRRR
YAP YAP YAP
YAP
A right curmudgeonly pair!

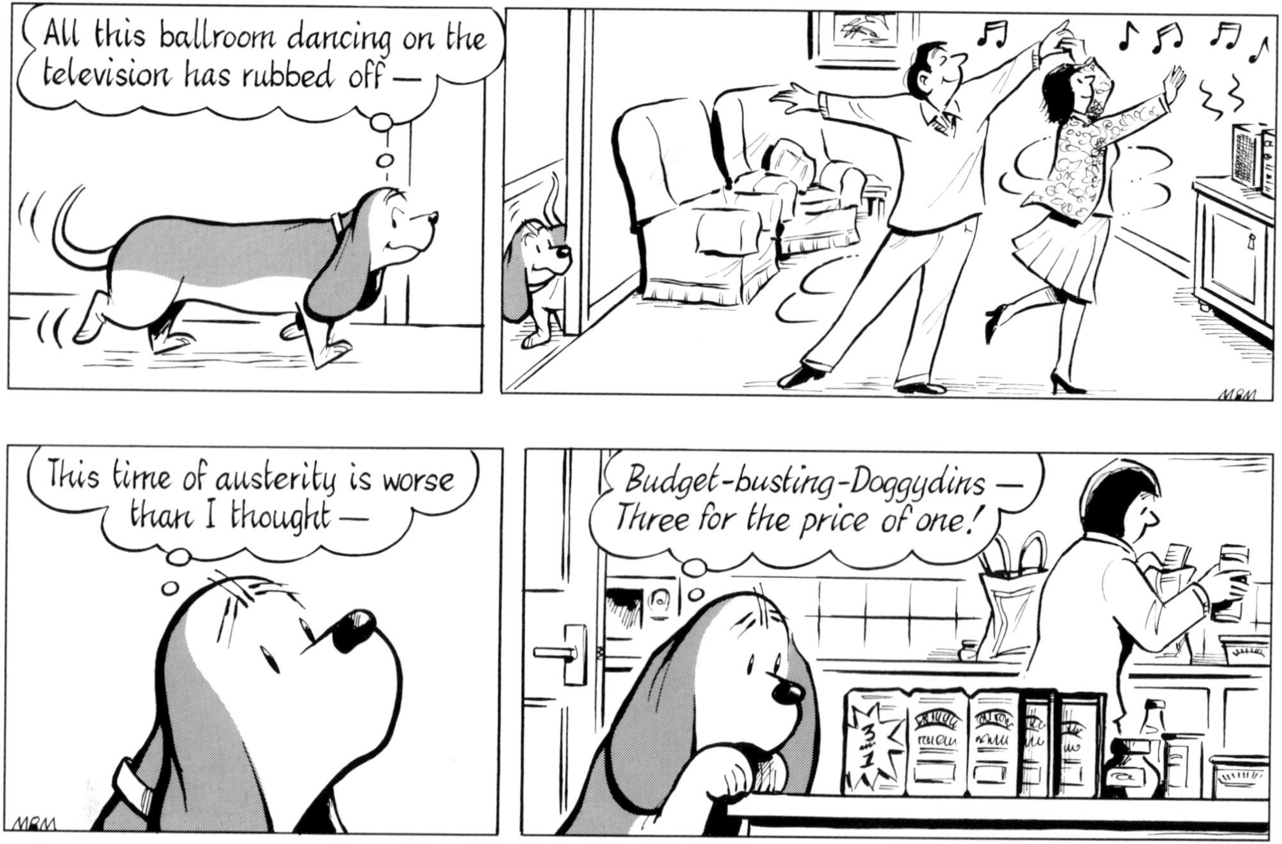
All this ballroom dancing on the television has rubbed off —
This time of austerity is worse than I thought —
Budget-busting-Doggydins — Three for the price of one!

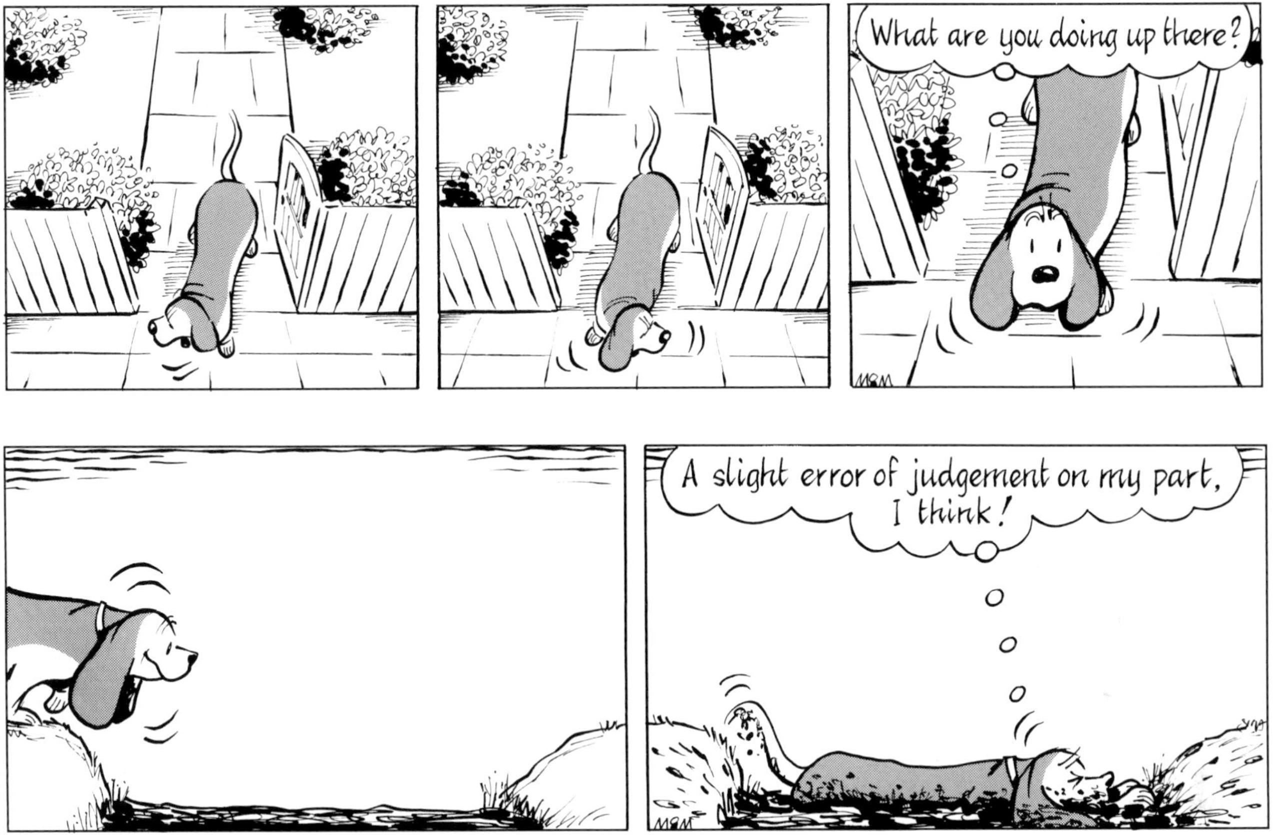
What are you doing up there?
M&M
A slight error of judgement on my part, I think!
M&M

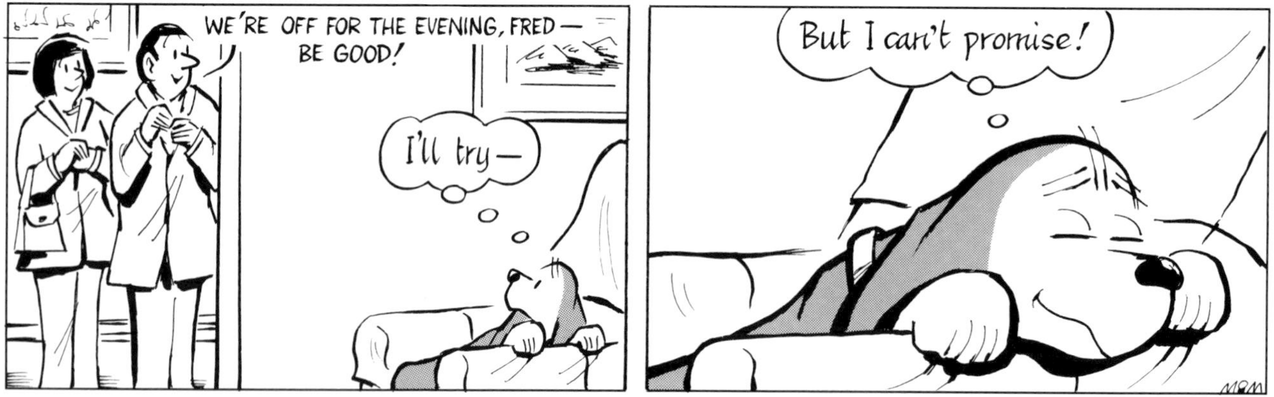
WE'RE OFF FOR THE EVENING, FRED — BE GOOD!
I'll try —
But I can't promise!

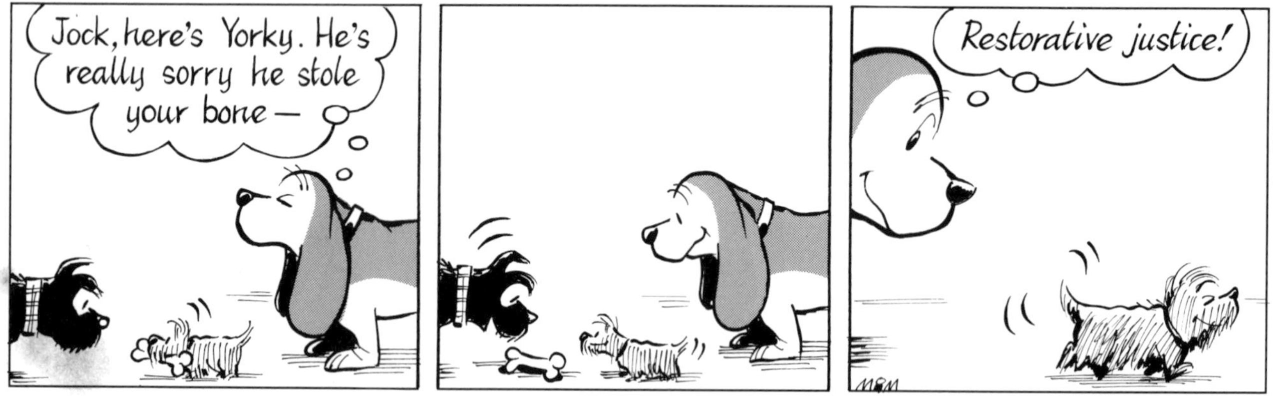
Jock, here's Yorky. He's really sorry he stole your bone —
Restorative justice!

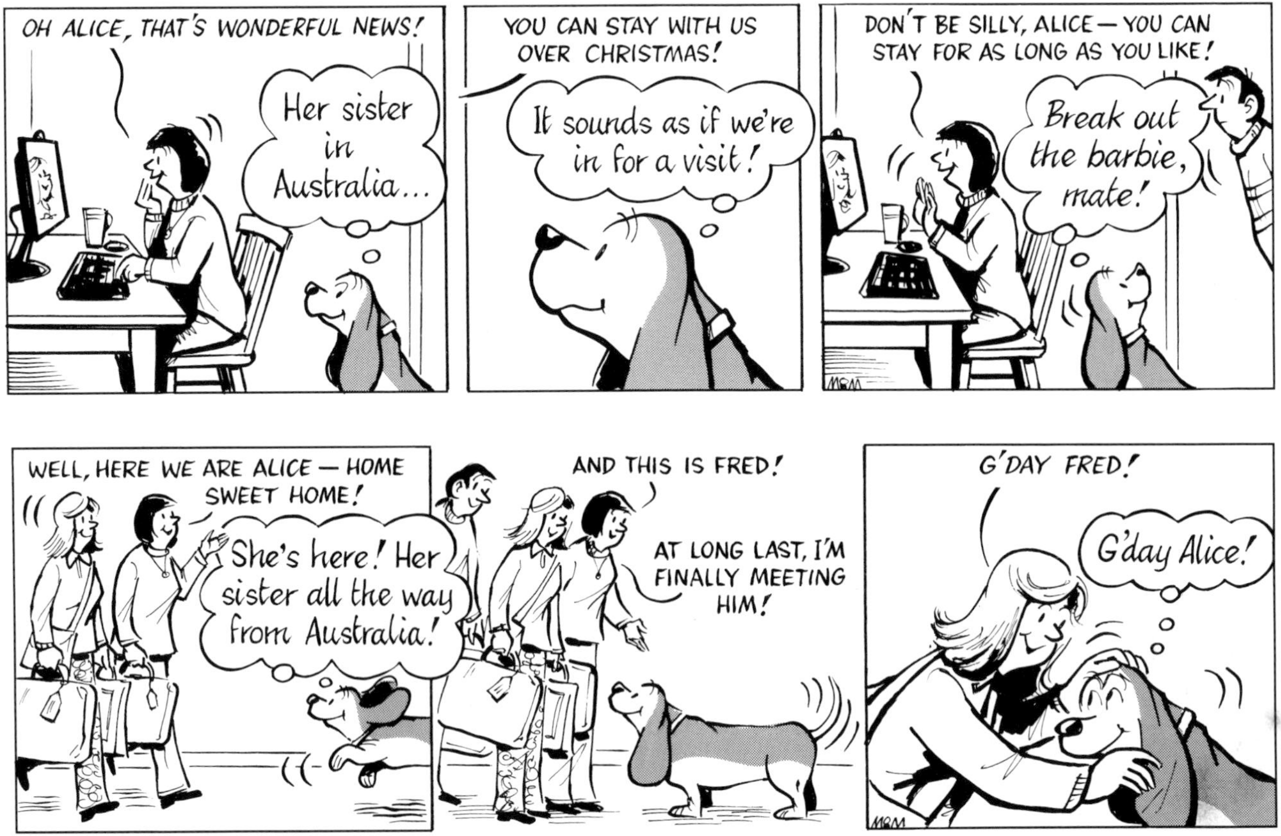
OH ALICE, THAT'S WONDERFUL NEWS!
Her sister in Australia...
YOU CAN STAY WITH US OVER CHRISTMAS!
It sounds as if we're in for a visit!
DON'T BE SILLY, ALICE — YOU CAN STAY FOR AS LONG AS YOU LIKE!
Break out the barbie, mate!
WELL, HERE WE ARE ALICE — HOME SWEET HOME!
She's here! Her sister all the way from Australia!
AND THIS IS FRED!
AT LONG LAST, I'M FINALLY MEETING HIM!
G'DAY FRED!
G'day Alice!

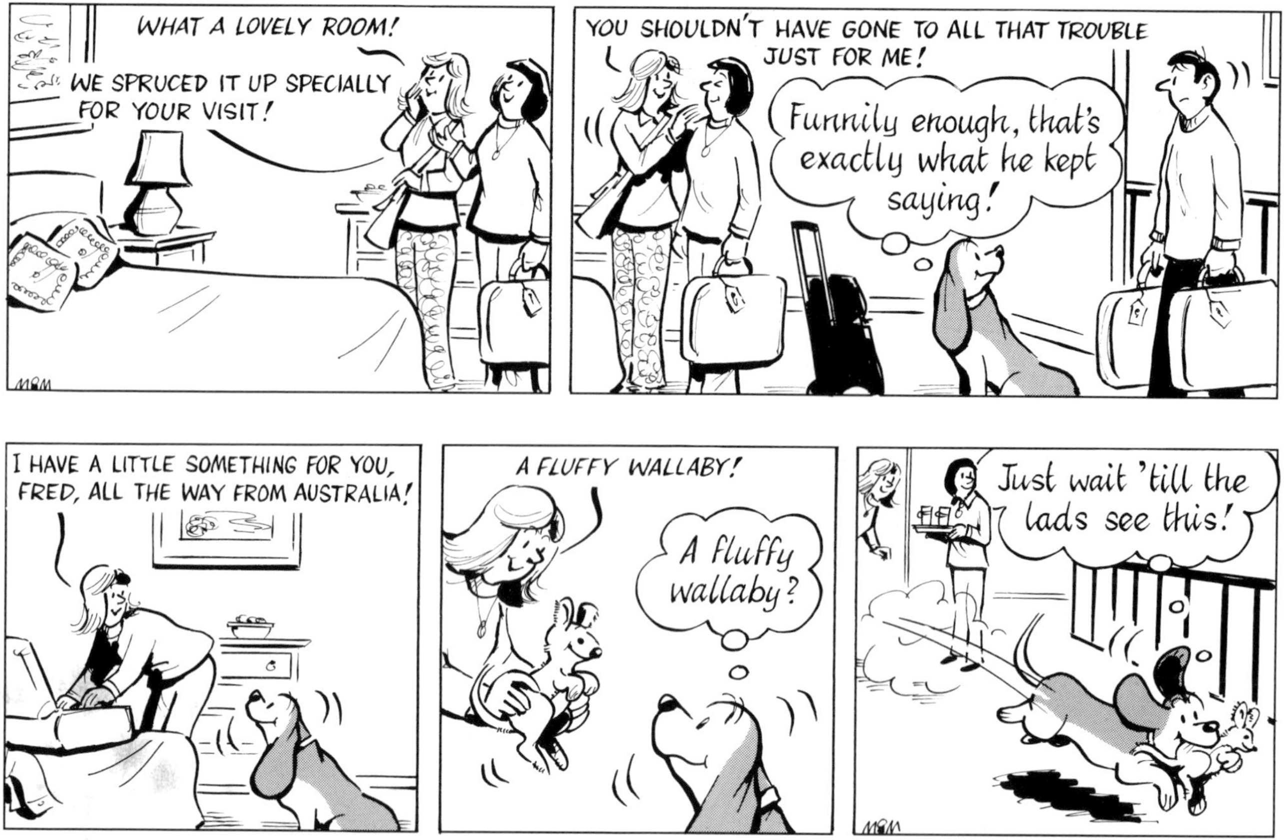

WHAT A LOVELY ROOM!
WE SPRUCED IT UP SPECIALLY FOR YOUR VISIT!
YOU SHOULDN'T HAVE GONE TO ALL THAT TROUBLE JUST FOR ME!
Funnily enough, that's exactly what he kept saying!
I HAVE A LITTLE SOMETHING FOR YOU, FRED, ALL THE WAY FROM AUSTRALIA!
A FLUFFY WALLABY!
A fluffy wallaby?
Just wait 'till the lads see this!
MGM

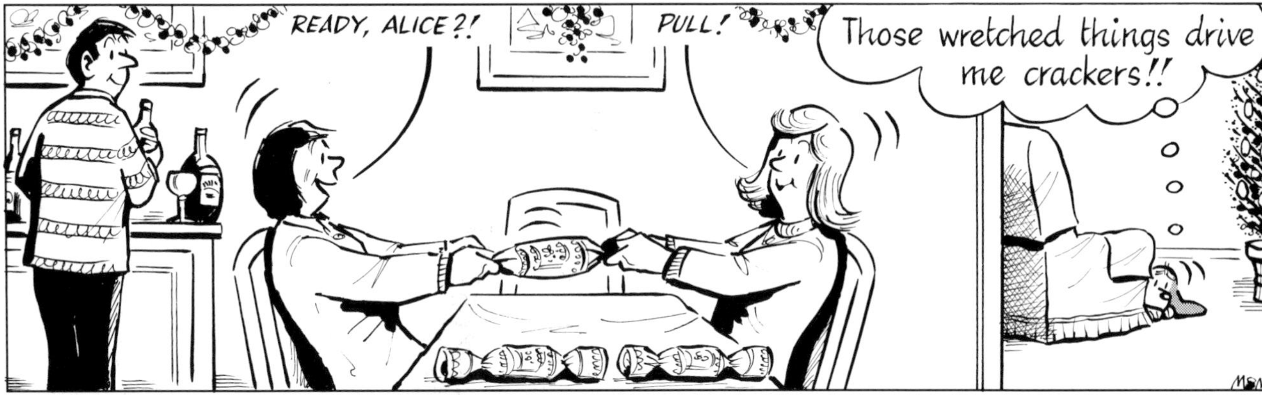
READY, ALICE?!
PULL!
Those wretched things drive me crackers!!
MSM

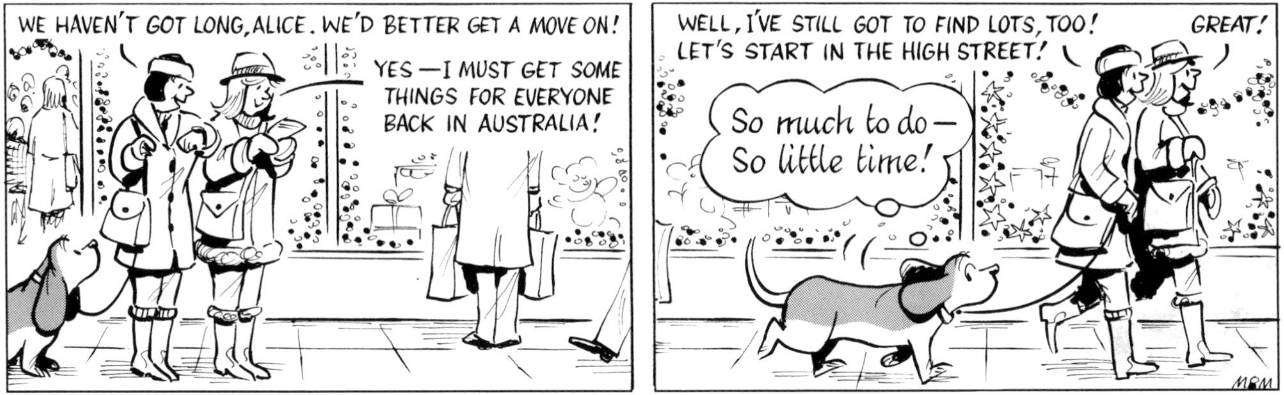
WE HAVEN'T GOT LONG, ALICE. WE'D BETTER GET A MOVE ON!
YES — I MUST GET SOME THINGS FOR EVERYONE BACK IN AUSTRALIA!
WELL, I'VE STILL GOT TO FIND LOTS, TOO! LET'S START IN THE HIGH STREET!
GREAT!
So much to do — So little time!
MSM

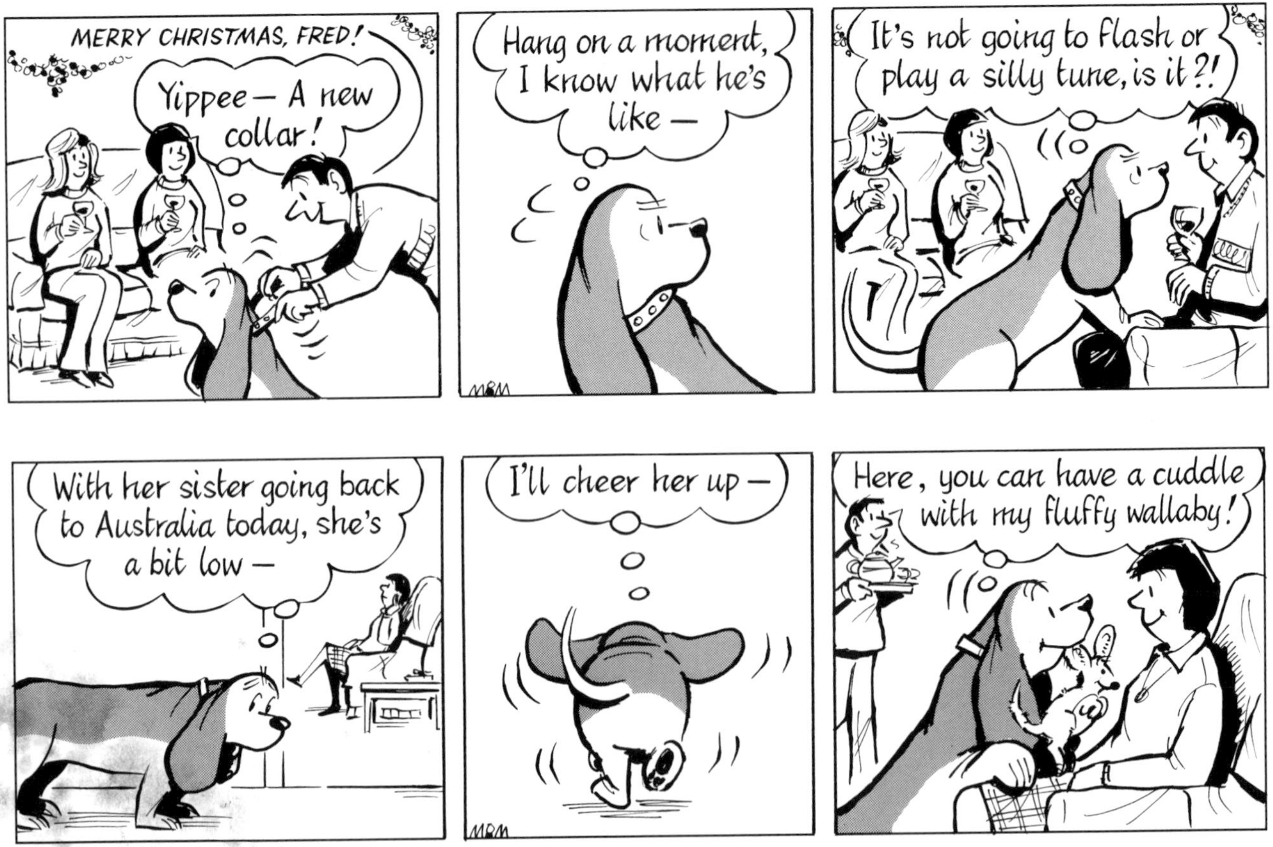
MERRY CHRISTMAS, FRED!
Yippee — A new collar!
Hang on a moment, I know what he's like —
It's not going to flash or play a silly tune, is it?!
With her sister going back to Australia today, she's a bit low —
I'll cheer her up —
Here, you can have a cuddle with my fluffy wallaby!

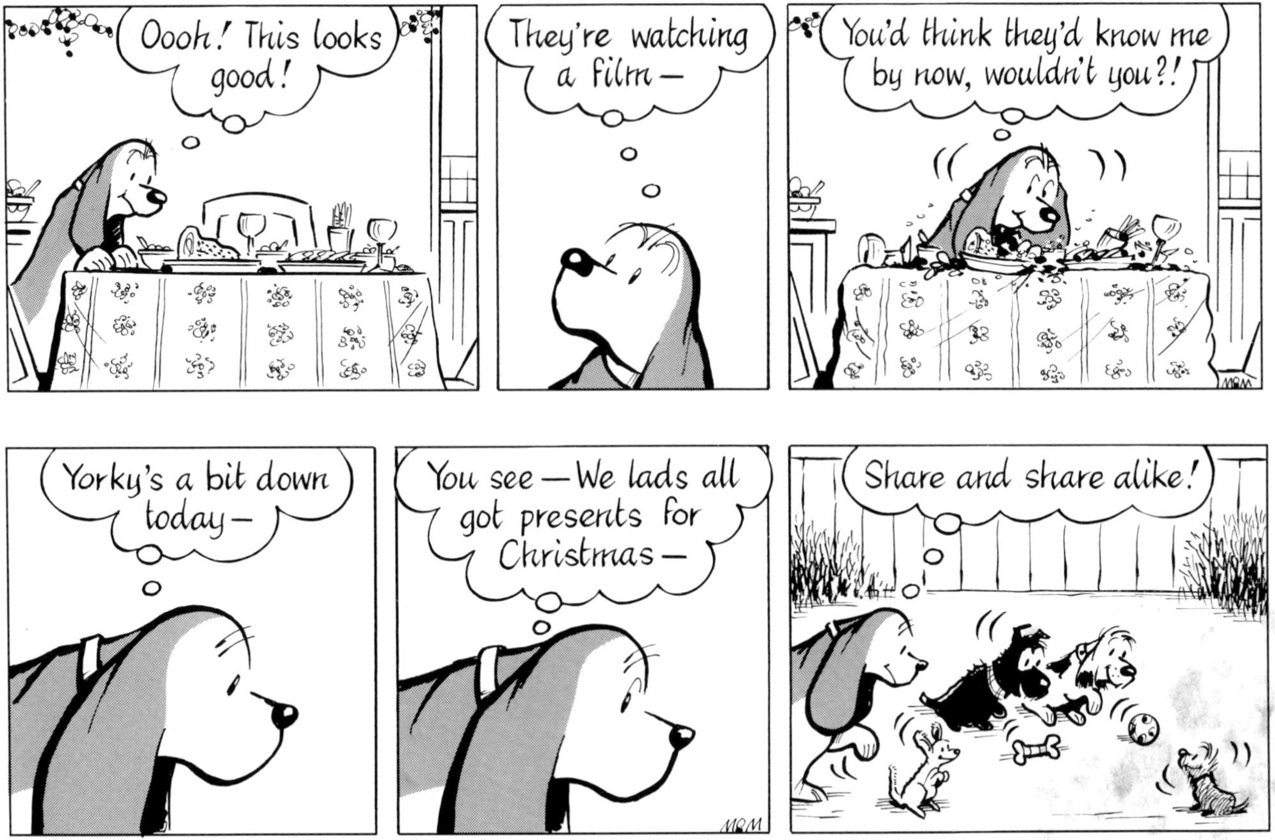
Oooh! This looks good!
They're watching a film –
You'd think they'd know me by now, wouldn't you?!
MGM
Yorky's a bit down today –
You see – We lads all got presents for Christmas –
MGM
Share and share alike!

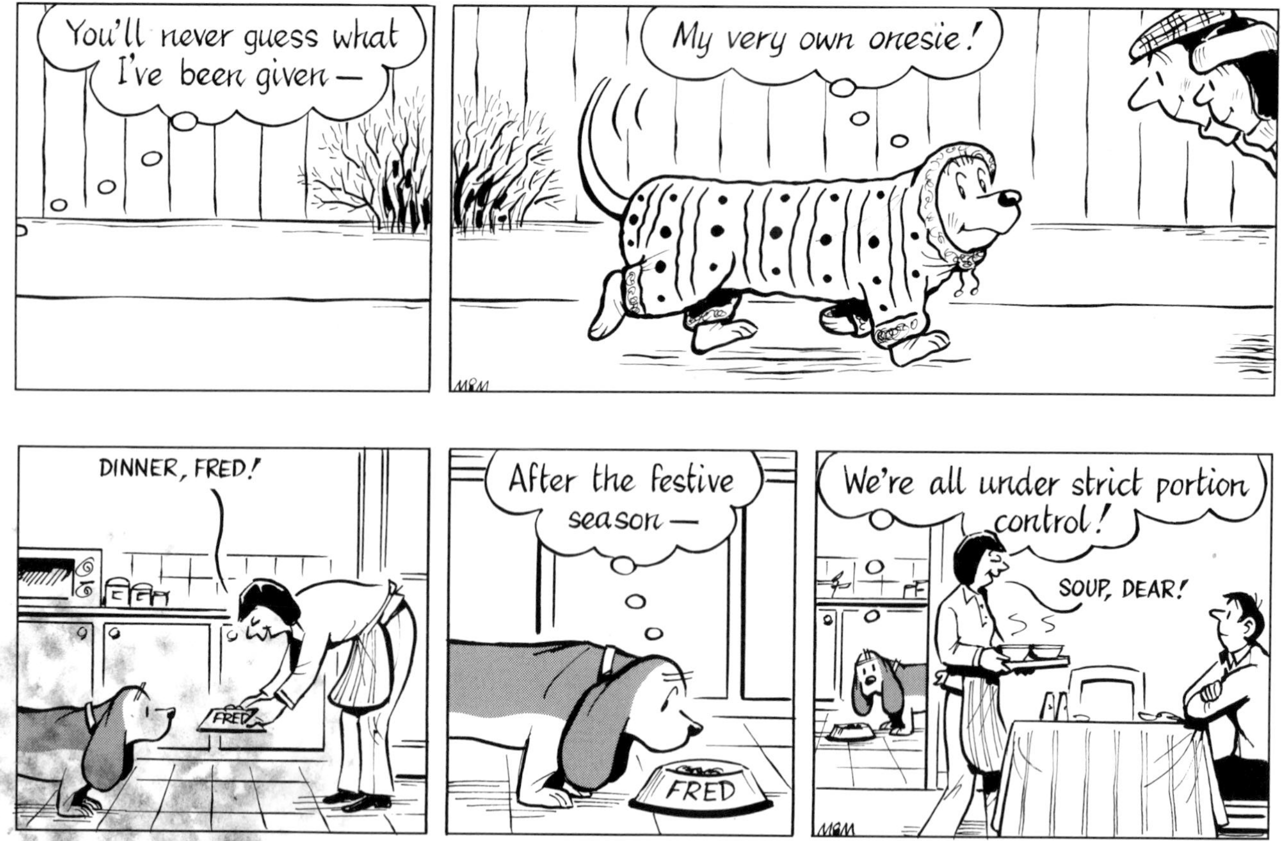
You'll never guess what I've been given —
My very own onesie!
MBM
DINNER, FRED!
FRED
After the festive season —
FRED
We're all under strict portion control!
SOUP, DEAR!
MBM